2 —

Don John of Austria

Don John
of Austria

SIR CHARLES PETRIE

Bt. C.B.E. M.A.(Oxon) F.R.Hist.Soc.
Hon.D.Phil (Valladolid)

*Corresponding Member of the Royal Spanish Academy
of History and of the Instituto Fernando el
Católico of Zaragoza. President of the Military
History Society of Ireland*

W · W · NORTON & COMPANY · INC ·

NEW YORK

Contents

CONTENTS

7

CONTENTS

9

Illustrations

PLATES

Between pages 160 and 161

MAPS

ACKNOWLEDGEMENTS

We are grateful to the following for allowing us to reproduce copyright photographs: The Mansell Collection for the portrait of Don John of Austria attributed to Antonio Moro (jacket), Charles V by Titian, Philip II by Titian, Veniero by Tintoretto, Elizabeth I and Pius V. The Mauritshuis, The Hague for the portrait of William of Orange. The Duke of Alba for the portrait of Don John (Frontispiece). The Trustees of the National Portrait Gallery for the portraits of Mary, Queen of Scots. The Museo Naval, Madrid for the portrait of the Marquess of Santa Cruz. *Hayat* magazine, Istanbul for the portraits of Ochiali and Sultan Selim II. Mme Jean Raindre for the portrait of François de Noailles, Bishop of Dax. The Trustees of the National Maritime Museum, Greenwich for the *Battle of Lepanto*.

Foreword

The sixteenth century is a good deal closer to the twentieth than any of the intervening ones. As in the present age men were divided by ideological differences – religious, not economic and political – but it came to much the same thing: ideologies cut across all other loyalties, and men felt that they had more in common with foreigners who held their views than with their own fellow-countrymen who differed from them. Then, again, international relations were on a wider scale than was to be the case until the First World War. The situation in the Americas, for example, had no small influence upon the Anglo–Spanish struggle in Europe, while the Turks could not deploy all their forces against the Spaniards in the Mediterranean until they knew what the Persians were going to do in the Middle East: at a critical moment during the Revolt of the Netherlands it proved impossible to reinforce the Spanish troops in the Low Countries owing to the failure of the Portuguese campaign in Morocco. Such instances could be multiplied almost indefinitely: by comparison, the wars of Louis XIV and Napoleon were very local affairs.

Above all it was an age of very great rulers, such as Elizabeth I, Philip II, William the Silent, Catherine de Medici, Charles V, Francis I, and Suleyman the Magnificent: indeed, it is no exaggeration to say that neither before nor since have there been so many outstanding Heads of State on the stage at the same time. Among these remarkable characters Don John of Austria was certainly not the least illustrious. Illegitimate son of Charles V and consequently half-brother of Philip II, he flashed across the international stage like a meteor, and crowded into the thirty-one years of his life more than most men in a much longer span. In any event a very sympathetic figure, the very brevity of his career lends glamour to it.

This biography consequently takes the reader into many fields. The suppression of the Morisco rising (very largely a Turkish Fifth Column Affair) in Spain itself; the defeat of the Turks in the naval battle of Lepanto, which saved Italy from becoming an Ottoman pashalik; the intrigue to marry Don John to Mary, Queen of Scots, and make him King of Ireland; and, finally, his death in the Netherlands in what was to prove the hour of victory. All these events have had to be re-examined in the light of recent research, which also proves conclusively that when the Turks first landed in Cyprus they were welcomed by the Greek inhabitants of that island.

No full-length biography of Don John in English has made its appearance since Sir William Stirling-Maxwell published his two volumes over eighty years ago. As a quarry his work is still invaluable, and I fully acknowledge my debt to him, but he was very prejudiced, and by no means always accurate. Of more recent years both the career of Don John and the Europe in which he moved have been the subject of careful study by scholars in Spain, France, and Finland, to whom every historian of the period is under a great obligation: their names and works are indicated during the course of my narrative.

I should like to express my grateful thanks to my colleagues of Valladolid University for many suggestions as to sources of information, and in particular to Señor Don Luis Suárez Fernández, who first introduced me to the Archives at Simancas. The Duquesa de Santo Mauro, and the Marqués and Marquesa de Santa Cruz, I have to thank for much kindness. The Director of the Spanish Institute in London, Professor Don Carlos Clavería, and his staff have been more than kind in the loan of books, and in the same connexion I would also like to thank Mr S. C. Holliday, Chief Librarian of the Royal Borough of Kensington and Chelsea. None of them, I may add, is in any way responsible for the opinions expressed in these pages. Finally, I should like to place on record that it was the late Duke of Alba who, many years ago, first aroused my interest in sixteenth-century Spain, for which I can never be sufficiently grateful.

As in my previous books of this nature, covering several countries, where the transliteration of names both of persons and places presents considerable difficulty, I have let myself be guided by usage rather than by uniformity.

CHARLES PETRIE

Don John of Austria

THE FAMILY TREE OF DON JOHN

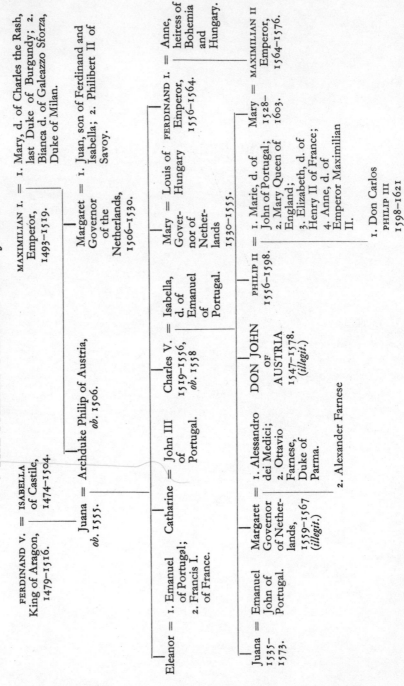

I

Birth and Background

DON JOHN OF AUSTRIA WAS BORN AT RATISBON OR REGENS-
burg in Bavaria, the son of the Emperor Charles V who was also
King Charles I of Spain. So much is certain, but the date of his
birth and the identity of his mother have been subjects of controversy. It seems most probable that his birthday was February
24th, 1547, for on the medal struck in honour of his victory at
Lepanto in 1571 his age is given as twenty-four. There is additional
corroboration in the fact that at a meeting of the Cortes of Castille,
held at Toledo in 1560, Philip II granted him a verbal dispensation
in virtue of which, although still under the age of fourteen prescribed by law, he was permitted to swear allegiance and do
homage to his nephew, Don Carlos, as heir-apparent to the
Spanish throne.

His mother was generally reputed to be Barbara Blomberg, the
daughter of a well-known family in Ratisbon, who was unmarried
at the time of his birth, and the evidence seems to prove that such
was indeed the case. But Faminianus Strada has recorded how he
was told by Cardinal de la Cueva that he had himself heard from
the Infanta Isabella Eugenia, the favourite daughter of Philip II,
that her uncle was the son, not of Barbara, but of a German
princess, who was later identified as the daughter of the Duke of
Bavaria.[1] Antonio Ossorio, on the other hand, queries this, and
says that the statement rests on nothing more substantial than the
fact that the princess in question was regarded as singular because
she neither got married nor entered a convent as was customary
in Germany in the case of girls of her rank.[2]

Whether Barbara was or was not Don John's mother the child
was in her keeping for a short time immediately after his birth,

[1] *De Bello Belgico Decades Duae*, vol. i, p. 653. Rome, 1632–47.
[2] *Vida de Don Juan de Austria*, pp. 7–8. Madrid, 1946.

though he was removed from her charge before he was weaned, for reasons which are obscure. She was, however, to cross the Habsburg path again, and it is difficult to believe that Philip would have bothered about her if she had not possessed some claim on him and his family, though it is, of course, at least arguable that he was in reality paying her hush-money on account of what she knew about his father's relations with the Bavarian princess. On his deathbed Charles bestowed on her an annuity of two hundred florins; by this time she had married one Jerome Pyramus Kegel, a gentleman of the Imperial Court, who obtained the post of Commissary at Brussels, and who died in 1569. It is at the beginning of her widowhood that contemporary records make mention of her, for the Duke of Alba was by this time Governor-General of the Netherlands, and Barbara's name occurs from time to time in his correspondence with his Royal master.

The Duke found the lady by no means easy to deal with, and in one of his letters to Philip he says that 'she is not a woman whom it is easy to bring to do what Your Majesty orders'.[1] Soon after her husband's death, Alba sent to inquire into her circumstances which he found were none too good financially. She had had two sons by Kegel, one of whom had been drowned in a water-butt at home, but the other seemed a lad of some promise. The Duke added that as Barbara was generally accepted as Don John's mother something would clearly have to be done for her. In this connexion, and in view of Don John's uncertain maternity, it is not without interest to record that in his notes on Alba's dispatches, the King always refers to her as 'my brother's mother', and never suggests that he had any doubts in the matter.

Barbara played so small a part in her son's life that her activities do not greatly concern his biographer, but some mention should, perhaps, be made of them. Certainly Alba found her one of his more exacting commitments. One of the earlier solutions which he attempted was to get her to transfer herself from Brussels to Mons, but this she refused to do on the ground that she did not understand French, from which Sir William Stirling-Maxwell has concluded, surely on insufficient evidence, that she was Flemish.[2]

[1] *Epistolario del III Duque de Alba*, vol. ii, no. 1098. Madrid 1952.
[2] *Don John of Austria*, vol. i, p. 4. London, 1883.

Finally she was persuaded to settle in Ghent, where she was provided with a house and an establishment consisting of a housekeeper and six women, a steward, two pages, a chaplain, an almoner, and four men-servants. One would have thought that this would have sufficed, but she wasted her substance in riotous living; what worried Alba even more was that she was – not unnaturally – always surrounded by suitors, and for reasons of his own Philip did not wish her to re-marry. In due course the King and the Duke lost patience, and it was suggested to Barbara that the ideal abode for her would be a convent in Spain. However, she replied that she knew only too well how women were immured in that country, and she would be cut in pieces rather than go there. By the autumn of 1571, Alba had become so exasperated that he was contemplating the possibility of inveigling her on board a vessel under the pretext of going to Antwerp, and of then taking her by force across the Bay of Biscay.[1]

So the situation remained until Don John himself arrived in Luxembourg in the autumn of 1576, and Barbara came to see him there. No record appears to exist as to the nature of their conversation, but it is reasonable to conjecture that it was not unconnected with Philip's desire to see the lady safely settled in Spain: it may even be that Don John lent his support to this proposition for, as he was now Governor-General of the Low Countries, he might well take a poor view of his mother's somewhat wanton widowhood at Ghent. However this may be, not long after – if not as a direct consequence of – this meeting Barbara betook herself to the Peninsula. Whether Don John had any influence over her is a moot point, but she would appear to have had some over him. For about this time she received a letter from Mary, Queen of Scots, asking her to secure the release of one of her followers by the name of Stanton, who had been wrongfully incarcerated by the Spanish authorities in the Low Countries: as a result of Barbara's intervention the prisoner 'was presently discharged'.[2]

The story of her subsequent career is soon told. She was at San

[1] cf. Gachard, L. P., *Correspondance de Philippe II sur les Affaires des Pays Bas*, vol. ii, nos. 884, 905, 912, 960, 969, 987, 1025, and 1054: Brussels, 1848–51; also *Epistolario del III Duque de Alba*, vol. ii, nos. 1098, 1116, 1160, 1239, 1290, 1408, and 1488, also vol. iii, nos. 1863 and 2026. Madrid, 1952.

[2] cf. Stirling-Maxwell, Sir William, *Don John of Austria*, vol. ii, p. 208. London, 1883.

Cebrian de Amacote when Don John died, and we are told that 'her grief was equal to her loss' – a somewhat ambiguous statement. After that she seems to have lived for a time in the neighbourhood of Laredo, and again near Ambrusela, but the evidence is conflicting when and where she died, nor is it of any importance. Her only surviving son by her husband justified the high opinion which Alba had formed of him, for he not only married a woman of position, but commanded a German regiment in the Spanish service. After his death his widow took up her residence in Valladolid, where she received an annual pension of 1,500 ducats from the Crown.[1]

If Don John was really the son of Barbara Blomberg it must have been from her that he inherited those characteristics of indiscipline and ostentation which were his two weakest qualities, for they clearly did not come from his father. Conceit was certainly not one of the Emperor's failings, and when he sent Philip the manuscript of his Memoirs he wrote, 'It is not such as I should have desired, but God knows I have not written it out of vanity.' It is true that he made war in style, as his weapons and accoutrements to be seen today in the Real Armería in Madrid abundantly prove, but when Charles was not in the field he cared little, unlike his contemporaries Francis I and Henry VIII, about fine clothes, and he chiefly affected the sober black of Spain. There is, indeed, a legend that he was once caught in a rainstorm wearing an expensive coat, whereupon he immediately sent a servant to fetch a less valuable one.[2]

It is difficult to resist the conclusion that justice has rarely been done to Charles V, and the reason is not far to seek – he touched life at so many points that it is almost impossible to visualize his career as a whole. The very extent of his dominions would be inconceivable were it not a fact. He became Holy Roman Emperor in 1519 after an election more memorable than any that had preceded it, and in which the Kings of England and France had been his competitors: when he ascended the throne he united in himself territories more vast than any that Europe had seen under one sceptre since the days of Charlemagne. Spain, Sardinia, Naples,

[1] cf. Vanderhammen, Lorenzo, *Don Juan de Austria*, folios 325–6. Madrid, 1627.
[2] cf. Wyndham Lewis, D. B., *Emperor of the West*, p. 58. London, 1932.

and Sicily in the Mediterranean, and Flanders and the Franche Comté farther to the north, were subject to him, while overseas in the New World another empire, of apparently inexhaustible wealth, had recently been added to his crown. Given the ability of the ruler of this vast heritage it is no exaggeration on the part of Bryce when he describes Charles V as 'far stronger than Maximilian or any other Emperor who had reigned for three centuries'.[1]

Imagination boggles at the thought of what such a man could have done with this inheritance had it not been for the ill-timed occurrence of the Reformation; for ill-timed it was to prove from the political standpoint whatever view may be taken of its religious aspect. As it was in Germany that Luther raised the standard of revolt, so it was the Empire that experienced the first impact of the centrifugal forces which were now unloosed. To quote Bryce once again: 'The Holy Roman Empire is but another name for the visible Church. . . . Mediaeval theory constructed the civil on the model of the ecclesiastical society. . . . The Roman Empire was the shadow of the Popedom – designed to rule men's bodies as the Pontiff ruled their souls. Both alike claimed obedience on the ground that Truth is One, and that where there is One faith there must be One government. And, therefore, since it was this very principle of formal unity that the Reformation overthrew, it became a revolt against the principle of authority in all its forms.'[2] A few pages earlier the same author had written: 'Hitherto it had seemed not impossible to strengthen the German state into a monarchy, compact if not despotic; the very Diet of Worms, where the monk of Wittenberg proclaimed to an astonished Church and Emperor that the day of spiritual autocracy was past, had framed and presented a fresh scheme for the construction of a central council of government. The great religious schism put an end to all such hopes, for it became a source of political disunion far more serious and permanent than any that had existed before, and it taught the two sections into which Germany was henceforth divided to regard each other with feelings more bitter than those of hostile nations.'[3]

[1] *The Holy Roman Empire*, p. 368. London, 1910.
[2] *ibid.*, p. 376. London, 1910.
[3] *ibid.*, p. 367. London, 1910.

It was with the repercussions of this revolution that the Emperor's sons, Philip and Don John, were to be called upon to deal.

Charles was not an extrovert, but he was a man of restraint rather than of gloom: he had been born in Ghent, and he never lost a phlegmatic coolness which, however, concealed a capacity for warm affection, especially where his family and friends were concerned. He possessed some very human characteristics, among them a lifelong horror of mice and spiders. In spite of the fact that he ruled over Spaniards, Italians, Germans, Flemings, Dutch, and Walloons he was no linguist; the only language in which he could express himself with comfort was French, though towards the end of his life he was pretty fluent in Spanish. He certainly came to understand the Spaniards very well indeed, which had not been the case when he first appeared among them. It is related that he once met a Spanish peasant on the road, and was subjected to a furious tirade against his methods of government in general, and his own repeated absences from Spain in particular: when at length the man discovered to whom he was speaking he merely added that had he known earlier he would have said a great deal more. Charles took it all in good part, for he had become at home with that democracy of the Spanish character which has always enabled a beggar to address a King as one gentleman to another.

Bartholomew Sastrow, the Lutheran notary of Stralsund, has left an attractive account of the Emperor at dinner, on this occasion at Augsburg:

> After placing the dishes on the table the pages took the covers off. The Emperor shook his head when he did not care for the particular dish; he bowed his head when it suited, and then drew it towards him. Enormous pasties, large pieces of game, and the most succulent dishes were taken away, while His Majesty ate a piece of roast, a slice of calf's head, or something analogous. He had no one to carve for him; in fact he made but a sparing use of the knife. He began by cutting his bread in pieces large enough for one mouthful, then attacked his dish. He stuck his knife anywhere, and often used his fingers while he held the plate under his chin with the other hand. He ate so

naturally and at the same time so cleanly that it was a pleasure to watch him.

When he felt thirsty he only drank three draughts. He made a sign to the *doctores medicinae* standing by the table, whereupon they went to the sideboard for two silver flagons and filled a crystal goblet holding about a measure and a half. The Emperor drained it to the last drop, practically at one draught, though he took breath two or three times. He took not the slightest notice of the crowd which came to watch the monarch eat. The dinner lasted less than half-an-hour, after which tables, seats, and everything else were removed, and there remained nothing but the four walls hung with magnificent tapestry. After grace they handed the Emperor the quills of feathers wherewith to clean his teeth, and he then rinsed his hands, and took his seat in one of the window-recesses. There everybody could go up and speak to him, hand him a petition, or argue a question.[1]

This account is at variance with the statement so frequently made by historians that Charles was a colossal eater, but he clearly ate all the wrong things from a dietary point-of-view, for richly cooked and salted dishes, washed down by heavy wines, cannot have been good for his gout.

The Emperor was an extremely cultured man, and a merciful one. It is true that he could be stern enough when he thought that occasion so demanded, and much has been made of his severity towards his birthplace of Ghent whose civic privileges he took away in 1540, but after all the city had not only risen against him, but had also invoked the aid of the King of France. On the other hand when he was in Wittenberg after his victory over the Lutheran princes, he visited the tomb of the reformer, when he was urged to have the body disinterred and thrown to the dogs. 'I war not with the dead,' he replied, 'but with the living: suffer him to repose in peace: he is already before his judge.'[2] Again, when he was about to embark upon his first campaign against Algiers a Moor came to him privately, revealed the fact that he was

---

[1] *Memoirs*, quoted by Wyndham Lewis, D. B., *op. cit.*, p. 56. It is to be noted that the fork had not yet made its appearance outside Italy.

[2] cf. Coxe, W., *History of the House of Austria*, vol. i, pp. 511–12. London, 1807.

Barbarossa's baker, and pointed out how easy it would be for him to poison his master; Charles dismissed the man with contempt.

As Don John's career unfolds itself it will be seen that he inherited more than one of his father's characteristics, if he developed some weaknesses of his own. His brother and sisters were Philip II; Mary, who married the Emperor Maximilian II; and Juana, who married the heir to the Portuguese throne, and shortly after his death gave birth to a child who was the ill-fated King Sebastian of Portugal. There was also another sister, illegitimate like Don John himself, namely Margaret, whose first husband was Alessandro dei Medici, and her second Ottavio Farnese, Duke of Parma.

Philip was to be the dominating factor in Don John's life, so it will be as well to see what manner of man he was, for it is difficult to resist the conclusion that, as was the case of his father, justice has rarely been done him. For many years it was the custom of English historians in particular, following in the footsteps of Sir William Stirling-Maxwell and Martin Hume, to say that Philip left his country ruined economically and on the downward path internationally. The line adopted was that because he had been the enemy of England he must have been a bad man. What these critics tended to ignore was that the golden age of Spanish civilization followed Philip's reign and did not precede it, while all the evidence goes to show that the economic decline really began after his death,[1] and was in any case a great deal slower than is usually stated.

As for Spain's position in the world, it was on balance a great deal stronger when the King died than it had been when he succeeded to the throne. It is true that England had slipped from his grasp, and that an attempt to subdue her by force had failed, but she was a nuisance rather than a menace; Philip had also lost part of that *damnosa hereditas* the Low Countries, but he had united the Iberian Peninsula, and thus completed the work of Ferdinand and Isabella, by the incorporation of Portugal in his dominions, while the Spanish possessions in the New World had

[1] cf. in particular Elliott, John: *The Decline of Spain*, in *Past and Present*, no. 20, pp. 52–75. Kendal, 1961.

been rounded off by the annexation of Brazil. The Crescent had been banished from the Western Mediterranean for ever, and the France of Henry IV was no more formidable than that of Henry II, while Spanish armies were to play a considerable part in French politics for many years to come; it was also largely his doing that Germany remained half-Catholic.

Philip was well aware of his own limitations, and he was under no illusion that he was a man of action. He could carry on a struggle for years against overwhelming odds should the necessity arise, but the taking of snap decisions on a battlefield was beyond the scope of a man who got diarrhoea under the stress of any sudden crisis[1]: therefore he took care both in war and in diplomacy to avoid any situation in which a snap decision might be necessary. This was the reason why he endeavoured to rule the world from his desk, and although he never spared himself the task was beyond him, as it would have been beyond any man. Von Pastor summed up the position very well when he wrote that Philip's 'natural autocracy was given a special character by the view he took of the heavy responsibilities which lay upon his shoulders. His unwearied assiduity at the council table would have been an excellent thing in the ruler of a small State, but in the case of a monarch who was master of half the world it could not fail to become a grave disadvantage, all the more so as it was united to a great want of decision.'[2]

Philip's character was extremely complex. Even in childhood he seemed outwardly older than his years, for he was reserved in his manner, and deliberate in his speech, yet what he had to say was well worth hearing, and even as a boy he was rarely off his guard.[3] There was, however, a softer side to his nature which only showed itself to his intimates, and which may well have been the cause of their affection for him. He was also popular with servants, which is always a good sign. He wrote poetry for his own delectation, he was a great lover of music and the visual arts, and he was liable to be moved almost to tears by the song of the nightingale on a summer evening. He was also very fond of children.

---

[1] cf. Walsh, W. T., *Philip II*, p. 195. New York, 1937.
[2] *Lives of the Popes*, vol. xvi, p. 357. London, 1899.
[3] cf. Cabrera de Córdoba, L., *Felipe II, Rey de España*, lib. I, cap. 1. Madrid, 1619.

Don John's favourite sister was Juana, who had married Prince Emmanuel John of Portugal, but he had died before succeeding to the throne. Known as Princess of the Brazils she acted as Regent for Philip II during his absence in Flanders; later she saw much of Don John, who became very fond of her. When she died in 1573 at the age of thirty-eight her brother was at Favignana, an island off Sicily, and as soon as he heard of her death he gave orders that the yards, masts, oars, and bulwarks of his squadron were to be painted black or covered with black material; thus funereally dressed the ships moved along the Sicilian coast, receiving the salutes of the shore-batteries.

Don John had little direct contact with his sister, Mary, who was born in 1528; she was married to Maximilian II when her brother was only a year old, and thereafter she remained in Vienna until the Emperor died in 1576, by which time Don John himself had only two years to live. Her husband was a good-natured, garrulous man, who, when other topics failed, would entertain the members of the *corps diplomatique* with the history of his dyspeptic symptoms, and warn them from his own experience against an excessive consumption of salad and prawns. Mary herself has come down the ages as a somewhat colourless figure, though with more than normal good looks and of considerable personal accomplishments. When she became a widow she retired to a convent in Spain, where she lived to an advanced age, and died in the early years of the reign of her nephew, Philip III.

Don John's third sister, Margaret, was a much more distinguished figure. She was the illegitimate daughter of Charles V, and was his eldest child, having been born before his marriage. Her mother came of a respectable family called Van der Genst of Oudenarde, and Margaret was brought up by her aunt, the Queen-Dowager of Hungary. She was first married to a Medici, who fortunately for her was assassinated during the first year of their married life, and secondly to Ottavio Farnese, Duke of Parma and Piacenza, by whom she became the mother of the celebrated Alexander. Motley has written that 'her personal appearance, which was masculine, but not without a certain grand and imperial fascination, harmonized with the opinion generally entertained of her character. The famous moustache upon her upper lip was supposed to indicate authority and virility of purpose, an impression which was confirmed by the circumstance that she was liable to severe attacks of gout, a disorder usually considered more appropriate to the sterner sex.'[1]

Such was Don John's immediate family circle, but some years were to elapse before his relatives knew anything of him, or he of them. As we have seen, for some obscure reason he was removed, while still at the breast, from Barbara Blomberg, and he was Governor-General of the Netherlands before he saw her again, for the Emperor placed him in the charge of Luis Quijada and his wife, Magdalena de Ulloa.

A better choice could not have been made, and it attests Charles's excellence as a judge of character, for no child could have been cared for by his parents more tenderly than was Don John during his infancy and childhood. Quijada was head of a noble family in Old Castille which since the early Middle Ages had provided many loyal servants to the Crown. The father of Luis, Gutierre, had been a close friend of Philip I, and two of his brothers had been killed fighting for Charles V. Luis himself had begun his career as a page in the Imperial service, and after serving as a soldier on various fronts he had become Vice-Chamberlain in the Emperor's Household under the Duke of Alba. About the time of Don John's birth he married, and settled his wife at his family seat of Villagarcia, near Valladolid; he then returned to his duty with the Emperor in Germany.

The evidence regarding Don John's early years is both scanty and conflicting, but it would appear probable that soon after Quijada's return Charles told him that he wished his son to be brought up in Spain. The two men then discussed the boy's education, and Quijada put forward alternative proposals – either he could be entrusted to the care of his wife at Villagarcia, or to that of Bautista Vela, who was curate of Leganes, a village just off the road from Madrid to Toledo.

The problem of how to get Don John to Leganes without Quijada being under the necessity of making the journey at a time when he could ill be spared from his master's side was solved by

[1] *Rise of the Dutch Republic*, Part II, ch. 1. London, 1856.

29

the request of one Francis Massi, a favourite violinist of Charles, to return to Spain with his wife, who had some property near Leganes. This fitted in with the Emperor's plans admirably, and Massi was asked not only to take the child to the Peninsula, but to give him board and lodging at Leganes while he was receiving instruction from Bautista Vela. Massi and his wife were told that he was the son of Adrian de Bues, and they were required to sign the following document:

I, Francesco Massi, viol player to His Majesty, and Ana de Medina my wife, we acknowledge and confess that we have taken and received a son of the Señor Adrian de Bues, groom of His Majesty's chamber, whom we have taken at his request, that we should take, keep, and bring him up as if he were our own son, and that we should not tell any person whosoever whose son he is, because the said Señor Adrian desires that neither his wife nor any other person should by any means know of the child, or hear him spoken of.

Wherefore I, Francisco Massi, and Ana de Medina my wife, and our son, Diego de Medina, we swear and promise to the said Señor Adrian that we will not tell or declare to any living person whose the said child is, but that I shall say he is mine, until the said Señor Adrian shall send me a person with this paper, or the said Señor Adrian come in person. And because the Señor Adrian desires to keep this matter secret, he has asked me to do him a kindness, to take charge of the said boy, which we do with very good will, I and my wife; and I acknowledge to have received of the said Señor Adrian for the purpose of conveying this boy on horseback, and for his equipment and maintenance for a year, the allowance which he gives me, one hundred crowns. It is also agreed that the said year shall count from the 1st. of August of this present year 1550.

In consideration of which payment I hold myself content and reimbursed for this said year; and for this reason I hereby sign this paper, I and my wife; and because my wife cannot sign I ask Oger Bodoarte to sign her name for her. And henceforth the said Señor Adrian is to give me fifty ducats for every year for the boy's maintenance. Done at Brussels on the 13th. day

of the month of June, one thousand five hundred and fifty
years.[1]

Before Massi left for Spain he had an audience of the Emperor
who said to him, 'I hear that Quijada has given you a commission.
Remember that I shall consider the fulfilment of his wishes as good
service done to myself.' The musician was also given a pension,
and he and his young charge would appear to have arrived in
Spain in the summer of 1551, Don John being then four-and-a-
half years old.

[1] cf. Weiss, M. W., *Papiers d'état du Cardinal de Granvelle*, vol. iv, pp. 499-500.
Paris, 1841-52.

2

Early Years

A MORE REMOTE SPOT THAN LEGANES FOR DON JOHN TO spend his early years would have been difficult to find, for although it is only a few miles from Madrid that city was not yet the capital of Spain: the population consisted of peasants who cultivated the fields in the immediate vicinity of the village. Of Bautista Vela, who was responsible for the boy's education, very little is known except that he would appear to have been extremely negligent where this duty was concerned: it is true that he was not aware of the identity of the child, or he might have paid more attention to one who in the future was to be not without influence in the distribution of mitres and red hats. The result was that such tuition as Don John did receive was at the hands of the sacristan, Francisco Fernandez, but his store of knowledge was soon exhausted. The boy was then transferred to the village school at Getafe, some three miles away, which he attended daily with a number of his companions from Leganes, with whom he was on a footing of complete equality.

This bucolic existence continued for nearly four years, during the course of which Massi died, but his widow took charge of Don John, to whom she was sincerely attached. It was clear, however, that unless the boy was to remain in ignorance of his origin, and to live the life of a peasant all his days, he must be removed from his surroundings; so, after some consultation with Quijada, the Emperor took action in the spring of 1554.

Philip II was about to marry Mary Tudor in accordance with that matrimonial policy of the Habsburgs which has been so well summed up in the lines:

Bella gerant alii, tu, felix Austria, nube,
Nam quae Mars aliis, dat tibi regna Venus.[1]

He had left everything in connexion with the marriage to his father, who had made all the arrangements, had wooed the bride, and had won over her principal advisers – in short had done all the courting. Now that Wyatt's rebellion in protest against the marriage had been put down there was no reason for any further delay, so Charles sent one of his chamberlains, Charles Prevost, to Valladolid, where Philip was acting as Prince Regent, to tell him to go to England, and when this part of his mission had been accomplished Prevost was to proceed to Leganes whence he was to remove Don John to Villagarcia.

Prevost duly delivered his message at Valladolid, and then set out for Leganes. He made the journey by coach, a form of vehicle which was just coming into use in Northern Europe, but which had not hitherto been much seen in Spain, so as it rumbled across the Castilles it and its occupant attracted a good deal of attention. Great was the astonishment of the inhabitants of Leganes when it stopped outside the door of Ana de Medina, and their surprise was in no way diminished by the respect with which Prevost treated her young foster-son, whom they seem to have known as Jerome. How much he had been told, or how much he guessed, about the boy's identity must remain a mystery, but he was not taking any chances; he invited Don John to dine with him, and he placed the child on his right at table. Then the two left Leganes, amid the tears of Ana de Medina and the shouted farewells of the urchins of the village who had been Don John's playmates for the previous three years. Prevost took his charge first of all to Valladolid, where the Princess of the Brazils was now acting as Regent in place of Philip, who had duly departed to England; but he made no attempt to present Don John to Juana, who consequently continued to remain in ignorance of his existence: instead his time in the capital was mostly spent at the

---

[1] The authorship of these lines is attributed to Matthias Corvinus, King of Hungary. They may be loosely rendered in English:

Others must fight for lands, and chase their foes and harry them,
But Austria when she wants the same will merely go and marry them.

tailor's in being fitted out with a wardrobe more suited to the life he was henceforth to lead.[1]

Don John's removal to Villagarcia marked the turning-point in his life, and during the years that he spent there he had the advantage of those quiet domestic surroundings which are so frequently denied to those born to the purple. Quijada himself was away with the Emperor, but the boy could not have been in better hands than those of his wife, who was a remarkable woman judged by any standards. She was, it may be added, remembered long after her death, for in 1723 her biography was written by Juan de Villafañe, a Jesuit, under the title of *La Limosnera de Dios: Relación histórica de la vida y virtudes de Doña Magdalena de Ulloa Toledo Ossorio v Quiñones, muger de Luis Mendez Quizada, Fundadora de los colegios de Villagarcia, Oviedo v Santander de la Compania de Jesus*, and published in Salamanca.[2] Doña Magdalena was of the bluest blood in Europe, and claimed descent from the Imperial House of Palaeologus. Born in 1525, she was thus only twenty-nine when Don John was placed in her charge, and as she had no children of her own she was only too ready to be a mother to him. She was given no inkling of his identity, but was merely told in a letter from her husband that he was 'the son of a great man, the writer's dear friend'.

Doña Magdalena's first care was the education of her ward, for she soon discovered that this had been neglected both by the sacristan at Leganes and the schoolmaster at Getafe. He had, indeed, first to be taught to read and write properly, and when this was done he received instruction in all the other subjects, including Latin, which were then considered necessary. His spiritual upbringing she attended to personally. In those days almsgiving and the relief of the indigent poor were the duty of the individual rather than of the State, and Quijada and his wife certainly did not neglect their obligations in this respect. Doña Magdalena took the opportunity of using Don John as the channel for her charity, and thus early accustomed him to give consideration to the wants of others less favourably circumstanced than himself.

[1] cf. Vanderhammen, Lorenzo, *Don Juan de Austria*, folio 11. Madrid, 1627.

[2] A more recent work is by Camilo Maria, Father Abad, S.J., *Doña Magdalena de Ulloa*. Comillas, 1959.

However fond she was of the boy she would have been less than human had she not speculated on his origin, and wondered on occasion whether he might not be the fruit of some *liaison* of her husband. These suspicions were strengthened for a brief space when one night the castle took fire, and Quijada, who happened to be on leave at the time, rescued Don John before attempting to save her. Nevertheless she accepted his explanation that the boy was of such outstanding importance that he must be the first to be saved, and it is more than probable that from that moment she began to guess his real origin: however this may be, she henceforth lavished an even greater affection upon him.[1]

He was a spirited boy, and there are a number of stories which bear witness to the fact: he also early developed an interest in military matters, and he and his young companions formed themselves into troops and companies much as if they had been Boy Scouts in the twentieth century. Don John would not appear to have got into any more serious trouble than the average boy of his age, and it can justly be claimed that in the Quijada household his youth was normal.[2]

Meanwhile events were taking place in the outside world which were to have an immediate impact upon him, for his father had decided to abdicate. 'Fortune is a strumpet,' the Emperor declared, 'and reserves her favours for the young.' The fact was that a reign which had held out great hopes was closing in disappointment, and Charles had failed to attain his main objectives. Far from heresy having been suppressed in Germany it was more flourishing than ever; he had failed to persuade the Electors to accept Philip as his successor in the Holy Roman Empire, and had seriously annoyed his brother, Ferdinand, in the process; and in spite of his campaigns in North Africa the menace of Islam in the Western Mediterranean was increasing almost every day: above all, his own health was deteriorating. So he handed the Netherlands to Philip, who was already King of the Two Sicilies and Duke of Milan, and, since his marriage with Mary Tudor, King of England: that was in 1555. In the following year the crowns of Spain and

[1] cf. Villafañe, Juan de, *Limosna de Dios*, p. 43. Salamanca, 1723.
[2] cf. Ossorio, A., *Vida de Don Juan de Austria*, pp. 10-13. Madrid, 1946.

the Indies were also transferred to Philip, and in 1558 Charles's brother became his successor in the Empire.

All this was effected with the maximum amount of pomp and circumstance, in which, incidentally, Don John was to delight, though Philip rather endured it as a regrettable necessity. The somewhat florid verse of Sir William Stirling-Maxwell was not unsuited to the occasion:

At Bruxelles, in the ancient hall within the castle gate,
Where valiant Dukes of Burgundy erst kept their royal state,
Upon the dais richly dight, beneath the canopy,
The throne was set, and all a-row stood chairs of honour three.
Fair Flanders' looms had spread the walls with storied hangings
    o'er;
And Caesar and Don Philip came, with trumpet blown before,
With Mary, Queen of Hungary, high lady wise and wight,
And Savoy's Duke of iron mould, and many a lord and knight
Of broad Brabant and proud Castille – great chiefs of war and
    peace,
Grave magistrates of towns and states, knights of the Golden
    Fleece.

Having divested himself of his Imperial and Royal functions Charles left the Netherlands and settled at Yuste in Estremadura, where Quijada, with his wife and Don John, joined him. This was in July, 1558, and as the Emperor died on the 21st of the following September the boy cannot have seen very much of his father. Vanderhammen indeed says that he went in and out of Charles's room as he pleased since he was lodged in an ante-room of Quijada's house,[1] but as the latter was a mile from Yuste this observation is open to question. The Emperor certainly saw the boy on several occasions, and expressed satisfaction with the way he had been brought up, though Don John himself does not seem to have been in any way impressed by the proximity of his august parent, for it is on record that he engaged in apple-stealing activities, and was pelted by the farmers in whose orchards he was caught. He appears to have been one of the group who stood beside the dying monarch's bed, though whether Charles at this

[1] *Don Juan de Austria*, folio 19. Madrid, 1627.

time acknowledged him as his son is more doubtful: that he was present at the Emperor's funeral would appear to be proved.

Not unnaturally rumours had by now reached Valladolid that Charles had left a son who was living in the household of Quijada, and before long the Princess Regent heard of them; she thereupon ordered the Secretary of State, Juan Vázquez, to find out if they were true. Quijada, mindful of the instructions which he had received from his old master, decided to hedge, so on October 18th, he replied: 'As to what you say of the lad who is in my charge, it is true that he was entrusted to me, years ago, by a friend of mine; yet there is no reason for believing that he is the son of His Majesty, as you say it has been rumoured at Valladolid, because neither in His Majesty's will, of which a copy was read to his confessor and me in his presence and by his order by Gaztelu, nor in the codicil which he afterwards executed, was there any mention of the lad; and the fact being so, I have no other reply to make.' This does not seem to have satisfied Vázquez, for six days later Quijada wrote to him again: 'You seem to think what is said about the boy as certain as the fitting up of the house at Alcalá for His Majesty's reception. Ask the agent the value of a certain rent-charge, and what I said to him about it, when I wanted to buy it for this child.'[1]

All the same Quijada was far from happy in his own mind that he was doing the right thing, so he decided to write to Philip on the matter. Up to this time his extant letters to the King contain only three possible references to Don John. The first is to be found under date of July 12th, 1558, in which he reports his safe arrival at Quacos, near Yuste, together with his wife and 'the rest'. The second appears in a postscript to a long letter, dated September 17th, written during and chiefly relating to the Emperor's last illness, when he says, 'As to the other, which Your Majesty knows to be in my charge, all the care in the world shall be taken until the time when Your Majesty may come, or send me some verbal order to give Your Majesty further information on the matter.' The third allusion is plainer, and occurs in a letter of recommendation of one Oger Bodoarte, who had been

[1] cf. Gachard, M., *Retraite et Mort de Charles V*, vol. i, pp. 435 and 441. Brussels, 1854-5.

instructed by the Emperor to buy an annuity for Barbara Blomberg and was consequently in the secret, but even there Quijada only refers to Barbara as 'the mother of the person whom Your Majesty knows'.[1]

The curiosity of the Princess Regent, however, began to act upon him to such an extent that he felt matters could not be left where they were, so he wrote to the King in these terms:

> Twenty days after the death of His Imperial Majesty, Juan Vázquez, on the part of the most serene Princess, wrote to me that I should advise him whether it were true that I had under my charge a child, desiring me also to know that he was said to be the child of His Majesty, and that I should advise him, in a public or private manner, of the fact, in order that, if the thing were true, provision should be made for fulfilling whatever directions had been left on the matter.
>
> To which I replied, that it was true that I had the charge of a boy, the son of a gentleman a friend of mine, who had placed him under my care years ago; and that, as His Majesty had made no mention of him either in his will or codicil, the report must be taken for an idle rumour; which was the only answer I could give, either in a public or private manner. And although I am aware that Your Majesty knows what the state of the case is, and the inconveniences which may result from any such publication of it, yet for the sake of explaining why I have written as aforesaid, and because I know through other channels that the matter has been talked about, I have thought it right to advise Your Majesty of what has passed, in order that it may be evident that I have done my duty.[2]

Quijada's next task was to discharge the Emperor's servants, settle his bills, and carry out the hundred-and-one duties entailed upon one in his position in such circumstances: these functions having been duly performed he with his wife and household returned to Villagarcia, doubtless with many speculations on his part regarding what the future might have in store for the boy who had been committed to his charge.

[1] *ibid.*, vol. ii, p. 506.
[2] *ibid.*, vol. i, p. 446.

He was soon to learn. Hardly had he arrived at Villagarcia than he was summoned by the Princess Regent to Valladolid to meet the other executors of her father's will, and arrange the details of its fulfilment. While he was there he wrote, on December 13th, a letter to the King which speaks for itself.

I find the affairs of the person, whom Your Majesty knows to be in my charge, so publicly spoken of here that I am greatly surprised; and I am even more surprised by the minute facts which I hear on the subject. I came hither, fearing that the most serene Princess might press me to tell her what I know about it; but, not being at liberty to tell the whole truth, I determined to hold my tongue, and say nothing more than I had already said and had advised Your Majesty of from Yuste. But Her Highness has had the great goodness, up to this time, not to speak a word to me about the matter; and so I have no trouble in making answer to those who ask me questions, only this – that I know nothing of what people say, and that if there is anything in it, it ought to be known to the Princess. But His Majesty's wish, that Your Majesty may know it, was, that this matter should be kept secret until Your Majesty come hither, when Your Majesty's pleasure might be done.

I do nothing likely to excite observation, or beyond what was done in the life of the Emperor; but I take great care that the lad should learn and be taught all that is necessary and belonging to his age and quality; for, on account of the obscure manner in which he was nurtured and has lived since he came into my charge, the greatest pains must be taken with him. And therefore I have thought it right to inform Your Majesty of what is passing, and of his late Majesty's intentions, that Your Majesty may be aware of it, and instruct me how to proceed. Ten days ago he had a bad attack of double tertian fever; but, God be thanked, I came yesterday from home, and left him free from fever and out of danger.[1]

The only written declaration of the Emperor with regard to Don John was contained in a paper which may be considered as

[1] *ibid.*, vol. i, pp. 449–50.

a codicil to his will, although it did not form part of that document:

Besides what is contained in my will, I say and declare that, when I was in Germany, and being a widower, I had, by an unmarried woman, a natural son, who is called Jerome, and that my intention has been and is, for certain reasons moving me thereto, that if it can be fairly accomplished, he should, of his free and spontaneous will, take the habit of some order of reformed friars, and that he should be put in the way of so doing, but without any pressure or force being employed towards him. But if it cannot be so arranged, and if he prefers leading a secular life, it is my pleasure and command that he should receive, in the ordinary manner each year, from twenty to thirty thousand ducats from the revenues of the kingdom of Naples; lands and vassals, with that rent attached, being assigned to him.

The whole matter, both as to the assignment of the lands and the account of the rent, is left to the discretion of my son, to whom I remit it, or, failing him, to the discretion of my grandson, the Infante Don Carlos, or the person who, in conformity with my will, shall at the time it is opened, be my heir. If at that time the said Jerome shall not have already embraced the state which I desire for him, he shall all the days of his life enjoy the said rent and lands, which shall pass to his the legitimate heirs and successors descending from his body. And whatever state the said Jerome shall embrace, I charge the said Prince my son, and my said grandson, and my heir, whosoever it may be, as I have said, at the opening of my will, to do him honour and cause him to be honoured, and that they show him fitting respect, and that they observe, fulfil, and execute in his favour that which is contained in this paper. The which I sign with my name and hand; and it is sealed and sealed up with my small private seal; and it is to be observed and executed like a clause of my said will. Done in Brussels, on the sixth day of the month of June, 1554.

Son, grandson, or whoever at the time that this my will and writing is opened, and according to it, may be my heir, if you do not know where this Jerome may be, you can learn it from Adrian, groom of my chamber, or, in case of his death, from Oger, the porter of my chamber, that he may be treated conformably to the said will and writing.[1]

This document, together with three others, would appear to have been handed by Charles to Philip when the Emperor left the Netherlands for Spain in September, 1556; folded up with it was the receipt given by Massi, and it was sealed with the Emperor's seal, being endorsed, 'This my writing is to be opened only by the Prince, my son, and failing him by my grandson, Don Carlos; and failing him by whosoever shall be my heir, conformably to and at the opening of my will.' The other three documents were unsealed, and were in no way concerned with Don John. The whole packet contained an endorsement by Philip in his own handwriting and signed by him with the words 'If I die before His Majesty this packet to be delivered to him; if after him to my son, or, failing him, to my heir.' In all the circumstances Sir William Stirling-Maxwell well summed up the position when he said that the arrangement was 'creditable to the good feeling and good sense of Charles V'.

By now it had become obvious that the secret of Don John's identity could not be preserved much longer, for rumours were flying all over Valladolid. The Princess Regent's curiosity was not to be baulked, and it was arranged between her and Quijada that she should make the acquaintance of her brother at an *auto-da-fé* which was to take place in the capital in May, 1559. Doña Magdalena de Ulloa came to Valladolid for this event, and she brought Don John with her. When the ceremony was over the Princess Regent asked the boy to accompany her to the palace, and when he proceeded to do so he naturally attracted the attention of the crowd, who broke through the line of pikemen and musketeers in their eagerness to see the reputed son of the Emperor. When the day's events were at an end he went back to Villagarcia.

There he remained for the next few months, but there was, on Quijada's orders, a slight difference in the treatment accorded to

[1] cf. Weiss, M. W., *Papiers d'état du Cardinal de Granvelle*, vol. iv, pp. 496–8. Paris, 1841–52.

him, and the seat of honour was henceforth on all occasions reserved for him: at the same time, on Philip's express instructions, no change was made in the boy's dress, nor was he informed of the reason why he had suddenly been transformed into a subject of private and public consideration and curiosity. On July 8th, 1559, Quijada wrote a letter to the King which throws some light on Don John's life at that time. It was in reply to one from Philip asking him to hand over a mule which the Emperor had borrowed in Flanders, and taken to Spain. Quijada answered that this she-mule, a blind pony, and a little he-mule had been put aside by him, at the desire of his late master, for the use of 'the person whom Your Majesty is aware of'. He continued:

Some time ago the most serene Princess desired me to give up this she-mule to Dr Cornelio; but I excused myself for not doing so, for the above reason, which likewise prevented these three animals being sold with the rest. And Your Majesty may be sure that if it had not been His Majesty's desire, I would not, on my own authority have interfered in the matter. The mule is very useful, and the more so because she is very gentle, and the rider somewhat frolicsome. The person in my charge is in good health, and, in my opinion, is growing, and, for his age, of an excellent disposition. He proceeds with his studies with much difficulty, and there is nothing which he does with so much dislike; but he is learning French, and the few words that he knows he pronounces very well; yet to acquire it, as Your Majesty desires, much time and more application is needed. Riding on horseback both in the military style and in that of the manège is his chief delight, and when Your Majesty sees him you will think that he tilts in good style, although his strength is not great.[1]

Philip must certainly have formed a good opinion of the brother whom he had not yet seen, for when on August 29th he held a Chapter of the Golden Fleece in the old castle of the Counts of Flanders at Ghent he included him among the fourteen new members of the Order. Of these, nine were invested on the spot,

[1] cf. Gachard, M., *Retraite et Mort de Charles V*, vol. ii, pp. 513–14. Brussels' 1854–5.

and the badges of the remaining five were to be transmitted to them in their absence: these latter were Francis II of France, and his brother who was to succeed him as Charles IX; Eric, Duke of Brunswick; Joachim, Baron Neuhaus, Grand Chancellor of Bohemia; and Don John. The insignia for Don John were to be taken by the King to Spain, and conferred by him in person.

Philip arrived in Valladolid in the middle of September, and at once made arrangements for his brother to be presented to him. For some obscure reason this was to be done while he was out hunting. Quijada accordingly made the necessary arrangements, and on the morning that he and Don John were to meet the King he told his wife of the boy's identity. Quijada seems to have loved a mystery, for just before the monarch made his appearance he dismounted, and told Don John to do the same. He then knelt down in front of the boy, and asked leave to kiss his hand, saying, 'You will soon learn from the King himself why I do this.' Don John hesitated, and then held out his hand. At this moment a groom appeared with a fresh horse, which Quijada told him to mount: this the boy did with alacrity, and laughingly said to his guardian, 'Then since you will have it, you may also hold the stirrup.'

Don John was only twelve, and he must have wondered what all this portended, but he was not given long to ponder upon the question for shortly afterwards the King approached. Quijada and his charge dismounted, and the latter was ordered to kiss the Royal hand. 'Do you know who your father was?' Philip asked, but his new-found brother was too much abashed to reply, so the King got off his horse, and embraced the boy warmly with the words, 'Good, you are the son of a great man. The Emperor Charles V, who is now in Heaven, was the father of both of us.' He then made an announcement to his entourage and the brothers rode back to Valladolid together; during the ride Philip remarked, 'Never have I hunted game more to my liking.'[1]

For the future Don John was treated like royalty, and he had his own establishment in Valladolid, at the head of which was Quijada. It was all very much in the grand Burgundian style

[1] cf. Ossorio, A., *Vida de Don Juan de Austria*, pp. 14–15. Madrid, 1946.

which had been introduced into Spain by Philip I, and somewhat reluctantly adopted by Philip II, though there is no reason to suppose that it was in any way displeasing to Don John. In attendance, service, and privilege he was treated as an Infante of Castille, but in one or two matters there was a difference: for instance he was addressed as His Excellency instead of as His Highness, he did not live in the Palace, and he was not allowed to sit within the curtains of the Royal tribune in the Chapel Royal.

He was not, however, destined to see much more of Valladolid, for Philip went on a visit to Aranjuez and Toledo, and took his brother with him. On February 2nd, 1560, the King met at Guadalajara his third wife, Elizabeth of Valois, and he never used Valladolid as his capital again; indeed, it was not until the last years of his life, in 1592, that he returned to the city of his birth.[1] For some time the removal of the capital had been under consideration, and what seems to have turned the scales against Valladolid was the alleged insalubrity of its air. The King would have preferred Toledo, but before long he came to the conclusion that it was unhealthy too, and his choice then fell on Madrid, to which he accordingly removed himself, and where a huge house belonging to Don Pedro de Porras, which later became the residence of the Duke of Lerma, was assigned to Don John. Shortly afterwards, it may be added, on September 21st, 1561, the old capital suffered the disaster of a fire, when no less than 440 houses went up in flames.[2]

It was at this time that Don John may be said to have had his first lesson in politics, for at Toledo the King met the Cortes of Castille with two objects in view, one of them was to obtain a subsidy and the other was in order that they might take the oath of allegiance to Don Carlos as heir to the throne. After a detailed analysis of the financial state of the kingdom when he succeeded his father, and a description of the Turkish menace, Philip concluded with a request for a subsidy sufficient to build a fleet for

[1] cf. Arribas Arranz, F., *Años de Carlos V y Felipe II en Valladolid*, p. 19. Madrid, 1945.

[2] cf. Arribas Arranz, F., *El Incendio de Valladolid en 1561, passim.* Valladolid, 1960.

the defence of the Mediterranean seaboard. The *procuradores* thanked him for the frankness of his exposition, and promised to do what he wanted, but all the same several months elapsed before they voted him the extraordinary sum of 1,200,000 ducats spread over the following three years. The taking of the oath to Don Carlos raised no complications.

Don Carlos was the only child of Philip and his first wife, Maria of Portugal, and as he was born in July, 1545, he was only some eighteen months older than his uncle. His mother died a few days after his birth, and as his father was for the most part out of the country he was brought up by his aunt Juana, the Princess of the Brazils. Rightly or wrongly, she seems to have come to the conclusion that the boy was delicate, and in consequence she spoiled him, to the neglect of his education. Anyhow, when Charles V was at Valladolid on his way to Yuste, although he admired his grandson's spirit he was far from happy at his wayward and overbearing temper, and he told his daughter that if she would take a stronger line with her nephew the Spanish nation would have reason to thank her. All the same there would not up to that time appear to have been anything abnormal about Don Carlos, and his faults could be attributed to his upbringing.

He seems by all accounts to have behaved with becoming propriety when the oath of allegiance was taken to him at Toledo, for when his aunt and Don John went to kneel to kiss his hand he would not allow it, but affectionately raised and embraced them. Don John, it is to be noted, was on this occasion officially announced as 'the most illustrious Don John of Austria, natural son of the Emperor-King'. It is true that a slight incident marred the obeisance of the Duke of Alba at the ceremony, for whether owing to thoughtlessness or design he was proceeding to omit the kissing of the Prince's hand when Don Carlos left him in no doubt that he had better comply with the normal custom. The young man, however, can hardly be blamed for acting in this manner in such circumstances: for after the anarchy of the preceding century, largely caused by the turbulence of the nobles, it was essential to the Crown that they should not only be kept in their places, but that they should appear to be kept in their places.[1]

[1] cf. Gachard, M., *Don Carlos et Philippe II*, vol. i, p. 69. Brussels, 1853.

Early in November, 1561, Philip decided that it was time that his son and his brother received some more regular education, so he sent them both to the University of Alcalá, and with them went Alexander Farnese, Prince of Parma, who was the same age as Don Carlos. Alcalá was a new university compared with Salamanca and Valladolid, for it had been founded by Cardinal Ximénes as recently as 1510, but it had already attained considerable fame as a seat of learning, and was causing its older rivals to look to their laurels.[1] Alcalá was also to have another claim upon the attention of posterity, for it was there that Cervantes had been born fourteen years before, though he was no longer living there when Don John, his future commander at Lepanto, took up his residence in the town.

Don John and his nephew were housed in the palace built by Ximénes for his successors in the primacy of Spain, but at the moment it was empty because the existing Archbishop of Toledo, Bartolemé de Carranza, had fallen foul of the Inquisition, and was being held *incommunicado* at Valladolid: Parma, it may be added, occupied other quarters in the town. The studies of the three young men – or boys which is what they really were – were supervised by Honorato Juan, who had himself been a pupil of Vives, and was eventually to be rewarded for his labours with the see of Osma. Of the three students the least promising was Don Carlos, and the most was probably Alexander Farnese, who had a charming personality in addition to a very good brain. Don John seems to been more at home on the sports field than in the classroom, but he stayed at the university until he was well into his eighteenth year.

Sir William Stirling-Maxwell is sceptical with regard to his studies there. 'The training of Honarato Juan and the professors of Alcalá does not seem to have imbued Don John with any abiding love of letters. No trace of such tastes is to be found in the remains of his familiar correspondence. To his friend Rodrigo de Mendoza,[2] to whom he unbosomed his inmost thoughts and hopes, he wrote about his mode of conducting political affairs, his

---

[1] The University was removed to Madrid in 1836.

[2] Gentleman of the Bedchamber to Philip II, and grandson of the fourth Duke of Infantado: died 1586.

prospects, his mistress, his horses and his horse-furniture; but the existing letters do not contain a single allusion to books. The sole evidence that he ever opened one, that has met my eye, is a passage in a letter to Secretary Sayas, in which he desires that a copy of Fray Luis de Granada in Spanish may be sent to him. But as the request is coupled with a desire that a confessor should also come to him, "if possible by Christmas", it is probable that the volume was rather for devotional purposes than for literary recreation'.[1] If this is a correct estimate he would seem to have changed little from the days when Quijada had written that "he proceeds with his studies with much difficulty, and there is nothing which he does with so much dislike".'

During this period an event took place of which the repercussions resounded round the chancelleries of Europe as they have since done in the pages of history. One evening in the spring of 1562 Don Carlos was descending a flight of stairs when he missed his footing, fell the last five or six, and struck his head against a door at the bottom. Whether this was in consequence of an assignation with the porter's daughter, a subject upon which a good deal of ink has been wasted, is quite immaterial; he was found insensible, and was critically ill for some weeks afterwards. Whether his ultimate, though incomplete, recovery was due to medical skill, and if so to which of the doctors who attended him, or whether it was the result of ghostly intervention, has been argued down the ages, and the late W. T. Walsh devoted no less than thirteen pages to arguing the point,[2] which is surely not of great importance. Whether the behaviour of Don Carlos was more unpredictable before or after his illness is disputable, but it seems clear that the blow on the head did some permanent injury to the brain.

Meanwhile now that Don John, who was no longer to be known by the name of Jerome, was in close proximity to his brother, the King took steps to carry out the Emperor's intention that the young man should enter the Church, and early in 1564 he asked Pope Pius V to confer a Cardinal's hat on him. The Pope promised compliance, but shortly afterwards a quarrel arose between the

[1] *Don John of Austria*, vol. ii, pp. 351-2. London, 1883.
[2] *Philip II*, pp. 323-38. New York, 1937.

Papal and Spanish Courts on an entirely different matter; in consequence diplomatic relations between Madrid and the Vatican were suspended, and the proposal remained in abeyance, much to the satisfaction of Don John. In the following year the Turks attacked Malta, and Don John asked to be allowed to join the expedition which was being organized for its relief. Philip refused, on the ground that he was far too young, and that in any case he was destined for the Church. For the first, but not for the last, time Don John determined to defy his brother.

Accompanied by only two attendants he slipped quietly away with the intention of going to Barcelona and embarking upon the fleet which was gathering there: however, he went down near Zaragoza with a tertian fever, to which he would appear to have been prone, and was there overtaken by a messenger from the King, who also brought a letter from Quijada, urging him to return. Don John proved obstinate, and insisted on continuing his journey to Barcelona, only to find on his arrival there that the fleet had already sailed: this meant that the only way of reaching Sicily where the main expedition was being fitted out was to travel overland through France, and as the French Government favoured the Turks such a journey would be attended by manifest risks. At this point, too, a formal order arrived from Philip that he was to return to the Court at once under pain of disgrace, and in these circumstances Don John felt that he had better not run counter to his brother's wishes any longer, so he reluctantly did what he was told. Philip, whose forbearance where Don John was concerned was always remarkable, received him kindly, and told him to go and kiss the Queen's hand, which he proceeded to do, only to be laughingly asked if he had found the Turks to be doughty warriors.[1] Nevertheless the escapade had done the young man no harm in the eyes of his fellow-countrymen, for in spite of a personal feeling of frustration he had proved that he had inherited his father's spirit.

At this time he also had impressed upon him the need for tact where his immediate relatives were concerned, for, as relations between the King and Don Carlos became increasingly more strained, his own position became increasingly more difficult. It

[1] cf. Gachard, M., *Don Carlos et Philippe II*, vol. i, pp. 169–70. Brussels, 1863.

is not easy to discover the exact terms on which the two young men were with one another, and stories of differences between them have been handed down to posterity just as they were bandied about Madrid. On one occasion we are told that Don Carlos shouted at his uncle, 'I cannot argue with an inferior. Your mother was a harlot, and you are a bastard,' to which came the ready reply, 'At any rate my father was a greater man than yours.' According to one version Don Carlos at once rushed off to complain to his father, according to another the King at that moment appeared on the scene as the *deus ex machina* that he is depicted by Calderón in *El Alcalde de Zalamea*; however this may be, he is reported to have composed the quarrel with some such words as, 'Don John is right, and you are wrong. His father and mine was a far greater man than yours has ever been or ever will be.' On another occasion Don John is said to have been apprehensive of a physical assault on the part of his nephew, and to have asked his brother what he should do if such were made: 'Forget that he is my son,' was the King's reply.[1]

That there were quarrels between the two young men may be taken for granted – they would have been more than human had such not been the case at their age – but it is easy to attach too much importance to them: after all Don Carlos was apparently becoming extremely unbalanced even before his accident, and after it he was at times quite impossible. What does seem clear is that Don John rarely lost his self-control, and whatever quarrels he had with his nephew would not appear to have originated with him.

It was another matter when the heir to the throne became implicated in politics, and between his brother and his nephew, Don John had no doubt where his duty lay. The crisis came at the end of 1567. Earlier that year, in the hope that an occupation might work a cure in his son, Philip had appointed him to be President of the Council of State, but he proved to be quite unfitted for any such responsibility, though it may unfortunately have given him a taste for politics. Whether or not he was in negotiation with the malcontents in the Low Countries has never been proved, but the balance of probability is that he was; otherwise

[1] cf. Ossorio, A., *Vida de Don Juan de Austria*, pp. 16–22. Madrid, 1946.

it is not easy to see why the idea of going there should have occurred to him. At any rate on Christmas Eve he informed Don John of his intention to leave Spain for Germany. Philip was at that time at the Escorial, and his brother at once went there to tell him what was afoot. Thereafter events moved rapidly: the King proceeded to consult a small panel of casuists and jurists about the action he should take, and in consequence of the advice they gave him he had Don Carlos arrested on January 19th of the following year. From that moment he was dead to the world, which saw him no more, and on July 25th, 1568, he died: there is not a shred of evidence that he was murdered on his father's orders, as Philip's detractors have maintained.[1] Of one thing there can be no doubt, and it is that Don John took the only possible course in these tragic circumstances: to have connived at the plans of his nephew would have been High Treason, and wholly contrary to the interests of Spain.

Young men with no fixed occupation are liable to go astray where the opposite sex is concerned, and Don John was no exception, for it was at this time that he had a *liaison* with an aristocratic young lady, Maria de Mendoza, and as a result of it he became the father of a baby girl to whom was given the name of Ana. The King had of late become rather strait-laced in matters of this sort, so the child was hustled off into the country where she was looked after by Magdalena de Ulloa at Villagarcia *para no dar motivo de disgusto a Felipe II*.[2] There she remained for several years until she was placed in a convent of Augustinian sisters at Madrigal, where, in 1594, she became involved in a very singular intrigue.

In September of that year a mysterious individual who called himself Gabriel made his appearance in Valladolid, and at once proceeded to act in a highly suspicious manner; he seemed to be about fifty, and was at great pains to impress upon those whom he met that he was far from being the humble person they took

---

[1] cf. Petrie, Sir Charles, *Philip II of Spain*, pp. 158–61. London, 1963.

[2] Ossorio, A., *Vida de Don Juan de Austria*, p. 30. Madrid, 1946. The King did not know of her existence until after his brother's death when he was informed of it by Parma with the laudable intention of furthering the child's interest: Philip then authorized her to add 'of Austria' to her Christian name, cf. Mul-acén, Marqués de, *Don Juan de Austria, Politico e Innovador*, pp. 63–64. Madrid, 1944.

him for. One day in evidence of his claim he produced some jewellery, including a beautifully painted miniature of a nun with a pet dog on her lap. 'Look,' he said, 'how beautiful she is, the greatest beauty in Spain; and though she is a nun she can marry if she pleases, and the mightiest of princes could not marry anyone more lovely.' 'But,' queried one of the women who was listening to him, 'how can she marry if she is a nun?' 'Oh!' replied Gabriel, 'there are no laws to bind Kings; besides, when this lady entered the cloister she protested that she did so against her will.' This was the sort of talk which might lead to trouble with the Inquisition, quite apart from any suspicion that Gabriel might be a thief, or at any rate a receiver of stolen property, so he soon found that the circle of his acquaintances had become considerably restricted.

All the same Spain is not a country of the reticent, even in Castille, and gossip about the mysterious stranger went the rounds of Valladolid, until one day at the beginning of October a woman of easy virtue reported to the *alcalde* that Gabriel, who was a client of hers, was in possession of a suspiciously large amount of money, with which he was extremely free; not that she objected to this as she was presumably one of the recipients, but she was afraid that the money was stolen, and she did not wish to be implicated if the theft came to light.

The *alcalde* agreed that the circumstances were extremely odd, so he sent two of his *alguaciles* to arrest this man of mystery, but when they reached his lodgings they found that he had left, and they were further informed that it was not his custom to spend more than a night or two in any one place. This was highly suspicious, so the search was intensified, and at about two o'clock in the morning Gabriel was found at a very low-down *posada*; he was told to get up, dress, and accompany the officers to the Town Hall, and while he was putting on his clothes they noticed, with an acumen worthy of Sherlock Holmes, not only that his linen was remarkably fine for one of his station, but that the collar and cuffs of point lace were fastened to the shirt in the manner affected by the rich, and were not detachable for greater convenience in washing as in the case of the poor. Needless to say the room was searched, and a number of remarkable objects came to light, among them some gifts from the Royal Family – one of them from the King himself – to Ana of Austria, the daughter of Don John.

When in due course Gabriel was examined before the *alcalde* he was at once called upon to account for all this wealth. 'I am,' he declared, 'a pastry-cook, in business in the town of Madrigal, eight leagues away, and my name is Gabriel de Espinosa. The jewels are the property of the Princess Ana of Austria, who is a nun in the convent of Madrigal, and Her Highness has entrusted them to me for sale.' He was next asked why he had changed his lodging, to which he replied, 'Because I found the hostess dirty.' This did not satisfy the *alcalde* who clearly was not public health-minded, and he interjected, 'But why should a mere pastry-cook care whether the hostess was dirty or not?' This touched Gabriel in a tender spot, and he retorted, 'It is precisely because I am a pastry-cook that it behoves me to be more scrupulous of cleanliness than another.' He had scored there, but the last word lay with the *alcalde* who had the power, and he forthwith committed him to prison. When Gabriel heard this he took a high tone, and said, 'Take care what you do, the King will not approve if you thus treat a person of honour.' The *alcalde* was not impressed, and merely observed, 'You have given yourself out as a pastry-cook, and as such you shall be treated until we find out that you are anything better, and you shall then receive such honour as you are entitled to.'

The scene next shifted to Madrigal, where a few hours later a packet of letters addressed to Gabriel were seized by the authorities, and their contents were sufficient evidence that something sinister was afoot.

Two of the letters were from a Portuguese Augustinian friar, Miguel dos Santos, a notable figure of the time, who was now confessor of the convent of Madrigal. In earlier days he had been Provincial of his Order in Portugal, and chaplain to King Sebastian, Philip's nephew, who had perished, or at any rate disappeared, at the disastrous battle of Alcazar-el-Kebir in 1578. When the contest for the vacant Portuguese throne took place two years later, Friar Miguel had supported Don Antonio against Philip, and when the Pretender's cause had gone down before

Alba, he had suffered a term of imprisonment, which was, however, modified by this assignment to Madrigal where it would
have appeared that he was politically harmless.

The other two letters were from Ana of Austria herself to
Gabriel de Espinosa. They marked her as an ambitious and
romantic young lady, as became the daughter of Don John and
the granddaughter of Charles V. She had never had any inclination towards a religious vocation, and she had often been sought
in marriage, among others by the son of the Duke of Alba; but
for reasons of State her uncle was determined that she should not
marry. At the same time she was given many privileges within
the convent of Madrigal, and was treated as a Royal personage:
nevertheless she was rarely allowed outside, and such conversa-
tions as she had with male visitors had to be conducted with two
grilles between her and them. Ana was only twenty-six, and,
according to all accounts, extremely attractive: Philip was not
taking any risks.

If the fact that these important people should be in correspondence with a pastry-cook was astonishing the contents of the letters
themselves were little short of sensational, for Gabriel was referred
to in them as 'His Majesty', and there were mysterious allusions
to a small girl who was under the care of Ana of Austria. The
letter from Ana to Gabriel was couched in the most impassioned
strain. 'I am yours, sire, as you know already,' she wrote. 'The
faith I have pledged to you I will keep as sacred as my baptism,
through life and death for ever, for death itself shall not tear it
from my soul, which shall cherish it for all eternity. I am so sure
that Your Majesty belongs to me, and will never forget me, that I
would fain beseech you to divert yourself and take pleasure, for
your life does not belong to you alone, but to us all.' There were
many pages phrased in this vein, and it also transpired that money
was to be raised by the sale of jewellery for the purpose of some
journey. The *alcalde* was not unnaturally mystified, so he decided
that the best thing was to send a full report to the King; meanwhile he saw to it that Gabriel was kept under lock and key in
spite of the objections raised by Ana of Austria.

Philip was not at all mystified, and he saw at once that the whole
affair was a plot to marry Gabriel and Ana, smuggle them out of

the country, and then have them recognized as the missing King Sebastian of Portugal and his Queen. To prevent this he took immediate action: all concerned were placed under the closest arrest, and were carefully isolated from one another. As there were difficulties in the examination of ecclesiastics by lay magistrates the King sent down to conduct the investigation his own almoner, Dr Llano Valdes, who was also the Apostolic Commissioner of the Holy Office, with full powers from the Papal nuncio and the Inquisition to submit any clergy to examination, and even if necessary to put them to the torture.

Dr Llano went to work with a will, and he certainly did not fail to use the rack, though how near he got to the truth is another matter. Ana of Austria was not, of course, tortured, and she seems to have given as good as she got, even to the extent of writing to Philip accusing the doctor and his secretary of carrying on a flirtation with a couple of pretty young nuns in the convent. Friar Miguel proved quite useless as a witness, for he incriminated everybody, but what he said on the rack he retracted when he was taken off it. Gabriel never revealed his real identity, and his answers, except in moments of delirious pain, were always enigmatical. Clearly there was a conspiracy to restore the independence of Portugal, but its exact nature probably remained as obscure to Philip as it has done to posterity.

In July, 1595, the sentences were promulgated, and their severity was proof of the importance which the King attached to the affair. Ana of Austria was condemned to strict seclusion and silence in a distant convent for eight years, without servants or attendants, and was to be for ever incapacitated from being the head of a community, while she was to fast on bread and water every Friday, and to be divested of all the honours and consideration hitherto paid to her rank. This punishment, it may be added, brought forth many protests in the highest circles in Madrid. She was not, however, destined to serve her full sentence, for three years later the King died, and Philip III took compassion on her: she was in consequence removed to the great Benedictine nunnery of Las Huelgas near Burgos of which she became perpetual abbess, and there she passed the remainder of her life.

Her two fellow-conspirators fared considerably worse. The

Friar was condemned to be degraded, led with ignominy through the streets of Madrid, and hanged in the Plaza Mayor, while Gabriel de Espinosa was to be hanged, drawn, and quartered in the main square of Madrigal, and his head affixed to a post: both these sentences were duly carried out. It is difficult to condemn Philip for acting so drastically in the circumstances: he knew better than anyone the strength of those centrifugal forces which are never far below the surface of Spanish life, and having completed the work of the Catholic Sovereigns by the incorporation of Portugal in his dominions he was not going to run the risk of having it undone. As for the methods by which the conspirators were examined and punished, repellent as these may be to the taste of the twentieth century, they would have fared no better had they plotted against a Tudor or a Valois.[1]

All this, however, is to anticipate, for Don John had long been in his grave before his daughter and her associates began to plot against his brother. Meanwhile he had evidently managed to conceal from that brother his *liaison* with Ana's mother, and he had impressed Philip most favourably with his discretion in the affair of Don Carlos: now, at the age of twenty-one, he had his reward, for he was appointed, in succession to the ageing Don Garcia de Toledo, General of the Sea, which meant, in effect, commander-in-chief of the Spanish Navy. At the same time he received the following letter from Philip for his guidance:

Brother,

In addition to the instruction which you have already received as to what concerns the charges of Captain-General of the Sea, and the duties and exercise of it, on account of the great love which I bear you, and my great desire that both in your position, life, and habits, you should possess the esteem and good reputation at which persons of your quality ought to aim, to this end it has seemed right to me to advise you of that which I shall here set down.

First, because the foundation and beginning of all things and

[1] The account of this conspiracy is based upon Hume, Martin, *True Stories of the Past*, pp. 75–99, London, 1910, and Ossorio, A., *Vida de Don Juan de Austria*, pp. 307–12. Madrid, 1946.

all good counsel is God, I charge you to take, like a good and true Christian, this beginning and foundation in all that you undertake and do; and that you direct, as to your chief end, all your concerns and affairs to God, from whose hand must proceed all good, and the favourable and prosperous issue of all your voyages, enterprises, and days in the field. Be also careful to be very devout and God-fearing, and a good Christian, not only in reality and in substance, but also in appearance and seeming, giving a good example to all; for by this means and on this foundation God will give you grace, and your name and reputation shall ever have increase. You shall take especial heed to frequent and give attendance upon confession, particularly at Christmas and Easter, and other solemn days, and to receive the most holy Sacrament, being in such place and situation as admits of it, and to hear mass every day that you are on shore, and to perform your private devotions and prayers, with much privacy, at an hour appointed for the purpose, fulfilling in everything the duty and observance of a strict Catholic and a good Christian.

Truth in speaking and fulfilment of promises is the foundation of credit and esteem among men, and that upon which the confidence of society is supported and founded. This is more required, and is much more necessary in men of very high rank, and who fill great public posts; because upon their truth and good faith depend the public faith and security. I urge it upon you most earnestly, that in this you take great care and heed, that it should be well known and understood in all places and seasons that full reliance may and ought to be placed in whatever you say; and that this is of the greatest importance not only to the public affairs under your charge, but also to your private honour and estimation.

Administer justice equally and rightly, and when necessary, with the rigour and example which the case may require; showing, when needful, firmness and constancy; and when the nature of things and people concerned admit of it, be also pitiful and benignant, for these are virtues very proper to persons of your quality. Flattery, and words having that tendency, are ill-favoured in those who speak them, and disgraceful and offensive to those to whom they are spoken. To persons who are inclined to hold such language, and to address you thus, maintain a countenance and bearing which may let all men see how little acceptable to you are such words and speeches. Treat in the same way those who in your presence speak ill and carp at the honour and the persons of the absent, that you may afford no opening for such discourse and talk, because it is not only prejudicial and injurious to third parties, but it concerns your authority and esteem to put a stop to it.

You must also live and walk with great circumspection as regards your own personal purity of life, because in this there is not only an offence against God, but it brings with it and causes many troubles, and it greatly interferes with business and the fulfilment of duty, and from it often spring other occasions of danger, and evil consequence and example. Avoid as far as possible gaming, especially with dice and cards, for the sake of example to others, and because in this matter of gaming people cannot and do not act with the moderation and restraint which is required of persons of your degree; and many occasions occur in which men of high position lose their temper and lower themselves, of which loss of dignity is the result. I charge you, that if you should ever game for amusement, you observe in the pursuit the decorum due to your person and authority.

Swearing, without very strict and compelling necessity, is much to be reproved in men and women of all classes, and it injures their reputation and especially that of men of high rank in whom it is most unbecoming and detrimental to their credit, dignity, and authority; wherefore I charge you to be very careful in this matter of swearing, and in no way to use oaths by the name of God, and other extraordinary oaths, which are not used and ought not to be used by persons of your quality; and that you let the same be understood by all the gentlemen and other persons who attend you, both by example and precept, that they may conform to the same.

In what belongs to your table, food, and service, let everything be done with becoming decency, authority, and neatness;

but also with great moderation and temperance, on account of the example you must set to all of the warlike profession which you have embraced, and because temperance and moderation are advantageous to your bodily health, and because your table will be the rule and standard of the tables of your officers.

Be very careful to say to no man a word that can injure or offend him, and that your tongue be an instrument of honour and favour, and not of dishonour to anyone. Those who do wrong and transgress, let them be punished justly and reasonably; but this punishment must neither be inflicted by your mouth with insulting words, nor by your hand. Likewise you must be very careful, that in ordinary intercourse and converse with men, you use modesty and calmness, avoiding heat of temper and loud words, which derogate and detract much from the authority of persons of your rank. You must also see that your own conversation, and the conversation held in your presence, may be honest and decent, as befits your quality and authority. In like manner, you must beware that in your intercourse with men, in general, of all classes, you preserve, with an affable, gentle, and courteous deportment, the becoming dignity which is due to your person and charge; and that, with that affability which gains men's love, you likewise maintain the reputation and respect which you ought to possess.

In winter, and at other times when you are not sailing and are on shore, and in the absence of the duties of your charge, to which your principal attention ought to be given, you may occupy yourself in active exercise, especially that which belongs to arms, in which you will also cause the gentleman who live with you likewise to engage, by which means they may avoid expense, pomp, and excesses; and that all addicting themselves to the true exercise of arms may by practice become expert cavaliers, and fitted for the purposes and occasions which may offer. In like manner you must avoid, and order others to avoid, waste and excess in dress, and equipment, and living, setting an example in what belongs to your own person and your servants.

These are the matters of which it has occurred to me to

remind you, trusting that you will act better than I have written. This letter is for yourself alone, and for this reason is written with my own hand.

In Aranjuez, 23rd. of May, 1568,
I THE KING[1]

---

[1] Vanderhammen, Lorenzo, *Don Juan de Austria*, folios 42–44. Madrid, 1627.

3

Arms and Armaments in the Mediterranean

SINCE THE DISCOVERY OF AMERICA, AND THE EMERGENCE of England and the Dutch as naval Powers, civilization was beginning to pass from the thalassic to the oceanic stage, but the transition was only in its early phases in the sixties of the sixteenth century, and the Mediterranean had not yet lost the pre-eminence which it had held since Classical times. For a variety of reasons, of which the most important were the restricted size of the inland sea and the absence of tides, the type of warship employed was very different from that required elsewhere, and it naturally followed that the method of warfare was very different too.

On the Christian side the Republic of Saint Mark was the leading maritime Power, although at any one time her fleet in being was never very considerable. Her practice was to keep afloat and in commission only a small number of vessels which spent their time cruising in the Adriatic and the Levant, and which visited, supplied, and relieved the garrisons of her various forts and dependencies scattered about the Eastern Mediterranean: in Venice itself there were an arsenal and dockyard containing at least two hundred vessels which in theory at any rate could be fitted out at very short notice. This policy had much to recommend it, especially on the score of economy, but it was subject to two serious disadvantages: in the first place it often proved difficult to man this reserve fleet if it were required to put to sea at short notice, and secondly it exposed the ships themselves to the risk of fire while they were in what today would be called 'mothball'. For example, in September, 1569, an explosion in the arsenal was followed by a vast conflagration during the course of which considerable damage was done to the vessels which were laid up.

There was in the sixteenth century another method of providing men-of-war, and that was hiring them from individuals, in other words what a later age would have described as recourse to private enterprise. This was not favoured by the Serenissima, and for a very good reason. The captains of such galleys were by birth or connexion members of mercantile houses; they were at least as greedy of gain as of glory; they were apt to consider their own profit more than any injury they might inflict on the enemy; and they too often preferred the preservation of their craft to the success of their cause. The escape of the Turkish fleet at Prevesa in 1538, although hemmed in by the superior forces of the Pope, the Emperor, and Venice, had been widely attributed to Andrea Doria's reluctance to risk his own galleys, and in due course the same charge was to be preferred against his nephew, Gian Andrea Doria.

The Spanish Navy was also of the first importance in the Mediterranean, and it had inherited a great tradition from the fleets of Castille and Aragon in the fourteenth and fifteenth centuries. More recently Charles V had shown himself fully conscious of the value of sea-power, but his position in this respect had been seriously weakened by his disastrous expedition to Algiers in 1541, and in his later years his commitments in Central Europe prevented him from retrieving the situation. Philip, it is true, took the matter in hand as soon as peace was restored by the Treaty of Cateau-Cambrésis, but his father's ill-luck pursued him too, for at Gelves in 1560 his forces sustained a severe reverse at the hands of the Turks when seventeen of his ships were sunk, and twenty-four were compelled to strike their colours; this was bad enough, but two years later another twenty-three vessels were lost in a storm off Herradura, and the result of these catastrophes was that in 1563 the Spanish Navy was estimated at no more than thirty-four sail. Philip, however, was the last man to be disheartened by failure, and he patiently set to work to repair the damage, with the consequence that by 1570 he had some hundred sail at his disposal. That was the number which he wished to maintain, for experience proved that an armaments race with the Ottoman Sultan was at once very costly and served no particular purpose.

A marked feature of the Spanish Navy, by contrast with the

Venetian, was the large proportion of hired vessels which it contained. Many of these were furnished by the mercantile aristocracy of Genoa, who had long been in the habit of investing part of their wealth in men-of-war with the object of hiring them out to foreign Powers or of using them in private enterprises against the Turks or the Barbary Corsairs. The disadvantages of these hired ships have already been noticed, but the vessels which Philip hired cost him considerably less than those which he owned: for example, for each of Doria's galleys he paid 6,000 ducats a year, while the annual cost of his own was 6,700 ducats, exclusive of all charges for risk and for interest on the cost of construction.

The French Navy during the latter part of the sixteenth century was a negligible factor in the balance of power in the Mediterranean, but the Order of St John possessed a few vessels, as did the Pope, the Duke of Savoy, the Medici, and the Republic of Genoa: these were usually in the pay of the King of Spain.

On the Moslem side the Ottoman fleet was largely furnished by the Barbary Corsairs, for the native Turk is a land animal, and has never taken very kindly to the sea. Suleyman I had never spared money in the construction of his navy, but it had not attained the standard reached by the other Mediterranean Powers, and so he had been compelled to call in the assistance of such tough seamen as Dragut and Barbarossa, whom he feared more than he trusted: in fact they were used by the Sultan, it was said, as a doctor uses poison, that is to say cautiously, in small quantities, and together with other ingredients.

Some of these sea-captains were Greeks, and two of the most famous of them, the brothers Barbarossa, came from Lesbos. An exception was Dragut, who was born on the Caramanian coast opposite the island of Rhodes, and he seems to have been the son of a Mohammedan farm labourer. Otherwise his career followed much the same pattern as that of his contemporaries who rose to high naval command in the reign of Suleyman. He took service in the fleet when he was little more than a boy, and in due course he contrived to purchase and man a galleon, with which he cruised the waters of the Levant, where his intimate acquaintance with the coasts and islands enabled him to seize and dispose of many prizes. In due course his exploits reached the ears of Kheyr-ed-Din

Barbarossa, who gave him a hearty welcome when he came to pay his respects at Algiers, and eventually appointed him to the command of twelve galleys. 'From henceforward this redoubtable Corsair passed not one summer without ravaging the coasts of Naples and Sicily: nor durst any Christian vessels attempt to pass between Spain and Italy; for if they offered it, he infallibly snapped them up: and when he missed any of his prey at sea, he made himself amends by making descents along the coasts, plundering villages and towns, and dragging away multitudes of inhabitants into captivity.'[1]

His luck, however, varied, and in 1540 Dragut was taken prisoner and handed over to Andrea Doria, on whose galleys he was compelled to toil at the oar. One day he was noticed by La Valette, later Grand Master of Malta, who had himself served in the same capacity in one of Barbarossa's ships, and knew Dragut well. 'Señor Dragut,' he called, '*usanza de guerra*', to which the cheerful reply came, '*Y mudanza de fortuna.*' In 1543 Barbarossa ransomed Dragut for three thousand crowns, and promoted him to high command, when he soon gave proof that imprisonment had but served to sharpen his appetite for Christians.

It was these Corsairs who made the Turkish Navy the effective force which it was to remain during Don John's career. Kheyr-ed-Din went to Constantinople in 1533 and was received by Suleyman: he spent several months in the shipyards there, and was by no means pleased with what he saw, so he secured the Grand Vizier's permission to institute the necessary reforms, for he had come to the conclusion that the Turks knew neither how to build nor to fight their galleys. The ships were not so fast as those of the Christians, while the Osmanli, instead of turning sailors themselves and navigating their boats properly, were in the habit of pressing shepherds from Anatolia, who had never handled a sail or a tiller in their lives, and of entrusting the navigation of their galleys to these inexperienced hands.[2] Kheyr-ed-Din soon changed all this. He was provided with an abundance of workmen and timber, and, inspiring the former with his own marvellous energy, he secured the construction of sixty-one galleys that winter; as a result he

---

[1] Morgan, J., *A Complete History of Algiers*, p. 439. London, 1731.
[2] cf. Gravière, Admiral Jurien de la, *Les Corsaires Barbaresques*, p. 13. Paris, 1887.

was able to take the sea in the spring with a fleet of eighty-four vessels. The momentum given to Turkish shipbuilding during the months that Kheyr-ed-Din passed in the dockyards of Constantinople was not lost while Suleyman was on the throne.

The control which, with the help of the Corsairs, the Ottoman Sultan came to exercise along the North African coast was both a defensive and an offensive advantage to him. In the first capacity it constituted a threat to their flank whenever any of the Christian Powers undertook an expedition against the Ottoman Empire which by now circumscribed two-thirds of the shores of the Mediterranean, and in the second it provided him with an advanced base for any enterprises of his own, such as supplying help to the Moriscoes. Previously this littoral had been divided between a number of Moslem dynasties which had grown up on the collapse of the Almohad Empire in the middle of the thirteenth century, and of which the principal occupation was piracy, so that they were a perpetual menace to those engaged in commerce in the Mediterranean. The conquest of Granada first brought united Spain face to face with the problems of North Africa, and for reasons of security she had occupied a number of strong places there, such as Peñon de Alger, Oran, and Tripoli. However, just at the moment when everything appeared to be going all right everything started to go all wrong. In the second decade of the sixteenth century Selim I conquered Egypt, and this event was the signal for the appearance of the Barbarossa brothers, of Dragut, and of Piale, who sometimes operated on their own and sometimes on behalf of the Porte. Under their pressure both the local dynasties and the Spaniards were forced to give ground. Barbarossa took Algiers as early as 1516, and three years later his brother was recognized by Selim I as Governor-General of Algeria, though it is to be noted that the Spaniards held Peñon de Alger until 1550 and Oran until the opening years of the eighteenth century.

In Tunis the fortunes of war were more variable. The Hafsids had reigned there for three hundred years, and on the whole their rule had been mild and just; but the twenty-second ruler of the dynasty, Hasan, seems to have been an exception, for he reached the throne over the bodies of forty-four murdered brothers, and when he got there the only example he set was one of vicious

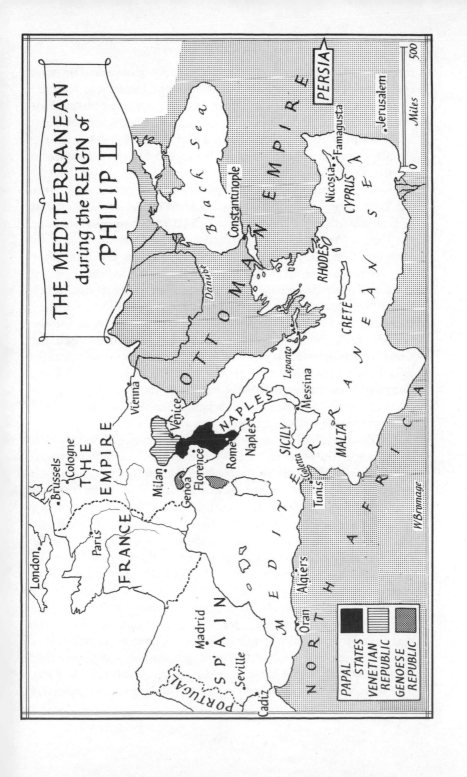

THE MEDITERRANEAN
during the REIGN of
PHILIP II

THE EMPIRE

FRANCE

London
Brussels
Cologne
Paris
Vienna
Milan
Venice
Genoa
Florence
Rome
Naples
Madrid
Seville
Cadiz

SPAIN

PORTUGAL

Danube

Black Sea

Constantinople

OTTOMAN EMPIRE

PERSIA

NAPLES

SICILY
Messina
Lepanto
Malta
CRETE
RHODES
CYPRUS
Nicosia
Famagusta
Jerusalem

AEGEAN SEA

MEDITERRANEAN

NORTH AFRICA

Oran
Algiers
Tunis
Goletta

W.Bromage

MALTA

0   500
Miles

PAPAL STATES

VENETIAN REPUBLIC

GENOESE REPUBLIC

feebleness. He was overthrown in 1534 by Kheyr-ed-Din who conquered Tunis in the name of the Sultan: Hasan was restored by Charles V in the following year, but the province remained for the most part in the hands of the Corsairs. Farther along the coast Tripoli had been detached from the kingdom of Tunis by the Spaniards in 1510, but it was added to the Ottoman Empire in the middle of the century.

These disasters changed the whole balance of power in the Mediterranean. Ferdinand and Isabella had hoped by the conquest of Granada to close the door by which Islam had so often invaded the Iberian Peninsula, and yet here were the Osmanli apparently sweeping along the coast of North Africa like the Ommeyad Caliphs in the seventh century. Nor was this all, for that Spanish command of the sea which had done so much to defeat the French in the Neapolitan campaigns had passed out of the hands of their successor, and the conquest of Egypt and the activities of the Corsairs had produced one of those rare situations when the Crescent was superior to the Cross at sea. In these circumstances it is hardly surprising that to the statesmen of Valladolid the Ottoman power should have appeared in the not inappropriate guise of a crescent, one horn of which pointed at Vienna and the other at the Straits of Gibraltar.

The fleets with which these various Powers fought one another consisted for the most part of light vessels propelled by oars, and they differed very little from those of Classical times. The war-galley of the sixteenth century was a craft of between 120 and 150 feet long, with a breadth of beam from fourteen to twenty feet, and provided with two or three masts. On the poop and forecastle, which were raised considerably above the deck, the guns were placed, and the musketeers fired their pieces. The prow was armed with a strong sharp-pointed beak, or *espolón*, ten to fourteen feet long, and plated with iron, thus being rendered a formidable instrument of attack when the boat was being driven forward by twenty to twenty-six pairs of long oars of which each was pulled by three to six pairs of arms. The rowers sat on benches that were firmly fixed between the ship's side and a strong central division which passed from stern to prow. Along this division, on a level with the rowers as they sat at their oars, ran a gangway on which the officers on duty paced the length of the ship. The rowers were partially screened from shot by high bulwarks; their benches were about four feet apart; and their oars were from thirty to forty feet long, of which one-third was within and two-thirds were outside the vessel. The armament consisted of a large traversing gun on the forecastle, flanked by two or four smaller pieces, while there were from ten to twenty other cannon of small calibre mounted on the poop. The large gun fired a ball of forty to sixty pounds, while the others were usually five- or ten-pounders.

The galley had a single deck, and below it the space was divided into six compartments as follows:

1. The cabin of the poop which was reserved for the use of the captain, the officers called the gentlemen of the poop, and distinguished passengers.
2. The second cabin where the inmates of the poop-cabin usually dined, and where they kept their wine and their effects.
3. The 'companion', where the salted provisions were stored.
4. The bread room.
5. The middle cabin.
6. The cabin of the prow. These last two formed one long compartment which was entered by two doors, one near the mast and the other near the forecastle: it was used for ammunition and marine stores, but it also contained berths for the sailors, as well as for the chaplain and the surgeon-barber.

A variation of the galley was the galleass, which was larger and of weightier construction. It was propelled by a similar number of oars, but they were placed at greater distances apart. The poop and forecastle were proportionately loftier and stronger, and in addition to the central gangway a narrow platform ran round the side of the vessel on which the musketeers could stand or kneel to fire through the loopholes of the bulwark. The galleass mounted between sixty to seventy guns, and of these three were heavy traversing guns which threw balls of fifty to eighty pounds in weight. The prow was armed with ten, and the poop with eight, smaller pieces, while the rest, thirty-to fifty-pounders, were placed between the benches of the rowers. The galleass was, indeed, a very effective instrument of war.

The galley and the galleass were both primarily dependent on oars, and looked back to Salamis; the ship relied upon sail, and looked forward to Trafalgar. It was of much more massive construction; of a more rounded form; and its hulk rose from the water to a height equal to one-third of its entire length. It possessed two gun-decks which ran the whole length of the vessel, over which the lofty poop and forecastle, also heavily armed, towered like fortresses. Then there was the brigantine, which was a small half-decked vessel with two masts, each carrying a large sail stretched on a yard longer than the mast; in addition there were thirty to thirty-four oars with one man at each: the armament consisted of two or three light guns. Lastly there was the frigate, which was a smaller type of brigantine, with fewer oars and a single mast.

In the sixteenth century a Mediterranean fleet was usually officered by an admiral and his vice-admiral; a commissary, who superintended the department of supplies and finance, and who had under him a purveyor, usually employed ashore; a paymaster; an auditor or criminal judge, whose place was in the last ship; a physician and his apothecary, who had charge of one or more hospital-vessels; and a butcher, whose business it was to select and kill fresh meat for the fleet.

Each ship was commanded by a captain, who had under his charge two or more young men of family, who were called gentlemen-of-the-poop, and who were serving their apprenticeship to the sea like the midshipmen of a later day; in the Venetian Navy it was the practice to allow two of these youths to a galley and four to a galleass. Next in rank was the master, who appears to have discharged the duties of first lieutenant, and after him came the boatswain and his mate, the pilot and his mates, and the driver of the galley-slaves: there were also, as we have seen, a chaplain and a barber-surgeon whose functions were what their names imply. Two artillerymen and their two assistants served the guns: there was an armourer to attend to the various weapons: and a staff of four carpenters looked after the galley itself. The crew consisted of eight sailors called helmsmen, together with eight first-class, and sixteen second-class, seamen.

Lastly, there were the wretches who pulled the oars. 'The galley-slavery of the Mediterranean was a marked and distinctive feature of the social life of the sixteenth century. For most of the southern States of Europe that branch of the naval service was used for purposes which are now attained by prisons, public works, and penal settlements.'[1] If the vessel were a Christian one the rowers would be Moorish or Turkish captives, or Christian convicts; if it were a Corsair they would all be Christian prisoners. In earlier days the galleys had been rowed by freemen, but then the boats were light, and a single man could pull the oar; but as the boats increased in size, and several men were needed for each oar, it was impossible to get freemen to do the work, and so recourse was had to slaves.

Think of six men chained to a bench, naked as when they were born, one foot on the stretcher, the other on the bench in front, holding an immensely heavy oar, bending forwards to the stern with arms at full reach to clear the back of the rowers in front, who bend likewise; and then having got forward, shoring up the oar's end to let the blade catch the water, then throwing their bodies back on the groaning bench. A galley oar sometimes pulls thus for ten, twelve, or even twenty hours without a moment's rest. The boatswain, or other sailor, in such a stress, puts a piece of bread steeped in wine in the wretched rower's mouth to stop fainting, and then the captain shouts the order to redouble the lash. If a slave falls exhausted upon his oar (which often happens) he is flogged till he is taken for dead, and then pitched unceremoniously into the sea.[2]

In the treatment which the galley-slaves received there was no difference in practice between the vessels of the Corsairs and those of the Christian Powers, and in neither was any respect shown to

[1] Stirling-Maxwell, Sir William, *Don John of Austria*, vol. i, p. 93. London, 1883.

[2] Such is the evidence of Jean Marteille de Bergerac, a galley-slave about 1701, as quoted by Gravière, Admiral Jurien de la, *Les Derniers Jours de La Marine à Rames*, p. 13. Paris, 1885.

education or rank. Side by side in common misery sat men like Dragut and the highest officials of the Sublime Porte on the one hand, and on the other a future Grand Master of Malta and a ruffian who stabbed for hire in the slums of Naples. It was not a sentimental age, and no contemporary seems to have expressed horror at a state of affairs where any man, however refined, was compelled to endure the vermin and ordure of his neighbour who might be half a savage. Indeed, when Madame de Grignan in the following century wrote an account of her visit to a galley, her friend Madame de Sevigné replied that she would 'much like to see this sort of Hell', and the men 'groaning day and night under the weight of their chains'. *Autres temps, autres moeurs!*

Some idea of the conditions obtaining in the Spanish service, which would seem to have been milder than elsewhere, may be obtained from the instructions issued to an admiral in the early years of the reign of Philip III. The officers in immediate charge of the convicts and slaves, if any of these managed to escape, were to supply substitutes at their own expense, or if that proved impossible they were to take the others' places at the oar themselves. Care was to be taken that the galley-slaves should be provided with good and sufficient food and clothing, and that they should not be employed, in port or during the winter, in work unconnected with the naval service. Neither convicts nor volunteers were to be detained beyond the terms for which they were condemned or had engaged to serve. Gentlemen, it was stated, were no longer to be punished by sentence to the galleys on account of the inconvenience which time had shown to arise from the practice, and if such persons were drafted they were not to be accepted. Adventurers serving as soldiers at their own expense were to be enrolled according to their capabilities and the needs of the service, and those of them who were too poor to maintain themselves might receive the King's rations.

Each galley was to be furnished with 11,000 ducats annually on account of expenses, and 1,000 more for extraordinary charges; this money was to be kept in a chest with four keys, and only disbursed under strict rules and close supervision. It was strictly forbidden to encumber the vessels with merchandise or unnecessary luggage. The arms were to be kept neat and clean, and were only to be issued to the soldiers when required for use. Extravagance was to be avoided in the wear and tear of flags, and in gilding and painting poops. The admiral himself was not to keep more than eight servants, that is to say the number that had been allowed to the Marquess of Santa Cruz, and these were to be able-bodied men enrolled among the soldiers, of whom forty served on board each galley. Officers and men were ordered to lead good and Christian lives under the inspection of the chaplain who was attached to each galley, and whose duty it was to confess them as well as to preach on suitable occasions; he was subject to the admiral's chaplain who dealt with general cases of heresy, but he was especially warned to see that men did not affect heterodoxy as a method of escaping from the oar.[1]

To understand the problem confronting Philip and Don John it must be remembered that although there were periods when Spain was at peace with the Sultan she was ever at war with the Corsairs, who never ceased to prey upon her coasts. Furthermore, they could always rely upon the co-operation of the Moriscoes in their depredations, and if there were any doubt upon this point we have the testimony of the Abbot Diego de Haedo, who lived in Algiers for many years during the latter part of the sixteenth century, and in 1612 published in Valladolid his *Topographia e historia de Argel* in which he says, 'They have utterly ruined and destroyed Sardinia, Corsica, Sicily, Calabria, the neighbourhoods of Naples, Rome, and Genoa, all the Balearic islands, and the whole coast of Spain, in which last more particularly they feast it as they think fit, on account of the Moriscoes who inhabit there; who all being more zealous Mohammedans than are the very Moors born in Barbary, they receive and caress the Corsairs, and give them notice of whatever they desire to be informed of.' Such being the case it was the obvious duty of the rulers of Spain to put an end to this nuisance: Philip II thought he had done so by the measures he adopted in his edict of October, 1570, but he was wrong, and it was not until his son expelled the Moriscoes from the country altogether that the object was achieved.

[1] *Instrucción al Conde de Niebla para el cargo de Capitán General de las Galeras de España, 1603. Documents Inéditos para la Historia de España*, vol. xxviii, pp. 393–418.

Thereafter, there was a marked diminution in the number of raids upon the coast of Spain, and with ships instead of galleys the Algerines tended to go farther afield, and to penetrate into the Atlantic: in 1631, Murād Reïs, a Flemish renegade, even sacked Baltimore in County Cork, and carried away 237 captives. 'It was a piteous sight,' wrote Father Dan, 'to see them exposed for sale at Algiers, for then they parted the wife from the husband, and the father from the child; then, I say, they sell the husband here, and the wife there, tearing from her arms the daughter whom she cannot hope to see ever again.'[1]

Where the land forces of the Mediterranean Powers were concerned the Spanish Army had been subject to many changes during the earlier years of the sixteenth century. In the Middle Ages it had conformed to the type usual in Western Europe, that is to say the predominant feature was the armed knight, while the infantryman mattered little, and was of no great account. There was, however, one distinctive feature, and that was the *jinete*, or light horseman, who proved extremely useful in action against the Moors, whose tactics were so similar to his own. It is also to be noted that the Spaniards had taken to the use of firearms much earlier than the French, English, or Italians.

The Italian wars soon proved that this system would have to be modified, for Gonsalvo de Córdoba realized that his *jinetes* were ineffectual against the massed columns of pikemen who on many a battlefield had proved themselves capable of withstanding the most determined charges of heavy cavalry. The consequence was that the hitherto despised infantryman once more came into his own, in the Spanish Army as elsewhere. For the sword, shield, and javelin which had been all that were needed in the conquest of Granada were substituted the pike and the arquebus. Under Gonsalvo de Córdoba the troops were organized in *coronelias*, of which each was in theory about a thousand strong, and was divided into four companies of two hundred and fifty mixed pikemen and arquebusiers with a certain number of 'sword and buckler' men. This formation, incidentally, introduced the word

[1] *Histoire de Barbarie et de ses Corsaires*, p. 277. Paris, 1649. This episode inspired Thomas Davis's well-known poem, *The Sack of Baltimore*. This was, of course, the period during which John Hampden was obtaining immortality for his refusal to pay Ship Money – a tax levied to prevent such happenings.

'colonel' in its various forms into military terminology, for the *coronelia* was commanded by a *cabo de colonela*, or 'head of a column'.

In 1534 the *coronelia* was replaced by the more famous *tercio*. Sir Charles Oman has written, 'Apparently the style came from the old military tradition that an army in array was divided into three divisions – van, main-battle, and rear. . . . A tercio, or third, was therefore a body sufficient to make up one of these normal divisions.'[1] It was really a brigade, for there were over three thousand men in each *tercio*, and they were all either pikemen or arquebusiers. The *tercios* were divided into ten or twelve companies, and the three senior ones were named Lombardy, Naples, and Sicily. The second of these acquired so bad a reputation for its lack of discipline that Philip ordered its disbandment in 1564, but it was re-formed some years later. In addition to the *tercios* the Spanish Army contained a number of regiments of very varying strength. The high proportion of foreigners in the Spanish service is also worthy of note, for on the death of Philip III in 1621 of the thirty-nine *tercios* then in existence only seven were Spanish, while of the others thirteen were Italian, eleven Walloon, two Burgundian, and two Irish, while there were also nine German regiments.

The human material, in so far as it was Spanish, could not have been better, for the Spaniards were sober and temperate, and they were more easily provided for than any other soldier of the day with the exception of the Turk: this was particularly important in the Neapolitan campaigns where the French were always at a disadvantage owing to their wastefulness and excess. Short in stature, but muscular and lissom, the Spanish soldier came mainly from mountainous districts, where seasons were very hot and very cold, and so he could stand climatic extremes, while his marching powers were remarkable. Uneducated the men might be, but they possessed great natural intelligence, and their musketry was always of a high standard. Their *esprit de corps* and sense of military honour were more exalted than in any other nation. At the same time Ferdinand V was unquestionably right when he said that Spanish troops required a very strong hand,

[1] *History of the Art of War in the Sixteenth Century*, p. 59. London, 1937.

73

and this was the more necessary because their pay was so frequently in arrears.

To turn to the Turkish Army is again to find the foot-soldier supreme in the latter half of the sixteenth century. Down the ages good Oriental infantry have always been rare, and that is what has made the Turk exceptional as a soldier – indeed the only Asiatic to equal him in this respect is the Japanese, and his merits were unknown outside Asia until a much later period. It must also be borne in mind that the Ottoman Government had been an army before it was anything else; fighting was originally the first business of the State, and governing merely the second. With the passage of time, and particularly after the capture of Constantinople, the necessity of administering vast territories transferred the preponderance to the governmental aspect, but even in the days of Suleyman the Magnificent the two great functions of the Porte were very closely united, and war took practically the whole government into the field. Substitute officials, it is true, had to be left behind to transact what public business was absolutely necessary, but these were paralleled by, and were usually identical with, the officers and soldiers who had to remain at home to preserve public order. So completely was the government an army that the more important judges went with it to war.

The outstanding feature of the Sultan's armed forces was the body of regular infantry known as *Yenicheri*, or 'new troops', a name which the West had changed to Janissaries. In Suleyman's reign they would not appear to have formed more than a quarter of the whole army, but on several grounds they enjoyed a special importance. Being recruited from Christian children[1] they were at an early age cut off from the mass of the population, and this accounts for their outlook in many ways. They were physically trained beyond comparison with their intellectual education; they were kept in poverty and idleness in time of peace; and they were comparatively irresponsible: such being the case it is in no way surprising that on occasion the Janissaries should have acted as an organized and very dangerous mob. They were liable to start a riot at short notice, or burn a section of Constantinople in

[1] The total number recruited in this way during three centuries has been estimated at half a million.

order to pillage the neighbouring houses, while on a campaign it was difficult to restrain them from plundering cities which had capitulated or from violating terms of surrender. On the battle-field, on the other hand, they were superb, and their *esprit de corps* made them equally feared at home and abroad. The Janissaries were not, however, all concentrated in the capital, for Busbecq has left it on record that they 'are scattered through every part of the empire, either to garrison the forts against the enemy, or to protect the Christians, Jews, and other helpless people from out-rage and wrong'. In spite of their bad reputation in Constantinople, it would appear that in small groups on garrison duty their severe training made them an efficient police.[1]

Where the Janissaries exercised the greatest influence was in matters connected with the throne, and they took the view that the death of a Sultan gave them an interregnum of licence before the accession of a new sovereign, which was why a Padishah's demise was concealed until his successor had assumed power. On these occasions they demanded donatives with increasing rapacity: Mohammed II gave them ten purses of gold; Bayezid II 2,000 aspers each; Selim I 3,000 aspers; and from Suleyman I they asked 5,000 aspers, but he reached a compromise by which they received one-third in cash, and the rest in increased pay. They also required to be 'refreshed' by liberal presents at critical moments in a campaign.[2] The source of this power to blackmail the Sultan was the fact that there was no fixed law governing the succession to the throne. It was a matter of fundamental custom that a prince of the House of Osman should rule, and it was almost as fundamental that a son of a Sultan should succeed him, though it was not until 1617 that the rule was established by which the eldest male of the Royal House became heir apparent. The reign-ing monarch naturally desired to choose which of his sons should follow him, and with this end in view when he gave them pro-vincial governorships he generally placed the favourite nearest the capital. The situation was further complicated after Mohammed II had issued a *kanum* by which the son who had reached the throne

[1] *Life and Letters*, vol. i, p. 86. London, 1881.

[2] cf. Hammer, Joseph von, *Geschichte des Osmanischen Reiches*, vol. iii, pp. 88, 148, and 158. Pest, 1834-6.

was legally empowered to execute his brothers, for as a result of this decree each knew that either he must obtain supreme power or die soon after his father; hence revolt was almost forced upon a man who found himself placed farther from the capital than a favoured brother.

These dynastic differences suited the Janissariea admirably. When Bayezid II grew old and feeble, his active and warlike son Selim opposed his wish to leave the Empire to Achmet; in the end Selim had his way, and Bayezid, forced to abdicate, met a death that was widely believed not to have been natural. The Janissaries turned the scale in this struggle, and henceforth they proved themselves a dangerous element whenever a Sultan had more than one grown son. Suleyman I had no brothers so their services were not required in his case, but during his reign he put two of his sons, Mustapha and Bayezid, to death, and in the case of the former it was unquestionably the young man's popularity with the Janissaries which marked him out for destruction, since only thus could the Sultan's own safety be assured in view of the precedent created during the last weeks of his grandfather, Bayezid II. It is always rash to speculate on these matters, but the Janissaries may unconsciously have done Christendom a great service on these occasions, for both Mustapha and Bayezid were princes of very considerable promise, and had either of them succeeded instead of the drunken and dissolute Selim II the issue of Lepanto might have been different, and a new assault on Vienna might well have been successful.[1]

In Suleyman's time the Janissaries numbered between twelve and fourteen thousand, but this number probably did not include the garrison in Egypt or the force which supported the rule of the Corsairs in North Africa, for one good turn deserved another, and if the Corsairs helped the Sultan at sea he in his turn ensured the continuance of their rule on land. As we have seen, in time of peace many of the Janissaries were scattered in provincial garrisons, so that probably not more than half actually resided in Constantinople, and of these such as were married lived at home, while the others were housed in two great barracks. They were

[1] cf. Lybyer, A. H., *The Government of the Ottoman Empire in the Time of Suleiman the Magnificent*, p. 95. Harvard, 1913.

organized in messes of ten, and ten messes constituted an *orta*, of which there were one hundred and sixty-five in Suleyman's reign. Each *orta* had its own officers, who had been promoted from the ranks, and above them all was the Agha of the Janissaries, who was a very important person indeed. This official had never been a Janissary, but had come through the colleges of pages, and he stood in a very special position in the State. He not merely commanded the Janissaries, but with the aid of his secretariat he directed their enrolment, the distribution of their pay, their promotion, the purchase of their supplies and clothing, and all the other business of the corps. The Agha was highly paid, and took precedence of all other generals save two whose corps were older than his.

The regular cavalry were all included under the general name of Spahis. Their organization was older than that of the Janissaries, and it had come down without a break from the earliest Sultans. The Spahis were divided into corps, and in Suleyman's reign their actual numbers were between ten and twelve thousand, or a little less than the number of the Janissaries; but since most of them were under an obligation to bring from two to six additional horsemen the total force which they could muster was from forty to fifty thousand. Attached to the regular army there were in addition various auxiliary corps of gunners, armourers, engineers and the like. There were also what were known as feudal Spahis, as well as contingents supplied by the Tartars of the Crimea, and vast numbers of irregulars, who were of little military value, but were the terror of invaded countries in time of war, for they carried fire, rapine, and the sword in all directions. When the Sultan took the field the number of troops who accompanied him was immense, and Gabriel d'Aramont, a French ambassador to Suleyman, wrote of 'the mass of his army, which is by common estimate of 300,000 men, as may be judged from the extent of the camp, which extends ten or twelve miles in length, contains at least 60,000 tents or more, with such order and obedience that, considering the great multitude, it is almost unbelievable'.[1]

[1] cf. Charrière, E., *Negociations de la France dans le Levant*, vol. ii, p. 68. Paris, 1848–60.

D'Aramont's tribute to Turkish discipline was echoed by all his contemporaries, and Bartholomew Georgevitz has left it on record that when he accompanied an Ottoman Army on a campaign against Persia he saw 'a captain decapitated with his horse and servant, because the horse, having been left loose, entered someone's field'.[1] Whatever might be the case with the irregulars, the regular army was held under an iron discipline for which it would have been difficult to find a parallel in the West.

On the other hand the Sultan had but one arm; although it was a long and a strong one, yet it could only reach a fixed distance, and it could but strike one blow. He could not fight a war on two fronts, for there was only one army, so there could only be one serious war. If, while hostilities were in progress on one frontier, conditions became critical on another, it was necessary to make peace on what terms could be had, and carry the army to the other extremity of the Empire. For example, Suleyman I concluded peace with Charles V in 1533 and with Ferdinand in 1547, in order to be free to act against Persia; had either Habsburg brother wished to go back on his word he could have marched to Constantinople with very little opposition. Had the Ottoman standing army been divisible, or separable from the person of the monarch, the Sultan could have kept up a steady pressure on both frontiers, and considerably extended his dominions both to East and West. From which it follows that if either Charles or Philip could have come to some agreement with the Persians their task both in Hungary and in the Mediterranean would have been a great deal easier. Even so Charles possessed two great advantages over Persia in the wars with Turkey. The first was that the Osmanli did not wish to pass the winter in the cold north, but they did not seriously object to spending it in Aleppo or Baghdad; this attitude may well have saved Vienna for Austria and lost Baghdad for Persia. The second advantage was that since the journey from Vienna to Constantinople was much easier than that from Tabriz, the Imperialists could have reached the Turkish capital while the Ottoman Army was in the east, whereas the Persians could not have got there while the Osmanli were in Austria. It is true that this advantage remained theoretical, for

[1] *De Turcorum maribus Epitome*, p. 45. Paris, 1566.

neither Charles nor the Shah was ever in a position to attempt such a stroke, but the knowledge that the possibility existed must have sent a cold shiver down the spines of successive Sultans.

Selim I[1] reigned for eight years, and during the course of them he nearly doubled the extent of his dominions, but it is significant that in all this warfare he never crossed swords with a Christian Power, for he realized the limitations imposed upon him by the Ottoman military system, and he wished to be assured of a secure position in Asia and Africa before he tried conclusions with the West. By 1518 such a state of affairs had been established, and the Sultan spent the last two years of his reign in organizing a navy. He died in 1520 on his way to Adrianople.

Selim was succeeded by his son, Suleyman I, known to Europe as 'the Magnificent', and to his own people as 'the Law-Giver'. He was probably the most outstanding of the Ottoman Sultans, and he has been not inaptly compared with Louis XIV:[2] in a century of great monarchs he was one of the greatest. He combined military capacity with statesmanship of a high order. With rare exceptions he stood by his engagements, and he was noted for his clemency and kindness of heart. It is true that there was a streak of cruelty in his character, though as an only son he was not under the necessity of committing fratricide to strengthen his throne: all the same he put two of his sons[3] and several of his relatives to death, while two of his Grand Viziers met the same fate. In this connexion it must be remembered that Suleyman inherited, and had to work, a system that 'carefully kept clear of all the human material that seemed to endanger its working or threaten its unity. There was no sympathy for weakness, no accepting of excuses, no suspension of sentence, no mercy. Suleyman did not always have the heart to execute promptly; but in the end he had no alternative, so remorseless was the system.'[4] In these circumstances it is much to his credit that he always did

[1] *vide supra*, p. 75.
[2] cf. Jonquière, Vicomte de la, *Histoire de l'Empire Ottoman*, vol. i., p. 194. Paris, 1914.
[3] *vide supra*, p. 76.
[4] Lybyer, A. H., *The Government of the Ottoman Empire in the Time of Suleiman the Magnificent*, pp. 88–9. Harvard, 1913.

everything in his power to restrain his troops after a victory in the field or the capture of a fortress. Suleyman's death, in 1566, was due to apoplexy, and it occurred in his tent before the walls of Szigeth, in Hungary, which he was besieging. What had happened was concealed from the army, and to preserve the secret the better the Grand Vizier gave orders for the execution of the doctor who had been in attendance upon the dead monarch. Indeed, it was not until news arrived that the heir to the throne, Selim, had reached Belgrade that the troops were informed that Suleyman was dead.

He proved to be the last of the able line of Sultans who in rather less than three hundred years had raised their possessions from nothing to one of the greatest empires in the world. They were a very virile race, for their reigns averaged about twenty-eight years which was far above the ordinary expectation of life in those days. With the exception of Bayezid II they were all able generals, and habitually led their armies in the field, while their high qualities of statesmanship were very marked. Many of them were addicted to literary pursuits, were students of history, and even had a reputation as poets, but in nearly all there was to be found an inclination to the cruel. It may be doubted whether in the history of the world any other dynasty in East or West has produced so long a succession of men with such eminent and persistent qualities.

What followed was anticlimax, for until the abolition of the Sultanate by Mustapha Kemal after the First World War the successors of Suleyman were mostly as much below the normal standard of monarchs as he and his predecessors were above it. One of the worst was Suleyman's own son, Selim II, generally known as 'The Sot' owing to his weakness for the bottle. He took practically no interest in affairs of State himself, which was bad enough, but he set a very bad example to others. Judges, cadis, and ulemas all took to drink, and poets gave expression to such unconventional views as that wine was sweeter than the kisses of young girls. These signs of impending decadence were not at first visible abroad, for the momentum given by the earlier rulers took some time to die down, while so long as statesmen like Sokolli, who was Grand Vizier from 1566 to 1578, were at the helm no Christian on the shores of the Mediterranean could sleep easily in his bed.

The situation which confronted Philip and his brother, therefore, in the summer of 1568 was at once confused and dangerous. On the credit side of the Spanish account were the relief of Malta and the death of Suleyman, together with the civil wars in France: these events meant that there was no longer an immediate Franco–Ottoman threat to the Western Mediterranean, but all the same there were ominous clouds upon the horizon, and in the background there were several very alarming factors.

Philip ruled over Spain, the Netherlands, the Franche Comté, Sardinia, Sicily, the Balearic and Canary Islands, the greater part of Italy, and most of the discovered New World. To hold together so vast a conglomeration of lands, nations and peoples something more than physical force or mere materialism was required, and a common centripetal factor was demanded – to be found in the Catholic faith. Therefore Philip set out to establish his hegemony on this basis, and in so doing he ran counter to the spirit of the Reformation which in essence was centrifugal, and which had already prevented his father from effecting the unification of Germany. As a result war became inevitable, and wars are costly undertakings, 'more especially', Major-General J. F. C. Fuller would have us believe, 'those that aim at religious compulsion instead of material gains'.[1] It was at this very moment that the wealth of the New World began to pour into the Old, with the most revolutionary consequences. At the date of the discovery of America it has been estimated that the stock of gold and silver in Europe amounted to £33,400,000, but in the following century it began to increase rapidly, and between 1536 and 1636 something like two hundred and fifty million of bullion entered Europe.

Force of circumstances caused this wealth to be spent mainly on war to combat the forces unloosed by the Reformation and to maintain the Spanish hegemony. It also stimulated the growth all over Europe of a new way of life, just as the release of the Persian gold by Alexander the Great had paved the way for Hellenistic and Roman capitalism. 'Because of war,' to quote Major-General Fuller again, 'this stream of bullion flowed into

[1] *The Decisive Battles of the World*, vol. i, p. 556. London, 1954.

the hands of the money-lenders of Genoa, Antwerp, and Augsburg. Gold and silver spent in the Netherlands financed the Baltic
States and became the magnetic centre of the reformed religion
which, by equating God and Mammon, ripened into a comfort-
able creed for bankers, traders, and merchants – the props of
bourgeois civilization.'[1] This development, as will be seen, primarily affected Philip's position in the north, but they must be
borne in mind in any consideration of his commitments in the
Mediterranean for they prevented him from following up a
success in that area such as the relief of Malta or – later – the battle
of Lepanto. What the Persians were to the Porte, the Dutch and
English were to the Catholic King.

[1] *ibid.*, vol. i, p. 557. London, 1954.

4

First Command

AT THE SAME TIME THAT PHILIP APPOINTED HIS BROTHER
to his first command he took care to surround him with competent
sailors whose experience would make up for his ignorance:
accordingly Don Luis de Requesens y Zuñiga was recalled from
the Rome embassy, and nominated Vice-Admiral of the Fleet
under Don John. Possibly a more important appointment to his
staff was that of the foremost naval commander of the day, Don
Alvaro de Bazán y Guzmán, first Marquess of Santa Cruz. Born
at Granada in 1526 he had displayed ability of the highest order
in naval warfare against the French and the Turks, but the most
remarkable events of his career still lay ahead. Quijada, it may be
added, being no seaman, for the first time had to entrust his old
pupil to other hands.

All fear of being forced to embrace a clerical career being now
removed, Don John lost no time in devoting himself to his new
duties. He reached Carthagena on June 2nd, 1568, and presided
at a council of war, at which Santa Cruz was the most important
figure, to discuss the plan of campaign. It was decided to send some
reinforcements to Gian Andrea Doria, who was watching the
Turk off Sicily, while Don John himself first of all cruised along the
Spanish coast, and then went through the Straits of Gibraltar to
meet a fleet which was expected from the Indies. There was no delay
in putting these plans into operation, and with a squadron of thirty-
three sail Don John made a sweep for pirates. During the course
of the next few months this took him as far west as Cadiz and as
far east as the Balearic Islands, while he also made an appearance
at Oran and Melilla. Beyond the capture of the odd corsair these
operations did not result in any great feat of arms, but they enabled Don John to serve his apprenticeship on that element with
which his name was for ever afterwards to be associated.

When he arrived at Madrid in September he was cordially received by his brother, but the rumours regarding the death of Don Carlos in the preceding July had by no means died down: on October 3rd the country was thrown into mourning again by the death of the Queen, Elizabeth of Valois, who died in premature child-bed, and even his most bitter critics have been forced to admit that Philip felt his loss deeply. In these circumstances Madrid held no particular attractions for a young man like Don John, quite apart from the fact, which has often been overlooked by his biographers, that he was extremely religious: such being the case it is in no way surprising that he should have spent the autumn in a Franciscan convent at Abrojo, near Valladolid, where he formed a close friendship with one of the friars, Juan de Colahorra, who was apparently noted for his austerities and for his gift of prayer: at this convent he was, too, within easy reach of his foster-mother at Villagarcia. He was there when the news of the rising of the Moriscoes in the kingdom of Granada reached him.

Like the majority of events in the sixteenth century this insurrection has rarely been considered objectively by historians, but as most of them wrote in an age which knew nothing of Fifth Columns, and little of militant minorities, perhaps they may be forgiven, which is not the case with their successors of more recent times who have slavishly followed in their footsteps.

As has been stated on an earlier page, the conquest of Granada by Ferdinand and Isabella coincided with a period of quiescence on the part of the Turks, for the Sultan of the day was the pacific Bayezid II, and there is no reason to suppose that the Catholic Sovereigns envisaged any serious threat to their new conquest from Constantinople. In due course, however, Bayezid II gave way to Selim the Grim, and Selim in his turn to Suleyman the Magnificent, and the situation was changed out of all recognition. In 1526 the Ottoman successes in Hungary aroused considerable enthusiasm among the Mohammedans and crypto-Mohammedans in the Peninsula, and the government of Charles V became not unnaturally alarmed; accordingly in the summer of that year an edict was issued which severely curtailed the liberties of the Moriscoes, and compelled them to abandon their national dress.

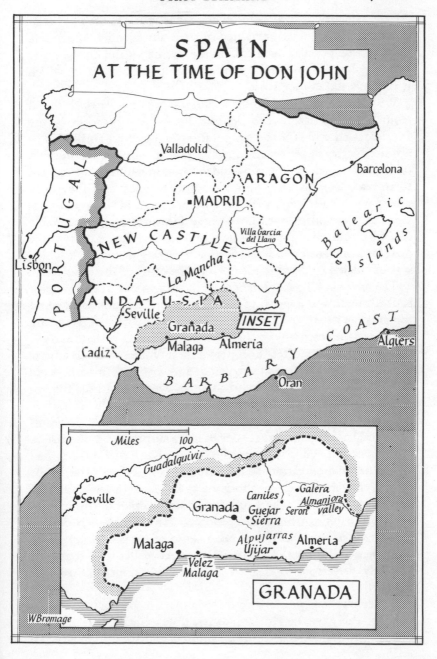

SPAIN
AT THE TIME OF DON JOHN

PORTUGAL

Valladolid

ARAGON

Barcelona

MADRID

NEW CASTLE

Villa Garcia
del Llano

Balearic
Islands

Lisbon

La Mancha

ANDALUSIA

Seville

Granada

INSET

Cadiz

Malaga   Almeria

BARBARY COAST

Algiers

Oran

0   Miles   100

Guadalquivir

Seville

Caniles

Galera
Almanjora
valley

Granada   Guejar   Seron
Sierra

Malaga

Alpujarras   Almeria
Ujijar

Velez
Malaga

WBromage

GRANADA

All the same for several decades after that relations between conquerors and conquered remained superficially friendly: at any rate there was no popular outbreak on the one hand, and on the other even the Inquisition turned a blind eye upon practices of which it certainly did not approve.

With the accession of Philip II and the growing Turkish threat from North Africa to the Spanish littoral the position of the Moriscoes changed for the worse. In 1560 they were forbidden to acquire Negro slaves on the ground that if they did the number of infidels in the country would be continually increased, and three years later an order was issued to the effect that they were not to possess fire-arms without a licence from the local Captain-General: in modern eyes both these measures seem reasonable enough from the point-of-view of security, but in 1567 the government went a good deal further by acting in a manner which was calculated to drive the loyal into the arms of the disaffected.

The national songs and dances of the Moriscoes were now proscribed; their weddings were to be conducted in public according to Christian ritual, and their houses were to be kept open during the day of the ceremony so that anybody could enter them and see that no unhallowed rites took place; their women were to appear in public with their faces uncovered; and, lastly, their baths were to be destroyed on the ground that they were being used for immoral purposes. To insult the Moriscoes the more this edict was published on the anniversary of the capture of Granada by Ferdinand and Isabella, and, what is even more surprising, it was issued in the name of Philip who, while he was King of England, had always urged moderation on his wife and her advisers. The whole episode merely serves to show how the most level-headed of statesmen, and Philip the Prudent certainly comes into this category, are liable to throw discretion to the winds when danger threatens the State: all the same, a sense of proportion must be preserved, and the lot of a Morisco subject of Philip II remained infinitely preferable to that of an Irish Celt under the rule of Elizabeth I.

A year was to expire before the edict was to be put into execution, and this gave the Moslem leaders time to make their preparations. They decided that a rising should take place on January 1st,

1569, and in preparation for it one of their first steps was to appeal for help to their co-religionists in North Africa, with whom they were anyhow in close touch. 'We are beset,' they wrote, 'and our enemies encompass us all around like a consuming fire. Our troubles are too grievous to be endured,' and the letter concluded dramatically with the words, 'Written in nights of tears and anguish, with hope yet lingering – such hope as still survives amidst all the bitterness of the soul.'[1] Unfortunately the letter fell into the hands of the Marquess of Mondejar, the Viceroy of Granada, who thereby received advance warning of what was afoot. The appeal did not fall wholly upon deaf ears, and the Pasha of Algiers allowed his subjects – or rather the Sultan's – to serve as volunteers with the Moriscoes, thereby anticipating the procedure of the twentieth century.

Luckily for the Christians their opponents proved no more amenable to discipline than had been the case when they were defending their independence against Ferdinand and Isabella, and they refused to bide in patience until the date fixed for the rising. In the middle of December, 1568, a detachment of fifty Spanish soldiers were murdered to a man, most of them in their beds, in a small village in which they had halted for the night, and the rebel leader, Farax Aben Farax, decided to strike while the iron was hot: accordingly, on the night of December 26th, 1568, he attempted to carry Granada by a *coup de main*, and once more the streets of that city rang with the cry, 'There is but one God, and Mohammed is his prophet.' He met, however, with no response from the ten thousand Moriscoes there, but merely with the rebuke, 'You are too few, and you come too soon.' Foiled in their attempt to seize Granada the rebels retired into the countryside, and the Alpujarras were henceforth the centre of the revolt, which spread to the neighbourhood of Almería in the east and of Velez Malaga in the west. It is to be noted that the Moriscoes in other parts of Spain, notably in Murcia and Valencia, made no move to join in the struggle.

News of these events filtered through to Don John at Abrojo, and soon served to direct his thoughts from the next world to

[1] cf. Marmol Carvajal, Luis del, *Rebelión de Los Moriscos*, vol. i, p. 219. Granada, 1600.

that in which he was living. In this he was encouraged by his secretary, Juan de Quiroga, and by his new friend, Juan de Calahorra, who both urged him to go to Madrid, and offer his services to his brother. He took their advice, and wrote to Philip as follows:

S.C.R.M.

My obligation to serve your Majesty, and natural faith and love to your Majesty, induce me, with the greatest submission, to propose that which appears to me fitting. I informed your Majesty of my arrival in this Court, and of the cause of my coming hither; and I did not think that there was any occasion to trouble your Majesty with letters of so little worth as mine.

I have now heard of the state of the rebellion of the Moriscoes of Granada, and of the distress in that city, on suspicion becoming certainty; and as the reparation of your Majesty's reputation, honour, and grandeur, insulted by the boldness of these malcontents, touches me very nearly, I cannot restrain myself within the obedience and entire submission of myself in all things to your Majesty's will, which I have always evinced, nor help representing my desire, and entreating your Majesty that, as it is the glory of kings to be constant in the bestowal of their favours, and to raise up and make men by their power, your Majesty will use me, who am of your making, in the chastisement of these people, because it is known that I may be trusted beyond most others, and that no one will act more vigorously against these wretches than I.

I confess that they are not people who deserve to be made of great account; but because even vile minds grow proud if they possess any strength, and this is not, as I am advised, wanting to these rebels; and because this power should be taken from them: and the Marquess of Mondejar not being sufficiently strong for this purpose (he having, as I am told, fallen out with the President, and being but little and unwillingly obeyed); and as some person must be sent thither, and my nature leads me to these pursuits, and I am as obedient to your Majesty's royal will as the clay to the hand of the potter, it appeared to me that I should be wanting in love and inclination and duty towards your Majesty, if I did not offer myself for this post. Although I know that those who serve your Majesty are safe in your royal hands, and ought not to ask, yet I trust that what I have done may be considered rather a merit than a fault.

If I obtain the position which is the object of my desire, I shall be sufficiently rewarded. To this end I came from Abrojo, which, but for the sake of your Majesty's service, and the importance of the occasion, I should not have ventured to do without the express command of your Majesty.

May our Lord preserve, for many years, the Sacred and Catholic person of your Majesty.

From the lodgings, this 30th. day of December, 1568, of your Majesty's creature and most humble servant, who kisses your royal hands,

DON JUAN DE AUSTRIA[1]

At first it did not seem as if the King was going to give his brother a command against the rebels, and that he preferred to trust to the local knowledge of the men on the spot, but when it became clear that the latter were divided among themselves he began to change his mind; the Council of State, too, advocated the appointment of Don John as likely to enforce unity among the Royal forces, so Philip gave way. All the same Don John was not given a free hand, or anything approaching one, which is understandable in the light of his youth and inexperience. A council of war was set up for his guidance, and it had to be consulted on any matter of importance. The members were the Viceroy of Granada; the Duke of Sesa, who was the grandson of Gonsalvo de Córdoba, whose military genius he had to no small extent inherited; the Archbishop of Granada, a prelate of the old school; Diego Deza, auditor of the Holy Office and President of the Chancery of Granada; and Quijada. It took some time to make all the necessary arrangements, and it was not until April 6th, 1569, that Don John took leave of the King at Aranjuez, and proceeded to the seat of war.

The first weeks of the revolt had seen it assume the form that was to characterize it until its termination. The rebels never at any

[1] cf. Vanderhammen, Lorenzo, *Don Juan de Austria*, folio 73. Madrid, 1627.

time held a large town, and it was only occasionally that they ventured on a raid upon the rich plain of La Vega, in which the city of Granada lay, or upon the towns on the coast. They chose as their King a young man of the name of Muley-Mohammed-Aben-Humeya, who was, or was alleged to be, a descendant of the Ommeyad Caliphs, but who, apart from personal courage, would appear to have had little to recommend him save his birth and his looks. From the beginning the campaign was marked by the most repulsive atrocities on both sides, though it must be remembered that it was the Moriscoes who started them. On the Government side Philip did not at first appreciate the seriousness of what was taking place, and he employed local levies in the fighting rather than regular troops. In all these circumstances he was extremely fortunate that Malta was not a Turkish base, for although the rebels were helped from North Africa it was not upon a large enough scale to affect the issue. If Selim II had been his father, or even if he could have torn himself from the bottle for a space, the verdict of 1492 might have been reversed.

On his brother's instructions Don John neglected nothing to make his official entry into Granada as impressive as possible, and hardly had he entered the city than he was surrounded by a great crowd of women whose menfolk had been massacred by the rebels. They clamoured for vengeance, and appealed for aid in their misfortunes – Don John promised both. On the following day the Moriscoes of Granada, who, as we have seen, had been too prudent to rise in arms, sent a deputation to him, doubtless in the hope that they might be able to take advantage of his youth and inexperience to secure some concessions for themselves. If so, they were soon undeceived. They were told that he had been sent to restore law and order; that those who had proved loyal would be protected; but that those who had taken part in the rebellion would be chastised with unsparing rigour. Finally, he directed them to state their grievances in a memorandum, but he also warned them not to include anything which they could not prove, or it would be the worse for them. He could hardly have been expected to have done anything else.[1]

[1] cf. Marmol Carvajal, Luis del, *Rebelión de Los Moriscos*, vol. ii, p. 21. Granada, 1600.

So far, so good, but when the council of war met the following morning all the disadvantages attendant upon a divided command at once made themselves evident. The Viceroy took the view that the rebellion was to all intents and purposes at an end, and that if matters were left in his hands he would soon secure a general submission of the Moriscoes. Deza would have none of this, and advocated much sterner measures: in his opinion hostilities would never cease so long as the Moriscoes of Granada were allowed to communicate with the insurgents in the mountains, and consequently to pass on to them information of what was happening on the government side. From this premise he argued that the first step was to intern them in a concentration-camp, and then to make such an example of those responsible for the atrocities in the Alpujarras as would frighten the insurgents into unconditional surrender. Don John and Quijada thought this was going a little too far, and were inclined to agree with Mondejar. Such being the case it was clear that the council was divided as to the policy which should be pursued, so the question had to be referred to Philip: in the meantime no policy was pursued.

The interval which elapsed before instructions were received from Madrid was used by both the government forces and the rebels to consolidate their respective positions. Don John made a careful examination of the fortifications of Granada, and he also did everything he could to improve the morale of the troops under his command, for as always in civil war, this was rapidly deteriorating: he was also at great pains to raise fresh forces, which presented no great difficulty for there was a widespread desire to serve under so popular a commander. The Moriscoes, too, were by no means inactive, and Aben-Humeya besought his coreligionists in North Africa to come to his aid before it was too late: they refused to espouse his cause officially, but they continued to encourage recruiting for his army. As for the Porte, it was too busy preparing to go to war with Venice to trouble about what took place in Andalusia, quite apart from the fact that it was still smarting under the reverse which it had sustained at Malta.

When Philip's instructions arrived it was found that the King had come down in favour of Deza, though only after considerable

91

hesitation, and orders were sent that all Moriscoes between the ages of ten and sixty were to be removed from the Albaicin to the interior of Spain on June 23rd, 1569. Whatever Don John may have thought of this policy it was his duty to implement it, and all the evidence goes to show that he did so with the maximum amount of humanity. There were, it may be noted, exceptions to the order for expulsion, for licences to remain were granted to those who held certain municipal offices, and to others who had sufficient credit and interest to obtain them: the Mudejares were likewise exempted from the general order.

Meanwhile hostilities continued with alternating successes on both sides, but without any decisive result being reached. In so far as a rebellion on the defensive has already failed the Moriscoes may be said to have shot their bolt, though from time to time they still won a victory in the field, but they never succeeded in enlarging to any extent the area which they dominated: on the other hand, within this area the same feuds broke out which down the centuries had been the main reason why they had lost their erstwhile wide dominions in the Peninsula. Their King was murdered, apparently as a result of private vengeance, and a successor was chosen in Aben-Aboo, who was possessed of great integrity and patriotism, though it was significant that he took care to obtain approval of his election from the Pasha of Algiers in the name of the Ottoman Sultan.

The government forces were equally hamstrung by divided counsels among their leaders, and the consequent necessity of referring all important questions to Philip for decision. Don John chafed increasingly against the restrictions imposed upon him, for his brother even demurred at him going out with a skirmishing party. 'I heard with regret,' the King wrote on September 7th, 1569, 'that you had been out the other day on one of these expeditions, because it does not befit you, nor is it your duty, which is to watch over the safety of the city. . . . If a large force went with you, the Moriscoes might appear on the other side, and do something which might be inconvenient; so you must do this no more. Even if the Duke of Sesa and Luis Quijada go with you, that is not right, for one of them ought to look after such things, and the other remain with you. I have also heard that you go and visit the sentinels, and watch the patrols on their rounds: this should not be done by you too often; only from time to time when circumstances require it.'[1]

This advice did not suit Don John at all, as his reply on September 23rd, clearly proves. 'If I had more experience and practice in my profession,' he protested, 'I should have nothing to reply to Your Majesty, but seeing that I am only learning the service in which I hope to die, it is not right that I should miss what opportunities there are of improving myself in it, and besides I know that it does not suit Your Majesty's affairs. I entreat you to observe how little it befits me, being what I am, or my age, that I should shut myself up, when I ought to be showing myself abroad.'[2] This threw the King back on the defensive, and on September 30th, he answered rather feebly, 'You must keep yourself, and I must keep you, for greater things, and it is from these that you must learn your professional knowledge.'[3] Don John followed up his advantage on October 4th. 'I am certainly most desirous,' he told his brother, 'to give satisfaction to Your Majesty, and do in all things as you wish; but at my age, and in my position, I see that Your Majesty's interest requires that when there is any call to arms or any enterprise, the soldiers should find me in front of them, or at least with them, ready to encourage them to do their duty, and that they should know that I desire to lead them in the name of Your Majesty.'[4]

Whether by themselves Don John's appeals for an active command would have had any effect upon his brother it is impossible to say, but the King's hand was soon forced by external events. Apart from the fact that some of the best Spanish troops were tied down in the Netherlands under Alba there were disturbing rumours about an expedition which was being fitted out in Constantinople, for it was said that its destination was Andalusia, where in any case it was reported that the number of mercenaries from North Africa had of late increased: the rebellion, in effect, might be contained, but it was every moment becoming more urgent that it should be crushed altogether.

[1] *Doc. Ined.*, xxviii, p. 25.
[2] *ibid.*, p. 26.
[3] *ibid.*, p. 28.
[4] *ibid.*, p. 29.

Accordingly Philip decided to give Don John his head, and no longer to confine his activities to the defence of Granada and the co-ordination of those of others. Orders were issued for the formation of two armies: one of them was to be commanded by Don John, and its special task was to pacify the country round the Almanzora valley; the other, under the Duke of Sesa, was to operate in the Alpujarras. Furthermore, the King decided that it would be better if he himself were nearer the scene of hostilities, so a little later, on February 17th, 1570, he arrived in Granada accompanied by the Archdukes Ernest and Rudolf.

In the Spain of Philip II good advice from Madrid to generals and administrators elsewhere was never lacking, so Don John was probably in no way surprised to receive a memorandum, probably written by Ruy Gómez, containing a number of hints for his guidance as a commander in the field.[1] In this document he was advised to be careful to secure accurate returns of his whole force, and of the men and boats employed in the transport service: he should insist on a daily roll of his ration strength, and of the amount of victuals required. If at all possible he should inspect his camp twice a day in company with Quijada, Requesens, and a small guard – the smaller the better, for 'as Quijada knows the Emperor was wont to visit his camp alone'. The gentlemen volunteers, of whom a great number had rallied to the colours once it became known that Don John was really taking the field, should be formed into two companies, and all their servants above the age of eighteen should have his own musket. Occasional false alarms of enemy attack should be given so that all ranks should have practice in getting under arms at the shortest possible notice.

As for Don John himself he was advised to set an example by the plainness of his dress; to stop whenever he found men at dinner, inspect their food, and partake of at least a morsel of it; and to go round the wards of the hospital twice a week. To a man who had been badly wounded he might occasionally give a crown or two, while it would be well to reward those who had committed acts of special gallantry with a handsomely trimmed cap or a sword. On the other hand bad or disorderly conduct ought to

[1] *Advertimiento á Don Juan de Austria, Doc. Ined.* xxviii, pp. 65–68.

be rigorously punished. Finally, Don John should always keep by him two or three hundred crowns in gold to meet any unforeseen emergencies and demands.

Now that he had power to act Don John showed that he was truly his father's son, for he lost no time in taking the offensive. Some four leagues from Granada lay the town of Guejar which was in possession of the rebels who used it as a base for their raiding parties. Don John decided that it must be taken before he operated farther afield, and to make success certain he moved on the place in overwhelming force in two columns, one commanded by himself and the other by the Duke of Sesa. As it turned out the Moriscoes made no effective resistance, and Guejar was taken by Sesa's column. All this happened on the days immediately preceding Christmas, 1569.

Don John returned to Granada, but he did not stay there long, for on December 29th, he set out for Galera, which a Spanish force under the Marquess of Los Velez, the Viceroy of Murcia, had been somewhat ineffectively besieging for some time. This proved a much stiffer proposition than Guejar, and it was not until the Spaniards had been driven back several times that the place was captured in the middle of February, 1570, with heavy loss. Philip was then at Guadalupe, where he received the following despatch from his brother.

S.C.R.M.

By Don Alonso Puerto-Carrero I advised Your Majesty of the taking of Galera, referring you, as to other particulars, to him, as a person who had been present at the whole operation and who could describe it, in order not to weary Your Majesty, while on a journey, with so long a letter. In this one I will write what remains to be said, and particularly I will reply to the five letters which I have received from Your Majesty by two posts, one of the 26th of last month, and the rest on the 1st, 3rd, 6th and 7th of this month. I had already on the 30th ult. written to Your Majesty the cause why up to that day I had not sent off any courier, but from henceforward, although there may be nothing of any moment, I will obey Your Majesty's order, and do as heretofore, which I deferred doing, expecting day after day that I should be able to send off the desired intelligence.

That on this second occasion the soldiers might have more room and a better road, though they had sufficient the first time (but there is no need to return to the discussion of that now), two mines had been constructed, and after these had been fired and had produced a reasonable effect on the front of the poop[1] and on the left side, the place was bombarded from four points, two on the front of the poop and two on the sides, to impede and keep back the Moors from its defence, and on another point below, towards the prow,[1] with two demi-culverins; and after this cannonade had been kept up without cessation for two good hours, as I had resolved to lay everything as low as possible, I sent to reconnoitre the place on two sides; when this was done, it having been seen that one of our soldiers had succeeded in seizing a banner, planted below the battery on our left, our troops advanced in the order and under the leaders agreed on the day before, as Your Majesty will see in the accompanying reports, in the best spirits.

At first, owing to the fear caused by the mines and the damage inflicted by our artillery, the Moors did not sally out in any great numbers to oppose them; yet in the place itself the defence was so obstinate that it was necessary to take it house by house, and the taking of it lasted from nine in the morning till night, fighting going on the while in the houses, in the streets, and on the roofs, the women fighting as well and as bravely as their husbands.

All were put to the sword, and really from what I have seen and see, it would appear that more than two thousand five hundred Moors are slain. Although I at first gave orders that women, boys, and girls should be killed, and a beginning had been made, yet seeing the evil looks with which the soldiers saw themselves deprived of their booty (which is by no means the thing which they count least) I forbade the slaughter to proceed further, and let each one take what he could get, and I believe there are few but have got something, so incredible

[1] The terms 'poop' and 'prow' are used in consequence of the resemblance which the rock-built town bore to a galley, whence its name Galera.

was the number of women, girls, and boys here, together with great store of clothing, wheat, and barley, which last I have caused to be purchased from the soldiers, the wheat at the rate of three reals the *fanega*,[1] and the barley at two reals. On our side no person of note is killed, nor do I believe that we have lost fifty in all, both in killed and wounded. The Captain Don Pedro Zapata was wounded, but he is recovering.

We have been considering what ought to be done with the place, and seeing how full it is of dead, and how shattered and destroyed by the batteries and mines (although the site is impregnable), we have resolved that it be burned and razed. To this resolution we are also driven because we have no soldiers fit for garrison duty, and it would be better to make the experiment of so employing them, if it is to be made, in some places where the appliances and the lodgings would be better; so I have ordered that the town should be fired at all points, and that if anything is left to be pulled down and destroyed, it should be done by the people of Guescar, to whom it is so important that the memory of the place, if possible, should perish, and that it should never again be inhabited, or that at least if it is to be inhabited, the site should be fixed lower down near the river.

In this work and in removing the artillery and all things pertaining to it, sending what is not wanted to Guescar, collecting what cannon-balls we could, and in attending to other urgent matters which had to be looked after, especially providing a store of victuals for the future, and reconnoitring the roads, I have been detained until now. To-morrow I hope to set out and sleep at Cuellar, which is three leagues off, and the day following I shall arrive at Caniles, which is a league from Baza, and four from Seron. This place it appears to me to be necessary to undertake first of all, in order that we may leave this district in security. As to Baza and its neighbourhood, and that which we may do and whatever may happen, I will advise Your Majesty. And because what we hear, from all quarters, confirms us in the belief that there is a strong force in the valley

[1] About 1.60 bushels.

of Almanzora, and that it is their intention to defend not only the towns but the open country, I once more entreat Your Majesty to consider that it would be well to make all these affairs especially in such important points as this secure, when security can be attained merely by augmenting your forces by three thousand men, especially as Your Majesty's person being so near, the respect and influence which attach to it must augment the strength and courage of all. I cannot here say precisely what number of troops I have; but at our second camp I shall hold a particular inspection, so that fraud will be impossible, and that I may ascertain exactly what soldiers we have with us, and inform Your Majesty of this and other things that may offer.

I have written to the Duke of Sesa to send three companies of infantry to Guadix, in order that they may replace another three whose men were beginning to disband, and that their officers might recover their health; although one of them who is called Madrigal is dead of disease, and his company has been given to Antonio Moreno, and the other two arrived here yesterday with three hundred and eighty soldiers. The weather has been fine and so it continues, although two days ago there was a change and some rain; I wish it may remain fair, that the troops may be the better disposed for what they have to do, and especially for the sake of the artillery, which always needs fine weather.

The possession of Galera has been given as Your Majesty ordered, and as to that of Castilleja the people of the Duke of Alba have been told what Your Majesty wrote.

According to Your Majesty's command, I shall not solicit the return of the Marquess of Los Velez, and in what concerns the charge of the cavalry I shall do the same, in so far as to wait to see if his son comes or not. As to putting it in the hands of another officer for a short time, I do not know to whom to entrust it, and Your Majesty may well believe that there is great need of a head to command whom the others will support and obey; therefore will Your Majesty consider the matter and order that which is best for your service, which it will be my business to execute?

As to the charge of *Maestre de Campo General*,[1] when the person holding that post is fitted for it, such an officer is necessarily brought into contact with the principal parts of the business of commanding and supplying the army. But supposing him to be wanting in these requisite qualities, Luis Quijada and the Grand Commander will supply the deficiency, and to those who hold the post of *Maestres de Campo* some portions of the duties may be committed.

As to the removal of the peaceable Moriscoes who dwell in this kingdom, according to what the Grand Commander of Castille has written, in order to leave the affairs of this kingdom in that security which for many reasons is desirable, he has already said that which we all think, and what in truth must be done; for these are the people who aid and abet the rebels, and supply them with intelligence, munitions, and provisions, as we well know and indeed see going on around us in Granada; and leaving for the present out of the question, whether the removal of them is required for the effect it may have in Valencia, I think that it ought to be done, time being suitable, and a sufficient force at hand, in the way and manner in which it was done at Granada, and that they should be sent as far away into Castille as possible, and that at their removal, leave, time, and assistance should be given to them to carry away, so far as possible, all their movables, and that they should also have licence to sell and dispose of their landed property, and that they should leave as many out of the whole number of these persons as might seem desirable to treat of the terms on which, when these troubles are quieted, they might be allowed to return to their houses and enjoy their former property; and that supposing it is determined to adopt this course, in ten or twelve days the Moriscoes might be removed from Benamaurel, Baza and its neighbourhood, Gor and Guadix, by means of a part of this army, and of the force that could come from Ubeda, Baeza, Quesada, and from some of the very districts whence the removal takes place; and they might march under the charge

[1] A *Maestre de Campo* was at this time the title of the Commander of a *tercio* and it was not wholly abandoned in favour of that of *Colonel* until the Thirty Years War. *Maestre de Campo General* would seem to imply something more exalted, and possibly in this connexion may have referred to a staff officer of very high rank.

of the escort until they had passed the frontier of the kingdom, and afterwards be transferred to the care of the cities of Castille and Andalusia.

There remains the principal point which it would be well that Your Majesty should decide, and take your determination accordingly, whether this policy may be the cause of dispelling the humours of those of Valencia and Aragon, and the kingdom of Murcia and other parts where they are found, which being a thing to be looked for in the people themselves, who keep their thoughts secret, it is impossible to be sure that the decision is a just one; nor being a matter so doubtful will it be prudent to anticipate that any step will have more success, than that which has been known and seen heretofore with the others, who so unexpectedly rose and resolved to execute that which they had taken in hand; whence it appears there will be difficulties in finishing the affair, so long as these rebels have in the dominions of Your Majesty a party who encourages, aids, and favours them. However, Your Majesty after giving directions that the *pros* and the *cons* should be considered, can order that which is best for your service.

From the Camp near Galera, February 16th, 1570.

Postscript. These rebels are so obstinate, and according to the intelligence which comes in from all quarters, so fixed in their determination rather to be cut in pieces than submit, or enter upon any good plan of reconciliation, that no man can promise any honourable arrangement with them. . . . But in case the contrary should happen, as, in spite of the opinion which is entertained and which they themselves give out, it may be that they may choose to submit themselves to the mercy and grace of Your Majesty, I wish that Your Majesty would advise me of what is to be done, that I may make no mistake in an affair of so much importance.[1]

Don John was thus at the front when his brother arrived at Granada, and this letter was given to the King by Alonso de Venegas: Philip thereupon took the opportunity of expressing

[1] The original of this letter is at Simancas.

publicly his approval of all that Don John had done and was doing. It was not, however, the dying rebellion of the Moriscoes that called for the Royal attention, for the intentions of the Sultan, or rather of the Grand Vizier, Mohammed Sokolli, were still uncertain, and it might well be that the great expedition which was being fitted out in Constantinople was intended to be used against Spain. Accordingly one of Philip's first actions after his arrival at Granada was to give orders for the strengthening of the garrisons in Murcia, and also for any necessary repairs to be done to the fortifications of Carthagena. It was only later that he received definite information to the effect that the Turkish armaments were directed against Cyprus, and he could thus breathe more freely.

The war against the Moriscoes might be petering out, but there was still some hard fighting to take place before it actually came to an end, and in one of these actions Don John displayed his gift of leadership and Quijada lost his life. In an assault on Seron the Spanish troops got out of hand, and a counter-attack by the enemy came within an ace of precipitating a disaster. Don John saw what was happening, and at once rode into the stream of fugitives: reining his horse across their path, he exclaimed, 'Soldiers, what are you flying from? Where is the honour of Spain? Is not your general with you? Turn your faces to this barbarous rabble, and you will soon see it retire before you.' While he was thus endeavouring to rally his men he was struck on the head by a musket-ball, and probably only the strength of his helmet, which turned the ball aside, saved his life. Quijada, who was beside him, was not so fortunate, for another musket-ball passed through his arm-pit, and he was evacuated to Caniles. The reverse was a severe one, for the Spaniards lost about six hundred men in killed alone, while the action seriously damaged the reputation which they had won at Galera.

Don John made no attempt to disguise his 'shame and regret' at 'the ill-behaviour of his troops', and he thus described to the King the incident which could only have the effect of prolonging the war:

Those who have long followed the wars never saw so much dismay and fear; and I could not have believed it had I not seen it, that a few Moors could have thrown soldiers into such utter confusion, that neither angry words, nor encouragement, nor anything else availed to induce them so much as to turn their faces towards the enemy. If Don Garcia de Manrique had not showed us a new way to retire, which he had found out the day before, we were on the brink of a very great misfortune; and in saving us from this, he has done Your Majesty service well worthy of recognition.

It happened that Luis Quijada, in doing all which ought to be done, and in using his utmost efforts to make the men stand fast, received an arquebus-shot in his left shoulder, from which he is in considerable danger; and to-day in trying to extract the ball the surgeons have made five incisions at the place where it entered, and also an opening at the other side, and with all this, although they have found the ball, they have not succeeded in getting it out, which is very unfortunate. The loss to Your Majesty's service is already much felt; for I was so much helped by his soldierly experience, his care and diligence, that I feel now of how great importance he is to the service of Your Majesty, whom I entreat to thank him for the services which he has rendered, and to give him orders to take more care of himself than heretofore, so that if he recover, as I hope in our Lord he may, though his state is critical, he may be again able to obey Your Majesty's commands.[1]

Don John's hopes were not to be fulfilled, for whether owing to the seriousness of his wound or the incompetence of his doctors Quijada died soon after his arrival at Caniles. Doña Magdalena de Ulloa was in Madrid when her husband was wounded on February 17th, 1570, but she is said to have been with him at his death on the 25th. He was, of course, given a full military funeral, with Don John as the chief mourner, and his body was taken to Baza where it remained until the church at Villagarcia was ready to receive it. Quijada's ancestors were buried in the Bernardine convent of La Espina, but he himself had long had in contemplation the erection of a family chapel at Villagarcia. In his will he took the matter a stage further by saying, 'Or if it should appear to Doña Magdalena

[1] *Doc. Ined.*, xxxiii, pp. 49–50.

more advisable to unite our estates and found a monastery of friars and nuns – always excepting barefooted nuns, for whom the country would be too cold – in that case I give powers to her and my executors to take order for such foundation, that we may be interred together, and have in death the good companionship which we have had in life.'[1] The building of this chapel was sufficiently advanced in 1572 for Quijada's remains to be transferred there from Baza. In the meantime when his widow set out on her return to Castille she was, on Don John's instructions, escorted by a squadron of horse, and he himself rode for several miles beside her litter.

There can be no doubt but that both the Royal brothers felt Quijada's death very deeply: it meant not only the loss of an old friend and wise counsellor, but also the snapping of a link with the Emperor. When he heard that Quijada had been wounded Philip wrote to Don John, 'I have heard with pain, you may suppose, of the misbehaviour of the troops, but with much more pain of Luis Quijada's wound. I shall not be easy till I hear that he is out of danger, and therefore I charge you to let me always know how he is. I know it will be quite unnecessary to tell you to take the greatest care of him.'[2] This letter crossed one from Don John announcing Quijada's death. 'Your Majesty has this day lost one of your best servants and ministers by the death of Luis Quijada, especially at a time when his presence will be so much missed in the affairs now in hand, the war having been hitherto conducted (as I have already written to Your Majesty) according to his advice and opinion, and when I feel myself so alone and in want of some person to whom we may have recourse in what we undertake, as Your Majesty may well understand, here at Seron, where I trust in God Your Majesty may have the victory; but I do not see how we can advance further without great risk; and in my judgement it would not be right to encounter such risk in a case of such importance, without great caution; and without more experience and soldiers than the Grand Commander and I possess, I think there would be so much danger, that I cannot help entreating Your Majesty very urgently to take steps to meet

[1] cf. Villafañe, Juan de, La Limosna de Dios, pp. 81–82. Salamanca, 1723.
[2] Doc. Ined., xxviii, p. 59.

it.'[1] To this Philip replied, 'I have never received a letter with greater grief than yours of the 25th, for I know well what you and I have lost in Luis Quijada. It is impossible to speak of him without sorrow, and you have great reason to lament him as you do. Our best consolation is that we are sure he must be in a better place, seeing how he lived and died.'[2]

The Spanish reverse at Seron had undoubtedly encouraged the Moriscoes, and the war was to drag on during the greater part of 1570, although the final decision was no longer in doubt now that the Sultan had decided to turn his arms against Cyprus rather than against Spain. Philip, on his part, was by no means deaf to his brother's appeal, for he reinforced him with two thousand men, and sent Don Francisco de Córdoba to take the place of Quijada. At the same time he was clearly alarmed by Quijada's death as evidence of the risks to which his brother was exposed, and he proceeded to take Don John severely to task for his rash conduct.

I have good reason to complain that you keep so ill your promise not to place yourself in jeopardy, as I know you did at Galera; how you kept it in this last day[3] is clear enough, because you tell me you were struck by an arquebus ball on the helmet, which has given me more pain than I can tell; you ought not to vex me thus, and to lower the credit of my arms, and add to that of our enemies, so greatly as would be the case if they were to shed a drop of your blood. I therefore distinctly order you, and will take it very ill if you disobey my order, not to do so any more, but to remain in the place which befits one who has the charge of this business and my brother, which is very different from that in which you have lately been found, as the Grand Commander will tell you . . . for everyone ought to do his own duty, and not the general the soldier's, nor the soldier the general's.[4]

A few days later he returned to the charge again.

[1] *Doc. Ined.*, xxviii, p. 54.
[2] *ibid.*, xxviii, p. 62.
[3] Presumably at Seron.
[4] *Doc. Ined.*, xxviii, p. 62.

It is well to be very cautious, as you say you are, for this is no affair where you ought to run any risk . . . and you must not be led away to any other view of it by the counsels of boys . . . I again wish to remind you how important your life is, seeing you are my brother, and that you are not to risk it as you have previously been in the habit of doing; for any accident that befalls you would be very prejudicial to my service, and to my authority and credit, as well as to your own . . . so you must take note of these things, and observe them to the very letter, since I speak to you as one who loves you, as it is right that I should, and desires that you should behave in all things like the son of our father.[1]

From these letters it would seem that Don John's behaviour in the Morisco war had caused his brother to form the conclusion that he was unduly rash and impetuous, and, as we shall see, he held to this belief during the whole of the younger man's life. Whether he communicated it to his ministers, or they arrived at it themselves, is difficult to determine, but at the beginning of March, 1570, Ruy Gómez wrote to Don John urging circumspection both in the field and in the council-chamber, for there had apparently been some slight difference with Requesens. 'Your Excellency,' he wrote, 'is reputed to be rash, and more desirous to obtain a reputation as a soldier than as a general; pray let this be changed, and listen to counsel.' He then went on to allude to the relations existing between Don John and the Grand Commander, and he admitted that Requesens was not so experienced a soldier that much could be learned from him, especially by a novice, but he stressed the fact that the other's good sense, diligence, erudition, and knowledge of the world, combined with his sense of duty, would keep him from doing anything seriously wrong. It was, however, of the utmost importance that no rumour should get round that Don John and Requesens were at loggerheads, for this would have the worst effect upon the discipline of the army. 'For God's sake let Your Excellency take care that nothing of this kind occurs; learn to act with him in everything, in such a way that no misunderstanding be suspected even by

[1] *ibid.*, pp. 62–64.

your intimates or your household. I say the same with regard to Don Francisco de Córdoba, now on his way to the army; he has had more experience of war in North Africa, and is a gallant gentleman.'[1]

Don John was not prepared to lie down under all this, and he lost no time in stating his case. To the King he wrote:

I give Your Majesty my word that on the day Luis Quijada fell I feared only that which did not happen. Under God, I believe that by taking my position in the path of the fugitives, I was the cause of preventing the greater part of our force from being cut to pieces. When a general sees that in no other way may such a disaster be prevented, how can he do his duty better than by taking such a post, whatever it may be?

To Ruy Gómez he went out of his way to be conciliatory, partly out of an innate courtesy, and partly, doubtless, because of the high place which the minister held in the King's estimation. Don John commenced his letter by assuring Gómez that he was grateful to his friends for telling him what they disapproved in his conduct, and he assured the minister that from him in particular no criticism would ever be taken amiss: he went on to say that he hoped Gómez would always write to him with perfect frankness, 'reprehending all that he deemed to deserve reprehension', for since he had lost his uncle there was no one in whom he trusted more, or who might find fault with him more freely. 'I can assure you, Sir,' he proceeded, 'that as regards what you advise about my doing the duty rather of a captain than a soldier, I keep it in my mind and will never forget it; and as to what happened at Seron, when my uncle, now in glory, was killed, I will give you a full account when it pleases God that we should see each other again, but will now say no more than this, that if you had been in my place and circumstances you would have done as I did.'

When Don John turned to his relations with the Grand Commander he made little secret of the fact that he chafed under the restrictions which were imposed upon him. He declared that as to listening to counsel, and showing proper respect to Requesens,

[1] *Doc. Ined.*, xxviii, p. 69.

he had never failed on either count; indeed he never took any resolution, great or small, without the advice and approval of his council, though at times it did seem to him that he was kept in excessive subjection by that body, but he would continue to bow to the views of its members so long as the King required such an attitude on his part. As for the Grand Commander, they were really on good terms, and any differences between them were more apparent than real, but in the future he would take care that even the appearance was avoided.

Don Francisco de Córdoba is, as you write, a worthy gentleman, and indeed does his duty with zeal and sincerity, and I can say the same of Hernando Tello; but the fact is, Sir, that many men in dealing with affairs like to have comrades, and there are others who prefer acting alone and care for nobody. These are not things to commit to letters, nor will I enlarge on a matter for which there is no present need. I pay all honour to those who are with me here; and if you hear anything else, rebuke me for it, as I once more give you full leave; yet I once more also beg not to be condemned without being heard.[1]

It is to be hoped that the precise implication of some of these observations was clearer to the recipient of this letter than it is to the reader of it today.

In that same month of March, 1570, Don John was provided with a new secretary, Juan de Soto, to fill a vacancy caused by death. Soto came with a strong letter of recommendation from Ruy Gómez, who described him as a man of prudence and experience, and one who was very knowledgeable in military and naval matters, having been secretary both to Andrea Doria and to the Duke of Alba. 'He is a man,' the minister wrote, 'with whom your Excellency may well take counsel on all matters. I entreat you to show him the favour which he deserves; for even if there were another Soto, not to let this one go, for I promise you he is a great treasure, and a man for bringing whom to your acquaintance you will one day give me many thanks.'[2] The appointment, it may be added, proved highly satisfactory to all concerned.

[1] *Doc. Ined.*, xxviii, pp. 72–76.
[2] *ibid.*, p. 70.

While engaged in stamping out the embers of the rebellion Don John was hampered by a number of difficulties which were none of his making. First among them was the lack of discipline among his soldiers, which impressed upon him the observation of Ferdinand V, quoted above, that Spanish troops required a very strong hand. Even the Gran Capitán, Gonsalvo de Córdoba, had had trouble of this nature, which arose chiefly from the fact that for months at a time the men went unpaid: in the case of Don John there was the further complication that the troops under his command were largely militia, and that they were engaged in a civil war, which is always destructive of discipline: much of the ferocity, for example, which marked the fighting in the Irish rising in 1798 was due to the rapid deterioration in this respect of even the best British regiments once they landed in Ireland. Such being the case it is in no way surprising to find Don John writing to Philip on March 12th, 1570, from his camp near Tijola as follows:

The shamelessness of these soldiers is unsufferable. If there are eight thousand here to-day, two thousand may be gone to-morrow, and neither hanging nor the galleys seem enough to keep any from deserting. The day we came here, two were hanged and four condemned to the galleys, but the rest go on as if that were nothing, and I am not much surprised, for there is not the least sense of honour amongst them, and they care for nothing but plunder and an easy life. The officers are much to blame for the faults of the soldiers, and certainly it is my misfortune that they should be so bad a set. . . . I often call them together, and after rebuking them I lament that we should be losing what our ancestors honourably won, and that they themselves should be losing their credit, not only with the world, but with Your Majesty, to whom it is my duty to report upon the conduct and character of every one of them. With all this and more, I cannot get them to do their duty. . . .

The chief cause which makes the men so ill-disposed and so lacking in courage is, I well know, their dissolute ways, their carelessness about their souls, and their easy consciences. Even in this matter, I assure Your Majesty what can be done is done, but for the souls of these soldiers, every man would need a priest for himself, and on service a very choice officer; and, besides all this, if they are not humoured and pampered, nothing can be done with them; and none but Your Majesty has the power to keep them from deserting.[1]

The attitude of a large section of the clergy also met with Don John's disapproval. It was extremely important to discourage the Moriscoes who had remained peaceful from throwing in their lot with the insurgents, but whenever any attempt was made by those in authority to separate the sheep from the goats the pulpits of Andalusia resounded with remonstrances against the King's clemency. The religious of all denominations have in the past borne a heavy responsibility for sectarian bitterness, and the Spanish Church, with its long tradition of crusading against the Moors, could hardly be expected to provide an exception. Don John, however, thought that the summer of 1570, when the Morisco rebellion seemed to be petering out, was hardly the time for such activities, and he wrote feelingly to his brother on the subject:

> What a pity and misery it is that soldiers whose duty it is to seek out and attack the enemy should be engaged in robbing and deserting as hard as they can; and that friars who ought to be interceding with Your Majesty for these unfortunate people, who have generally sinned from ignorance, should expend their energies in denouncing the pardon now offered, and meddling with the business of others at the very time when they are doing their own so ill.

Don John asked the King to give instructions to the bishops that preaching of this type should cease.[2]

The terms accorded to the defeated Moriscoes were admirably calculated to serve the end which the government had in view, that is to say to ensure that if a Turkish force ever did effect a landing on the Spanish coast it would not find an Islamic Fifth Column there to assist it. By an edict of October 28th, 1570, all the Moriscoes from the disturbed districts were to be removed

[1] ibid., pp. 81–83.
[2] ibid., p. 101.

into the interior, while their real estate was declared forfeit to the Crown; their movable property, on the other hand, they could take with them, if they wished, at a valuation. Orders were issued that in this dispersal families were not to be broken up, and the removal seems to have been affected in a humane manner; the districts chosen for re-settlement were as far from the coast as possible, and the most severe penalties were to be imposed on any Morisco who should attempt to leave his new abode without leave. It is doubtful whether the twentieth century would in similar circumstances have treated the Moriscoes any better, and eighty years later Cromwell treated the Irish much worse. In any event Philip was at last free to face the Turks without the fear of having a knife in his back.

When Don John's presence was no longer required in the field he returned to Granada, where the King went to the gates of the town to receive him. After a solemn *Te Deum* in the cathedral the two brothers went on to the palace, and there they had a private conversation which lasted far into the night.[1] It would appear that the matter under discussion was the prospective campaign against the Turks, and the appointment of Don John to the supreme command: if this were the case he was probably not unprepared for what Philip was going to say in view of a letter which he had recently written to Doña Magdalena de Ulloa.

Madam,

I kiss your ladyship's hands for the trouble you have had in always replying to my letters, which is the chief kindness you can show me, for that which I most desire is ever to be informed of your ladyship's health and welfare.

As to what I ought to say in reply to a letter which I received about the fifth of the present month I will do it in this. . . .[2] There is no doubt but that things are in such a state that whatever a man may determine one moment, he is obliged to change the next, and so all that can be said on this head is that in everything it is necessary to proceed according to the course of events. In one case only I should stand out, were they to choose

[1] cf. Ossorio, A., *Vida de Don Juan de Austria*, pp. 77–78. Madrid, 1946.
[2] Blank in the original.

to send me to Flanders, whither it would not suit me to go, it being so far off, and also because the quiet of that country is not to my liking. By letters of friends who are in the way of being well informed, I have heard that the Princess[1] is going thither, and the Duke of Medinaceli with her. I do not think the appointment unsuitable; indeed perhaps because I desire it, I believe it would be the best to make; God grant that it may be so!

This black war is not yet over; but it is now in such a state that, if no evil humours again arise, all that remains for me to do may be finished at the latest by the end of October. I long for it so much that even if the end were seen I doubt of it. May God so dispose it that it may be of benefit to me!

I have just now received a letter from His Majesty, in his own hand, in which he tells me of the need he has of me for this affair of the League and other matters. Of all these things I shall believe what I shall see. I am very glad that Don Juan de Mendoza has told your ladyship of the suspicions which have arisen in consequence of my having gone to Granada, whereof I have given your Ladyship such an account as can be given from such a distance. I believe His Majesty and his ministers are satisfied as to the truth, and that all our proceedings here are in better conformity with the interests of His Majesty's service than they could themselves have contrived by sending orders from Court; and about this whole business some things have been at different times written which have been useful for other purposes, for I having shown that I felt hurt at all these suspicions, and the Duke of Sesa and the Grand Commander, as participating in the matter, having done the same, we have given them to understand that if they think we are more careful and attentive with regard to our own liking and pleasures than to that work which we are appointed to do here, they are wrong in employing us under such hard conditions, and that we can do our duty but ill, if it is not left to us, as being on the spot, to do what ought to be done in this war, one of the things which ought to be done being that I should go to Granada, from whence things may be directed with greater convenience than

[1] The Princess of the Brazils?

from a place as unprovided as this is, and that I did not pretend to make this change of quarters on my sole judgement, but also on that of the gentlemen who assist me and who knew that it was the right thing to do. To all this other things were added, which have been treated of with all the plainness which the case requires, but I look forward to saying it to your ladyship by word of mouth some day, if God will.

Your ladyship tells me with your great and wonted kindness to consider well what I am doing, all eyes being now fixed upon me, and not to be too adventurous, but rather to avoid all occasions of risk. Once more I kiss your ladyship's hands for what you are doing for me, of which I entreat you never to become weary. To this, Madam, I will answer with the simple truth which I love so much, that since my uncle and father has been taken from me, I give to our Lord infinite thanks, endeavouring always to live as absent from one who did me so much kindness, and also I think that I have not governed myself so ill, nor laboured so little that, this loss considered, anyone will say of me the contrary.

As to holiday attire, although I might be inclined to use it, the toils of a nine months' campaign would be sufficient to unfit me for it, especially, Madam, as all times and conditions are not the same, and people who have sense and are not mere brutes change with age; though others there are in the world who in order to say an ill word catch at anything, I do not therefore wonder at what they say and murmur about me, seeing that they do the same about God himself; nor that even your ladyship should write that things have come to such a pass, that you do not dare to ask about me, seeing that in this respect the saints themselves do not live secure from the vexations of this world; wherein I will endeavour to steer my course as much as I can in conformity with the advice of your ladyship, whom I entreat ever to grant me a hearing, for there is no one whom I so much desire to satisfy as her to whom I owe my bringing up and the place in the world which I now hold, obligations which I will acknowledge even in my grave.

I beg your ladyship to excuse so long a discourse, since the inventions of this world are sufficient to cause that which a man least expects, and to let me know whether those of the holy abbess have gone so far as greatly to disturb your ladyship's feelings of justice.

I once more remind your ladyship that if there be in your neighbourhood any gentlemen's sons who may be suitable for my pages, I am in need of some, and that Balverde ought to see whether he knows any one to do the duty of Fran^{co} Lopez, for that I can from hence assure him that Fran^{co} de Leon, who assisted the Postmaster-General and is doing the duty here, possesses a good pen and ability. As to all this, I shall hope to receive your ladyship's opinion.

Here there is nothing new to tell, except that the troops which I have in the Alpujarra are achieving good exploits; many people have made their submission, and there are a few. . . .[1]

If this letter proves anything it surely is that ambiguity was not the prerogative of Philip alone, but that Don John could be at least as vague as his brother when necessity arose. Its interest lies in the light which it throws upon the writer's aversion from an appointment in the Low Countries, and upon the mother-and-son relationship which clearly existed between him and Doña Magdalena.

The end of the Morisco campaign meant that Don John had now served his apprenticeship to High Command in the field, and he had every cause for satisfaction with what he had achieved. He had brought a particularly unpleasant war to a successful conclusion, and the fact that it had taken him some time to effect this result was in no way his fault – equally important, no one thought it was. He had acquired a reputation as a gallant leader of men, and he had made himself popular with his troops, who, as we have seen, required a good deal of handling. At the same time he seems to have implanted in Philip, the ministers, and even in Doña Magdalena a suspicion that he was unduly rash; how far this was justified it is not easy to say, and it may have been largely due to the civilian's lack of realization of the fact that in the conditions of contemporary warfare troops, not least Spanish

[1] The remainder of this letter is missing. The MS. is in the Royal Academy of History in Madrid.

troops, had to be led from the front rather than from the base. However this may be, it was during the Morisco campaign that the King, and to a lesser extent Ruy Gómez, had sown in their minds the seeds of suspicion that Don John was rather a headstrong young man: they were to bear fruit later.

5

The Holy League

IF PHILIP WAS FOR SOME TIME LEFT IN DOUBT AS TO THE objective of the Turkish armaments he was assuredly too well acquainted with the international situation to be very surprised when he heard that they were directed against the Venetian island of Cyprus. The Porte had in the sixteenth century turned its attention to the sea: Suleyman the Magnificent at the beginning of his reign had captured Rhodes from the Knights of Saint John, and at the end of it he had tried – and failed – to deprive them of Malta in an attempt to secure the key to the Western Mediterranean. His successor, or rather his successor's ministers, decided that the time had come also to assert Turkish authority nearer home, and to deprive the Republic of Saint Mark of its advanced base in Cyprus, thereby, amongst other things, securing the safety of the pilgrimage to Mecca, which had been molested by crusading galleys based on the island's harbours.

Ever since the days of the Fourth Crusade the Latins had enjoyed a very bad reputation in the Near East, compared, for example, with the condition of the Greek Rayahs in the Sultan's dominions that of the Greek population of Chios under Genoese domination was pitiable in the extreme; for in addition to daily exactions and injustices they were compelled four times a year – that is to say at Christmas, Easter, Whitsuntide, and Circumcision – to attend a ceremony, best described as a feast of humiliation. Their clergy and chief citizens were summoned to the palace of the Podestá: when they were all assembled a herald, mounted on a stand, with a wand in his hand, read four prayers for the Pope, the Emperor, the Republic of Genoa, and the family of the Justiniani. At the end of each prayer the unfortunate Chians were required to show their approval by quasi-enthusiastic acclamations – for the Pope, of whom they knew no good; for the Emperor, of whom they knew nothing at all; for the Republic which had subjected them; and for the Justiniani, whom they detested as a financial company that ruthlessly pillaged them.[1]

Venetian rule was no better, and the Greeks of the Morea complained bitterly of the religious persecution of the Serenissima: indeed it was the universal cry of all the Christian population of the Near East from the middle of the fifteenth century to the beginning of the eighteenth, 'A thousand times rather the Turks than the Latins.' Such being the case when the Spaniards cooperated with the Venetians they automatically ranged the Greeks against them, and this deprived them of any popular support in the area in which they were operating, a state of affairs which was to prove a serious handicap for it meant that their preparations were always liable to become known to the enemy.

The lot of the Cypriots was no different from that of the other Greeks who were under Latin domination. They had not had a ruler of their own race since Richard I of England, on his way to the Third Crusade, had dethroned Isaac Comnenus, bound him in fetters of silver, and incarcerated him in the castle of Markappos in Syria. This was a mere episode in the history of England, but so far as Cyprus was concerned it had far-reaching results. It was the first step in the subjection of the Eastern Empire to the Crusaders, and it was followed fifteen years later by their capture of Constantinople itself, and the division of the Empire into feudal fiefs. For Cyprus it was the beginning of a domination by the West for nearly four hundred years, the introduction of the Feudal System of the Normans, and the establishment of the Roman Church in an island hitherto Greek in its institutions and Orthodox in its faith.

Richard I soon tired of his conquest, and sold it to the Templars, whose rule was marked by great severity: from them it passed to the House of Lusignan, who reigned from 1192 to 1489, generally with the title of Kings of Cyprus and Jerusalem, though the latter kingdom was in Moslem hands, and under their rule all political power was concentrated in the governing race. During their régime war broke out with the Mameluke Sultans of Egypt, and in 1426 King Janus of Cyprus was decisively defeated and cap-

[1] cf. Midhat Bey, Ali Haydon, *The Life of Midhat Pasha*, pp. 6–7. London, 1903.

tured: he was only released ten months later on the payment of an enormous ransom, the promise of an annual tribute to Cairo, and, most important of all, the recognition of the suzerainty of the Egyptian Sultan. The Lusignan dynasty really came to an end when the last King died in 1474, but his mother, a Venetian, remained on the throne for a further fifteen years while her fellow-countrymen consolidated their position in the island: at the end of that period she was persuaded to retire to Venice, and henceforth the banner of Saint Mark floated over Cyprus.

The policy of its new masters was to make the island as secure as possible, for it was clear that it would be highly vulnerable as soon as the Ottoman throne was occupied by a less pacific Sultan than Bayezid II. To reconcile the inhabitants the nobility and clergy were confirmed in their ancient privileges and possessions, and while the dominance of the Latin archbishop was maintained it was expressly declared by the Pope that the Orthodox Church was not to be molested for observing its traditional customs. Certain concessions, too, were made to the peasantry, and the taxes hitherto paid under the Lusignans were confirmed, while a promise was given that no further burdens would be imposed. All this was something, but in reality it did little or nothing to reconcile the Cypriots to Venetian rule.

As the sixteenth century progressed, and the Turks passed over to the offensive once more, it became obvious to the Venetian Government that if it wished to retain Cyprus it would sooner or later have to defend the island by force of arms, and in 1550 one of the most famous military engineers of the day, Giovanni Girolamo Sammichele, was sent to complete the fortifications according to the latest theories of defence. It was not that the Lusignans had neglected the defences of their kingdom – they were generally on too bad terms with their neighbours to run any such risk – but that the development of gunpowder had rendered their fortresses indefensible. Walls of masonry were no longer what was required, but thick ramparts of earth, not only to withstand the attackers' fire but also to provide a sufficient platform from which the defenders' cannon could sweep the ditch and the sloping glacis beyond it. Sammichele accordingly devoted his energies to the task entrusted to him, and he concentrated on

Famagusta where, however, he died before his work was complete. He was succeeded by Giulio Savorgnano, who performed the same service for Nicosia.

By this time the Mameluke Sultanate had ceased to exist, and Egypt was a province of the Ottoman Empire. Since the Serenissima continued to pay the tribute arranged with King Janus to Constantinople instead of to Cairo, it was only natural that the Porte should regard Cyprus as a Turkish possession, and consequently view with considerable disfavour the rehabilitation of the island's fortifications. That the Turks would have attacked Cyprus anyhow may be taken for granted, but they now also had an excuse, and when their preparations were sufficiently advanced they called upon Venice to hand over their possession to them: the Venetian Senate returned a defiant reply, and war was declared. This was in 1570.

It might have been expected that the Republic, as a great naval Power, would have met the Turks at sea, but no effort was made to do this: possibly the recent explosion in the arsenal[1] had too severely impaired the ships which were laid up, or possibly the somewhat low estimate of the Ottoman Navy given by the Venetian ambassador at Constantinople was not shared by the experts in Venice itself – however this may be the Republic refused to commit its fleet to action against the enemy without allies, and in this way it lost the first round of the contest without having struck a blow, having ignored the eternal truth that, at any rate before the arrival of the aeroplane, an overseas empire could only be retained by command of the sea.

On July 1st, 1570, the Turkish expeditionary force made its appearance in Cypriot waters, and anchored off Larnaca, where its commander, Lala Mustapha Pasha, at once established a strong bridgehead, and whence he sent reconnoitring parties into the interior to test the strength of the enemy defences. They soon discovered that they would meet with no opposition from the mass of the inhabitants who cordially disliked the Venetians, and were quite willing to co-operate with the Turks of whom they had had no previous experience. This meant that the defence of Cyprus devolved on the fortresses of Nicosia, Famagusta, and Kyrenia.

[1] *vide supra*, p. 60.

Having ascertained these facts Lala Mustapha waited at Larnaca until his whole force was assembled – it consisted of some 50,000 infantry, 2,500 cavalry, 30 pieces of heavy artillery, and 50 smaller guns.

On the Venetian side everything was in disarray. All the available forces were concentrated in Nicosia and Famagusta, and a small garrison was put in Kyrenia, but the Venetian resources were negligible compared with those of Lala Mustapha. The local militia were of varying quality, and in addition there were a mere 5,000 regular infantry: the cavalry hardly amounted to 500, because, we are told, the feudal nobles who were responsible for providing the horses to mount them had been replacing the horses by locally bred mules. The leadership was equally uninspiring. The lieutenant-governor had recently died, and his successor had not arrived from Venice, while the *proveditore*, one Nicolo Dandolo, was a weak character, and quite unable to grapple with the situation. An exception was the general of the militia, Astore Baglione, and he had strongly urged that the invaders should be opposed before they established their bridgehead, but his advice was rejected.

Lala Mustapha was at first in some doubt whether to make his main effort against Nicosia or Famagusta, but he finally decided in favour of the former. The Turks accordingly marched to that place – without encountering any opposition – and pitched their camp to the south-east of the town, on the high ground where the Asylum was later to be built. Thereafter the siege was undertaken in the approved method of the time. The first batteries were set up at a distance of about three hundred paces from the ramparts, on a front of about a mile extending from the Paphos gate to the Famagusta gate, in order to attack the four southern bastions of the town. Under cover of the fire from these batteries the besiegers occupied the old medieval ditch, which had not been completely filled in, and from there they pushed forward zigzag trenches that could not be enfiladed by the Venetians on the ramparts. By this means they edged their way to within eighty paces of the ramparts, and there set up a second line of batteries from which for four days they bombarded the four bastions, namely Podecatero, Costanza, Davila, and Tripoli.

The next move of the attacking forces was to drive trenches up to the counterscarp, where they threw up ramparts of earth, and also posted musketeers to drive the defenders from the walls. Under cover of this fire they drove deep trenches across the ditch, and protected them from the flanking fire of the Venetians by ramparts constructed of earth and brushwood: by this means they reached the corners of the bastions, and began to cut away the masonry so as to form a sloping approach along which to deliver an assault.

At this point the weakness of the Venetians became very obvious, and it mainly lay in the fact that the fire from the ramparts had proved insufficient to stop the construction of the enemy's trenches and the siting of his batteries, while there were insufficient troops in the town to deliver an effective counter-attack. All the same it was clear that something must be done now that the Turks were across the ditch and were beginning to demolish the bastions, and it was accordingly decided to make a sortie in order to destroy the works of the besiegers. It was made one midday when the Osmanli were sleeping in the shade, and at first achieved some success for two batteries were captured, but the Venetian soldiers got out of hand, and a strong counter-attack drove them back into Nicosia. This reverse put an end to any thoughts of further sallies on the part of the besieged, who henceforth contented themselves with constructing lines of defence across the four threatened bastions.

The siege had by now lasted for six weeks, and it was clear that Lala Mustapha had no time to lose if he was to capture the town before the end of the campaigning season. He offered the besieged terms of honourable surrender, but they were so convinced they would shortly be relieved that they refused to contemplate anything of the sort. Lala Mustapha's sources of information told him that no Venetian fleet was likely to arrive, so he decided to stake everything on one blow, and brought up the troops from his base at Larnaca, a step on which he had not hitherto ventured: the courage of the Janissaries was also stimulated by the promise of substantial awards to those who were the first across the walls.

The attack was made before dawn on September 9th, 1570, when the Venetian sentries must have been asleep. The Costanza bastion was stormed without any great difficulty, and its defenders driven into the main square of Nicosia: the Tripoli bastion met with a like fate, and its guns were turned on the Venetians in the square. Thereafter there was some particularly bitter street-fighting until the Turks were finally victorious. A city which resists to the last must expect to be sacked, and Nicosia was assuredly no exception to the rule: in the massacre which followed its capture some 20,000 people were butchered, including the governor and the bishop, and those not killed were sold as slaves or sent to work in the galleys.

The campaigning season was now drawing to an end, but Lala Mustapha still had some successes ahead of him: warned by the fate of Nicosia the Governor of Kyrenia surrendered without even a show of resistance, and the rest of the island, with the exception of Famagusta, followed his example. The Turkish general then moved on Famagusta, but when he found that it was going to be held against him he decided that it was too late in the year to begin a regular siege, so in October he settled down into winter quarters, and the Ottoman fleet returned to Constantinople.

Meanwhile the Serenissima had been conducting, but with little success, a diplomatic offensive to obtain allies. The Republic of Saint Mark enjoyed a very bad reputation for perfidy, and its record was particularly suspect where the Porte was concerned. She had often been at peace with the Sultan, when her neighbours were at war, and to her neutrality at critical moments might be attributed some of the most outstanding triumphs of the Crescent. Her territories had been respected when Calabria and the March of Ancona was being ravaged by the Barbary Corsairs. When the Knights of St John were driven from Rhodes the war-galleys of the Serenissima lay idle in the harbours of Cyprus and Crete, and when, a generation later, the Knights stood at bay at Malta the ambassadors of Venice were assuring Suleyman of her friendship. In these circumstances it is no wonder that most of the other Powers saw no reason why they should embroil themselves with the Porte for the sake of Venice. Shah Tahmasp I of Persia was, through his ministers, profuse in compliments and sympathy, but he took care to avoid any personal contact with the Venetian envoy. England had always been on good terms with Venice, but quite apart from the fact that she had no means of intervening in a Mediterranean quarrel Elizabeth I could hardly be expected to join an alliance of Catholic States. The Emperor Maximilian II had only recently made peace with the Sultan, and he had no desire to go to war again in the interests of Venice whom he had always found a very troublesome southern neighbour. Charles IX of France was too far off to provide any military aid, and he had no navy; moreover, he was the ally of the Sultan, and in any case his dominions were in a chronic state of civil war. In effect, only the Pope, and, through him, Philip in the end proved both able and willing to come to the aid of the sorely pressed Venetians.

Pius V, the title which Michel Ghislieri had taken on his elevation to the Papal throne in 1565, was one of the most outstanding Popes of the sixteenth century. He was now in his sixtyeighth year, and had been born at Bosco in the Milanese. He was of humble origin for his father had been a corn-dealer, and in early youth he used to travel with the mules that carried the grain from Lombardy across the Ligurian Alps to the ports of the Mediterranean. At the age of fourteen he was persuaded by some Dominican monks to embark on a clerical career, where his rise proved to be very rapid. At different times he held professorial chairs in the Universities of Bologna and Pavia, but what most struck those who came in contact with the future Pope was his force of character. One example of this will suffice. When he was Prior of Alva his convent was one day beset by three hundred hungry soldiers who were clamouring for food, and threatening to sack the building if their demand was not satisfied. The prior came to the gate, and told them that if they would behave in a peaceful and orderly manner they would be supplied with both food and shelter. The offer was accepted, and the prior established such an ascendancy over them that they not only carried out any instructions he gave them and protected the house from other possible marauders, but when they finally took their departure they left behind them an offering in acknowledgement of the hospitality of Saint Dominic.

Such was the background of the man who, with the support of Philip, became Pope Pius V, and in that capacity fulfilled all the high hopes which his supporters had formed of him. When the

Venetians made their appeal for help he eagerly seconded it, and although he had no navy of his own he promised to pay for the maintenance of twelve galleys if they would supply the ships. Furthermore, he sent an emissary of his own with that of the Serenissima to Spain so that the maximum pressure could be applied to the King to give a favourable reply to the Republic's request. They found Philip in Andalusia, and he received them most graciously, but he soon discovered that there was a considerable difference of opinion among his advisers as to the course which Spanish policy should take. Diego de Espinosa, who was not yet suffering from *folie de grandeur*, in particular expressed grave doubts concerning the wisdom of binding Spain by any formal treaty to a Power with such a bad reputation for duplicity as Venice. He was an able man with an extraordinary capacity for work which had primarily recommended him to his master, and although he did not carry the weight of Alba and Ruy Gómez in the Royal counsels the King always listened to what he had to say.

Philip himself shared to the full his ministers' distrust of the Republic of Saint Mark, but he took a wider view of the problem. Independent of any personal desire to appear before the world as the champion of Christendom he felt that the suggested co-operation afforded an excellent opportunity of weakening the maritime power of the Sultan, and thus of ensuring the safety of his own possessions in the Mediterranean. After considerable thought, therefore, he dismissed the Papal and Venetian emissaries with the assurance that notwithstanding his commitments in Granada and the Low Countries, he would come to the aid of the Republic, and with this end in view he promised to send commissioners to Rome to unite with those of the Pope and the Serenissima in drafting a treaty of alliance against the Porte.

At the same time a Spanish squadron, which was lying off Sicily under the command of Gian Andrea Doria – not, incidentally, a name likely to recommend its bearer to the Venetians – was ordered to put to sea and render what immediate assistance it could in the defence of Cyprus. Doria was joined by a small Papal squadron, and on the last day of August he made junction with the Venetians in Crete. A plan of campaign was drawn up, and was about to be put into execution when the news arrived of the fall of Nicosia. A dispute at once arose as to the course which should now be pursued, and several conflicting opinions were expressed, but no one had sufficient authority to enforce any particular view so a rupture took place, and the expedition was abandoned. The various squadrons returned to their respective bases, the Christian cause became the laughing-stock of the Mediterranean, and in Madrid, Rome and Venice a furious controversy arose in the endeavour to fix the responsibility for this disgraceful fiasco.

By this time Philip's undertaking to enter into an alliance with the Pope and the Serenissima was taking effect, and on July 1st, 1570, the plenipotentiaries were received in Rome by Pius V. Spain was represented by her ambassador to the Holy See, Don Juan de Zuñiga, with whom were associated Cardinal Granvelle and Cardinal Pacheco, Archbishop of Burgos; the Republic of Saint Mark contented itself with its ordinary ambassador, Michele Suriano, with whom was afterwards joined Giovanni Soranzo; while the Pope sent no less than seven Cardinals, of whom the more important was his nephew, Cardinal Alessandrino, who had begun life as apprentice to a tailor, and then, like his uncle, entered the Dominican order. His appointment was, incidentally, further evidence of the fact that in the sixteenth century – and for many years afterwards – high birth was no prerequisite for advancement in the diplomatic world, and Philip II fully realized that it is training, not class, that makes a good diplomatist. Henri IV was to take the same view, and two of his ablest ambassadors were Cardinal d'Ossat and President Jeannin, the one the son of a tanner and the other a foundling. Indeed, in the following century a French diplomatist went so far as to say, 'The majority of great noblemen are more suited for ceremonial missions than for negotiations. It is on the occasion of some baptism, marriage, death, or birth, or the ratification of a treaty, that they really shine. They can pay compliments as to the manner born, but they will neither take the trouble nor have the inclination to learn to transact business.'[1]

At their audience the Pope urged the plenipotentiaries to arrange as soon as possible the terms of an alliance against the

[1] cf. Cambon, J., *The Diplomatist*, p. 74. London, 1931.

enemy who was menacing all Christendom, and they made a dutiful reply, but when they assembled in private conference their mutual differences soon manifested themselves. The Spanish representatives made no secret of their suspicions of the Venetians, and Granvelle at once asked them for a set of proposals which he could place before Philip. To this Suriano replied that the Republic of Saint Mark was not present in the guise of a suppliant,[1] and that he had nothing to add beyond what had already been asked by the Pope. He then inquired why they should not adopt the chief points of the League of 1537, formed against the previous Sultan between Charles V, Paul III, and the Serenissima, and also the procedure of that day, namely to announce the formation of the alliance at the end of the first session, leaving the details to be adjusted later. Granvelle, however, would have none of this: the year 1570, he argued, was not 1537; times had changed, and the facts of the two cases were different; they were not met, like their predecessors, with a clear idea of the issues at stake, and therefore they must proceed cautiously.

The truth was that both the Spaniards and the Venetians were trying to turn the prospective alliance to their own ends, and only the Pope was single-minded in his desire to strike a blow at the infidel as such. Suriano's brief was to obtain access to the resources of Spain to save Cyprus, a course in which his Spanish colleagues were not in the least interested: Granvelle, on the contrary, desired that the League should be defensive against the Turks, but offensive against the Barbary Corsairs, while he gave proof of his suspicion of Venetian policy by requesting the Pope to excommunicate any party which might secede from the League. This, however, proved to be going too far, and he did not succeed in carrying either point.

In this atmosphere of mutual suspicion the conference, like so many conferences, pursued its weary and somewhat unedifying course; in the meantime all Cyprus, with the exception of Famagusta, passed into the hands of the Turks, and the allied fleets made their abortive cruise to Crete. As the weeks went by Philip did abate some of his reluctance to co-operate with the Serenissima, and that for a variety of reasons. In the first place the

[1] Which is exactly what she was.

Morisco rebellion was at an end, and he consequently had much freer hands than had previously been the case; while in the second the very considerable force which the Porte had mounted against Cyprus, and the rapidity of its success, had left him in no doubt as to the danger which threatened every Christian State in the Mediterranean. Above all, there was the risk that if he delayed much longer Venice might make a separate peace with the Turk.

As a matter of fact this was just what she had been trying to do. It was the French General Sarrail who said during the First World War that what he had seen of alliances somewhat diminished his respect for Napoleon, and the immediate reaction of the Venetian Government to the loss of Nicosia was to see what terms could be obtained from the Porte behind the backs of their allies. The Grand Vizier, however, would not hear of any compromise, and demanded the unconditional surrender of Cyprus. 'Peace is better for you than war,' he told the Venetian envoy. 'You cannot cope with the Sultan, who will take from you not Cyprus alone, but other dependencies. As for your Christian League, we know full well how little love the Christian Princes bear you. Put no trust in them. If you would but hold by the Sultan's robe you might do what you please in Europe, and enjoy perpetual peace.' As there was clearly nothing to be gained by these underhand negotiations, which in any case had already come to the ears of the Pope, the Republic decided that honesty was the best policy.

Even so acrimony continued to mark the relations of the pleni-potentiaries, and on one occasion Pius V, a testy saint if ever there was one, angrily ordered Granvelle out of his presence. The division of the expenses of the League was discussed at great length, and it was only with the utmost difficulty that the Venetian representatives were induced to contribute a third of the total amount, instead of a fourth as they had originally proposed. As may be supposed the right of naming the Captain-General of the League was fiercely debated. The Venetians claimed it in virtue of their position in the Levant, and the skill of their sailors: as against this Granvelle placed the rank of Don John, who was to command the Spanish forces, and the fact that Philip was making the largest financial contribution. As no agreement seemed possible the matter was referred to the Pope, who at first nominated Don

John to the naval, and the Duke of Savoy, who had won the battle of Saint Quentin for Spain, to the military command, but when it was remembered that the House of Savoy had an ancient claim to Cyprus it became obvious that this second appointment was hardly likely to be well received in Venice: therefore Don John was declared the *supremo* on both elements, and, after some more haggling, the Papal admiral, Marc Antonio Colonna, was appointed to be his second-in-command.

At long last, in May, 1571, the task was completed, and on the 25th of that month the Holy League was publicly inaugurated at Rome. On the previous day the Pope had written to Don John.

POPE PIUS V

To our well-beloved son in Christ, health and the apostolic benediction. Almighty God, the author of all good, has been pleased that, with his divine favour, the League should be concluded, which I, right dear son in Christ the Catholic King of the Spains your brother, and the Illustrious Republic of the Venetians, some months ago began to negotiate against the most cruel tyrant, the lord of the Turks: which having come to so good an issue, it appeared to us right to congratulate your nobleness on the occasion, as by these letters we do, being assured that our message will be welcome and agreeable to you, on account both of your piety towards God, and of your desire for the increase of the Christian world.

Greatly do we rejoice to behold you thus prosperously navigating this our sea, that together with the fleets of the other members of the League you may make a beginning of the destruction of the common enemy; and therefore do we entreat and warn you in Christ our Lord, that, imitating the virtue of the captains-general, your predecessors, you use your discretion diligently both to provide all things requisite to the success of the expedition and to avoid delay, which, in affairs of war, is so important and so praiseworthy.

We would further urge this upon you with many reasons, did we not know that the business carries with it its reward in the common benefit of the Christian world, and your particular honour, and that you need no further exhortation from our zealous and fatherly love, being assured that your nobleness will never be found wanting either to the one or to the other. Given at Rome on the 24th of May, 1571.[1]

On May 25th the Pope held a consistory in which the treaty was read by the datary of the Church. When this had been done Pius laid his hand upon his bosom, and swore to observe it; his example was then followed by the Cardinal of Burgos and Juan de Zuñiga in the name of the King of Spain,[2] and Michele Suriano and Giovanni Soranzo on behalf of the Republic of Saint Mark: the next day High Mass and a colourful procession celebrated the completion of the Holy League.

In substance the provisions of this treaty were the following:

The League was to be perpetual, not only against the Turks, but against Algiers, Tunis, and Tripoli. (This was a tribute to the diplomacy of Granvelle, for the Venetians had originally no such intention.)

The forces of the League were to consist of two hundred galleys, one hundred vessels of war, fifty thousand infantry – Spanish, Italian, and German – four thousand, five hundred light cavalry, and a fitting complement of artillery and munitions.

These forces were to be ready every year in March, or at latest in April, to proceed to the Levant, or on any other expedition, according as might have been agreed upon by the contracting parties, who were to meet every autumn in Rome to decide upon the campaign of the following year.

In years in which no combined enterprise was undertaken each of the contracting parties was to be at liberty to undertake any operation against the Turks on his own account. Algiers, Tunis, and Tripoli were considered to be especially under the observation of the King of Spain, and the Gulf of Venice under that of the Republic of Saint Mark; and in the event of either the King or the Serenissima undertaking an operation, each of these Powers was to have the right of calling upon the other to come to its assistance with fifty galleys, provided the Power, so called upon, was not at the time menaced by the Turk.

[1] cf. Vanderhammen, Lorenzo, *Don Juan de Austria*, folio 154. Madrid, 1627.
[2] Cardinal Granvelle had been sent to Naples where the Viceroy had recently died.

The contracting parties were reciprocally bound to defend each other's dominions from the attacks of the Turk with the exception of the Pope, whose towns and territories were nevertheless to be defended by the forces both of the King and of the Republic.

The expenses of the war were to be divided into six equal shares, of which the King was to defray three, the Republic two, and the Pope one. Of any other expenses, the King was to pay two-thirds and the Venetians one-third. The Republic undertook to furnish twelve galleys to the Pope, who was to arm and maintain them, and provide a contingent of three thousand infantry.

Each of the allies was to supply in larger proportion those materials of war which were most plentiful in his territory, the excess of these to be taken as an equivalent for a smaller proportional contribution by others.

Each was to be allowed to supply himself with corn, duty free, for the purpose of the League, at any port belonging to any of the other contracting parties.

In the conduct and administration of the war, each of the three Commanders-in-Chief was to have a voice, the execution of their plans being left to the Captain-General of the League. Don John of Austria was named Captain-General, and in his absence Marc Antonio Colonna, the Commander of the Papal forces.

The Captain-General of the League was not to use any personal banner, but only that of the League.

The Emperor Maximilian and the Kings of France and Portugal were to have it in their power to join the League, under conditions to be agreed upon, and the Pope was to use his influence with these sovereigns to obtain their co-operation.

The territory of Ragusa was not to be molested by the forces of the League, unless for some reason to be approved of by the Pope.

Any territories that might be acquired by the League were to be divided between the contracting parties according to the rules laid down in the League of 1537, excepting those in Tunis Algiers, and Tripoli, which were to belong to the King of Spain.

Other spoil was to be divided in the same proportions as the expenses of the League.

The Pope or his successor was to be the arbiter of any differences which might arise between the contracting parties.

Finally, none of the allies was to make a truce, peace, or alliance with the Turk without giving notice to all the rest, and obtaining their consent.[1]

It is not possible to read the clauses of this treaty without echoing the sentiments of General Sarrail. On the one hand were Spain and the Republic of Saint Mark, intensely suspicious of one another, and only working together in relative harmony owing to the pressure of a man nearly seventy; on the other were the resources of a vast Empire which stretched from Budapest to the Red Sea, and from the borders of Persia to those of Morocco, all under the control of a man of outstanding ability, namely the Grand Vizier, Mohammed Sokolli. It is by comparing the strength and weakness of the contending parties that one can best realize the magnitude of the task which faced Don John.

[1] cf. Arroyo, M. A., *Relación del Progresso della Armada de la Santa Liga*, folios 20–23. Milan, 1576.

6

Lepanto: The Preliminaries

THE NEGOTIATIONS LEADING UP TO THE FORMATION OF
the Holy League may have been unduly prolonged, but no time
was lost at Madrid as soon as Philip heard that it had been ratified.
This news reached him on the morning of June 6th, 1571, and at
three o'clock that afternoon his brother left the capital for the
seat of war, or in the words of G. K. Chesterton:

> Sudden and still – hurrah!
> Bolt from Iberia!
> Don John of Austria
> Is gone by Alcalá.

Part of his household of twenty-one had already preceded him,
and part were to follow immediately, while Philip would not have
been Philip if he had not supplied him with a memorandum containing the most elaborate instructions as to the way in which
everybody with whom he came in contact should be addressed:
etiquette meant a great deal in sixteenth-century Europe, and no
one was better versed in it than the Catholic King. He also pointed
out to his brother that he would be commanding troops who would
not necessarily take kindly to a Spanish general, and that tact
would be required upon a considerable scale.[1]

Those early summer days witnessed a veritable exodus from
Madrid to Catalonia, for the young and adventurous all wanted
to see service against the infidel under so dashing and popular a
prince, and in consequence he was followed by a very numerous
cavalcade. His journey had thus all the appearance of a Royal
progress; the castles of the nobility were thrown open with the
most lavish hospitality for him and his suite; at Zaragoza he was
received with a pomp and ceremony which could not have been

---

[1] cf. Ossorio, A., *Vida de Don Juan de Austria*, pp. 94–96. Madrid, 1946.

more elaborate in the case of the King himself: and, always deeply religious, he spent two days in the Monastery of Monserrat. It was all very different from his fugitive dash to Barcelona six years before in the vain hope of participating in the relief of Malta.

Among those who accompanied Don John to Catalonia was Maria de Mendoza, to whom there can be no doubt that at this time he was sincerely devoted. That his feelings were reciprocated is abundantly clear, but she seems to have been a very temperamental young lady, and she undoubtedly tried to play upon her lover's feelings in her endeavour to persuade him not to leave her: there was at least one scene between them at which they were both in tears, and finally Don John thought it well to take his leave of her in writing. He pointed out that the King's commands must be obeyed, but he confessed that he would be leaving his heart behind him in Spain. This would not appear to have had much effect upon Maria, but Don John was able to put to sea without any further *crises des nerfs* in public, at any rate on his part.[1]

On June 16th he had arrived at Barcelona, where he was welcomed on the same scale as elsewhere since he left Madrid, and he remained there until the 20th of the following month. If, however, his public reception was all that could be desired, he received a letter from Philip which betrayed the old mistrust that he would be too rash, and placed definite restrictions upon his freedom of action. The King and his ministers could not cure themselves of the suspicion that in the Morisco campaign he had shown more courage than judgement, and they had no intention of leaving the fate of an extremely costly fleet and of thousands of men in the hands of one whom they considered to be an impetuous and inexperienced youth; accordingly, Don John was told that in all his actions he must attach particular weight to the opinion of Gian Andrea Doria, and that he must not risk a battle without the unanimous consent of Doria, Requesens, and Santa Cruz.[2]

We have already seen how vulnerable Don John was to any suggestion that he lacked judgement, and this further evidence

[1] cf. Ossorio, A., *op. cit.*, pp. 97–98. Madrid, 1946.
[2] cf. Cabrera de Córdoba, L., *Felipe II, Rey de España*, vol. ii, p. 102. Madrid, 1619.

that the King still entertained doubts on this score clearly wounded him to the quick. On July 8th he unbosomed himself in a long letter to Ruy Gómez which was obviously intended to be shown to Philip, or at any rate its contents were meant to be communicated to him. The gist of his complaint is contained in one long sentence:

> I confess to you that this unkind treatment, of putting me on an equality with many others at the time that all are observing how I am treated has at times led me to think of giving up my post,[1] and seeking some other path wherein to serve God and His Majesty, since for this place which I now hold it is given me so clearly to understand that I am not fitted; yet if anything can console me it is the persuasion that, as I do not deserve the treatment I receive it proceeds not from His Majesty's will but from that of some person who tells him that if little authority be held by me His Majesty's authority will be the greater.

Whether this last sentence was meant as a sly dig at Gómez himself must be a matter of opinion, but the letter ends upon a very friendly note:

> Above all, whatever your opinion may be, I desire that you should tell it frankly and give me your advice, remembering how meritorious it is before God to act the part of a father to one who has no other father but you, and who is beset by a thousand persons who seek occasion in my youth and inexperience to ruin me, as if ruining me would be for their honour and advantage. Seeing how important this matter is to me, I once more commend it to you, and I commend myself to you, in whom my whole confidence is placed.

This was all very well, but Don John seems to have overlooked the fact that by stressing his 'youth and inexperience' he was in reality justifying his brother in that very restriction of his powers of which he so bitterly complained. However this may be, four days later he wrote to the King himself, presumably in the belief that by then Philip would have become acquainted with the contents of his letter to Gómez.

[1] Is the influence of Maria de Mendoza to be traced here?

133

S.C.R.M.

For the grace and favour which Your Majesty has done me in writing me a letter in your own hand, I kiss your hands many times. With it, I have received the instructions and other despatches for my voyage, and they have reached me in such good time that I regret the time which has been lost and the consequent prejudice to Your Majesty's service. I am every hour looking for the Marquess of Santa Cruz, upon whose arrival we may at once set sail, that being the only thing needed to enable us to proceed on our voyage.

As to what concerns following the instructions and advice of the persons whom Your Majesty has been pleased to appoint in order that they may afford me their aid and counsel, and especially the Grand Commander, I certainly will do it, for I know that to be my duty, and I am glad that it should be thus ordered that the affairs both of Your Majesty's service in general and of this which is entrusted to my charge should be assured by so much sincerity and prudence. In truth I neither desire nor look for anything else but that we should all strive after this sole object, postponing other points less important. At the least thus it is with me, and therefore Your Majesty need have no doubt but that I shall always proceed in conformity with this desire, and entreating Your Majesty to cause me always to be informed of that in which I may have shown any want of understanding, for, as I have at other times written to Your Majesty, I trust so little to my age, experience and opinion, that I see plainly the great need I have of the counsel of others; therefore I again entreat Your Majesty with all possible humility that you will ever admonish and reprehend me whenever you shall judge that, after I have been heard, I have failed to do what is fitting. For never shall that happen for want of goodwill, there being no man in the world to whom in that respect I will allow to have the advantage of me, as in reason I am bound. Of the Instruction which Your Majesty gave me with your own hand on the first voyage I made in the galleys, I am every day seeing the great value; and such will be the case still more now, according, as I think, to the wish of Your Majesty, to whom it is my aim to give satisfaction, there being in my eyes nothing more desirable than to obtain the favour and accomplish the wishes of Your Majesty.

I have answered the Pope; the Grand Commander thinking that it was not fitting to await Your Majesty's reply, and that my letter would do if it were so shaped that I might be prepared with a defence in the future when I may have to treat on similar matters.

Your Majesty has done me a very great favour in directing Antonio Pérez to send me a copy of that which has been written to the ministers in Italy, as to the manner in which I am to be received and treated, and not only will it be to me a pleasure to conform myself to Your Majesty's will in this matter, but I would be glad to have the power of divining your thoughts in all things else in order to follow them, as it is my duty to do. Yet with due humility and respect, I would venture to say that it would be to me an infinite favour and boon if Your Majesty would be pleased to communicate with me directly with your own mouth, which I here desire for two reasons. Of these the chief is, that in affairs of this quality it is not for the good of Your Majesty's service that any one of your ministers should be enabled to deliberate with me as to what your pleasure is, none of them being under the same obligations to give effect to it that I am. The other reason is, because I might have made, before leaving, certain arrangements directed towards the end of securing with less noise that which Your Majesty desires; and because something is due to me inasmuch as God has made me Your Majesty's brother, and I cannot therefore avoid saying so, nor help feeling hurt, that I should have been so little considered that at the time when all think I have deserved something better at Your Majesty's hands and look to see me obtain it, I should behold a proof of the contrary in your order reducing me to an equality with many others of your servants, a thing certainly in my conscience not deserved, having always held myself more ready for Your Majesty's service than for vanities or any other things.

God can bear witness of the pain which this occurrence has given me, for no other reason than because it shows how little satisfaction my services have given; and therefore I very often find myself thinking whether it would be more according to Your Majesty's pleasure if I were to seek some other mode of serving you, since in my present post I believe myself to be so out of favour that I cannot attain the accomplishment of that to which my desires here tend and strive. Meanwhile I will obey, as far as possible, whatever they may be, the orders which Your Majesty may give, although I fear the difficulty arising out of the flattery which they say prevails in Italy. Your Majesty may believe me that I wish neither for honour nor wealth unless for the purpose of therewith serving Your Majesty better; but the consideration of this matter does not concern me, it being my duty to execute that which I am ordered, in which I shall never fail in any case whatsoever.

Our Lord, etc. 12th July, 1571.

Petulant as is the tone of this letter it is impossible not to have some sympathy for the young man who wrote it, humiliated as only youth can be by his enforced dependence upon the judgement of others, and worked upon at the same time by the hysterical outburst of a woman – the mother of his child – to whom he was sincerely devoted.

While Don John was smarting under the treatment unjustly, as he thought, meted out to him by his brother, and was mingling his tears with those of Maria de Mendoza, it was every day becoming more certain that the Holy League would not receive any assistance from France. Charles IX assured the Serenissima that he had done everything in his power to dissuade his ally the Sultan from his aggressive policy towards her, and he expressed his regret that his own domestic troubles prevented him from rendering any active assistance, but he promised that he would join any alliance against the infidel as soon as he was assured that the Emperor and the other Christian Powers were combining, not for their private advantage, but for the honour and safety of Christendom as a whole.[1]

The truth is that the formation of the Holy League was causing the Most Christian King a good deal of disquiet. During the winter

[1] cf. Charrière, E., *Négociations de la France dans le Levant*, vol. iii, p. 198. Paris, 1848–60.

it had been customary in Paris to scoff at the whole affair, and to say that Madrid and Venice were squabbling over the command of an expedition which would never be assembled. Now, however, that the Holy League was a fact it could no longer be laughed out of court, and envoys were consequently sent to Rome and Constantinople for the purpose of embroiling the allies with one another, or of inducing the Sultan to dissolve their unity by moderating his policy. These intrigues produced no practical result beyond providing the wits of Madrid with the joke that the King of France had sent as his emissaries a soldier to the Pope and a bishop to the Sultan, as if he were going to fight the one and convert the other.[1]

The news, too, from the seat of war in the Levant was far from encouraging. In January, 1571, the Venetians had taken advantage of the absence of the Turkish fleet at Constantinople to reinforce and revictual Famagusta, and its garrison was brought up to a strength of 4,000 infantry, 800 militia, 3,000 citizens and peasants, and 200 Albanians, all under the command of Marc Antonio Bragadino. More than that the Republic of Saint Mark was unable to do unaided, so far had she fallen from her proud estate of former days.

With the spring came a revival of Turkish aggression. In April the invaders were heavily reinforced, and the first batteries were erected on a front of a thousand paces on the south side of the fortress, against the arsenal tower: by the end of May the Turks had driven their trenches up to the counterscarp, entered and crossed the ditch, and had begun to mine the ravelin and the arsenal tower. Some of these mines were discovered by the defenders during their own subterranean counter-measures, and the Venetians were only too glad to make use of the gunpowder they thus acquired, for their supplies were running perilously low.

All through June, while Don John was resisting the pleas of Maria de Mendoza and resenting the affront which he considered his brother had put upon him, this mining and counter-mining continued. On the 21st the besiegers succeeded in firing a mine

[1] cf. Carraciolo, F., Conte de Biccari, *I Commentarii della Guerra fatta coi Turchi da D. Giovanni d'Austria, dopo che venne in Halia*, p. 57. Florence, 1581.

under the arsenal tower which shattered the wall; the Turks thereupon swarmed over the debris, but after five hours of hand-to-hand fighting their attack was repulsed by the defenders led by Baglione. A week later much the same situation was repeated when a breach was blown in the walls, but again an attempt to carry the fortress by assault was repulsed. On July 9th the ravelin was captured, but it had been ruined by the Venetians in anticipation of such an event taking place, and in the resulting explosion more than a thousand Turks lost their lives, while nothing was left standing that could be of any use to either combatant. So it went on with the Turkish artillery and mines doing their worst, but with the defenders resisting every assault.

Nevertheless it was clear that the end could not long be delayed, for while the Turks were every day being reinforced, within the fortress men, munitions, and food were becoming ever shorter, and there was no sign of any relieving force. By the end of July the Venetian High Command had come to the conclusion that further resistance was impossible, and on August 1st it decided to surrender. It would appear that this move was by no means displeasing to Lala Mustapha, for not only was he losing heavily in the repeated assaults, but he knew better than the besieged that Don John was putting to sea, and he had no desire to be caught between the two fires of the garrison of Famagusta and a Spanish expeditionary force. Accordingly he was prepared to grant reasonable terms, which were that the fortress would be surrendered on condition that all lives were to be spared, that the garrison should be transported to Crete with their arms and property, and that the inhabitants should be allowed either to remain in safety or to go whither they wished.

At first all went well, and as soon as the terms had been signed Lala Mustapha sent forty vessels into the harbour, and on them the sick and wounded were embarked; by August 4th they had been followed by the rest of the garrison. At this point the first complication arose for Bragadino complained that the Osmanli were offering violence to such of the inhabitants as remained, and that in any case not enough ships had been provided. The Turkish commander-in-chief replied that he would take the necessary steps to enforce discipline among his troops, and that he would provide two more ships; he also said that he would like to meet Bragadino in person.

Thereafter everything went wrong. It is true that Bragadino was at first treated with the utmost courtesy, and for a space he and his conqueror seem to have chatted amicably enough together: then a quarrel arose, apparently because Lala Mustapha demanded hostages for the safe return of his ships, which the Venetian refused on the ground that this had not been provided for in the terms of capitulation. Whether Lala Mustapha had meditated treachery from the beginning, or merely had no control over his temper, is uncertain, but he took umbrage at Bragadino's attitude, and declared the terms of the capitulation to have been broken: he gave orders that all his Venetian guests were to be executed on the spot, with the exception of Bragadino, who on this occasion was merely deprived of his nose and ears, but after a fortnight of imprisonment and torture he was bound to the pillory in the square of Famagusta, and flayed alive under the eyes of Lala Mustapha: his skin, stuffed with straw, was then exposed to public ridicule and finally sent to Constantinople for the delectation of the Sultan. Some years later it was purchased by his brother for a large sum of money, taken to Venice, and laid in a marble urn in the church of SS Giovanni and Paolo.[1] With the fall of Famagusta for three centuries Cyprus passed out of history until it was once more brought on the international stage, this time by a British Prime Minister.

On July 26th Don John had arrived at Genoa with a fleet of forty-two ships and in company with the Archdukes Rudolf and Ernest, and the welcome which he received must have done much to compensate both for the resentment which he felt at his brother's lack of confidence in him and for his separation from Maria de Mendoza. For a Spaniard in the latter part of the sixteenth-century Italy was hardly a foreign country, so completely was it under the domination of Spain. That many Italians bitterly resented this state of affairs cannot be denied, but their memories of the French were at least equally unpleasant, and independence in any form was out of the question: if for any reason the Spaniards had been forced to withdraw Italy would have become an Ottoman pashalik, and that

[1] cf. Newman, P., *A Short History of Cyprus*, pp. 167–70. London, 1940.

sobering reflection did much to resign her more thoughtful inhabitants to the control of Madrid.

The actual Spanish possessions consisted of the Duchy of Milan, the Kingdom of the Two Sicilies, and what was known as the Stato dei Presidi. This last comprised the towns of Orbetello, Talamone, Monte Argentaro, Porto Ercole, and Porto Santo Stefano which Philip had in 1557 obliged Cosimo I of Tuscany to leave in Spanish hands as pledges for his loyalty, and they provided Spain with a ready means of access to the Italian peninsula should Genoa ever be closed to her. They thus possessed considerable strategic, but no other, importance. The Spanish Empire was governed by councils, and Italy was no exception, for the supreme authority was the Council of Italy, a mixed body of Spaniards and Italians which sat at Madrid, and had recently been reconstituted, but in actual fact the Viceroys in Milan and Naples had things very much their own way.

The Milanese was regarded primarily as a *place d'armes*. Its strategical importance was very great indeed, for it not only linked Spain with Austria, and, through the Franche Comté, with the Low Countries, but it served as a barrier against a French advance into Central or Southern Italy. In consequence, the Lombard towns were all strongly fortified, as were also the frontiers of the Duchy. There was a permanent garrison of about five thousand Spanish infantry, besides Italian troops, which included a native militia, for which each Lombard commune had to provide and equip its quota of recruits. The military power was always predominant over the civil, and although the Senate of Milan continued to exist, it was invariably beaten in any trial of strength against the Spanish Viceroys. There was, however, a considerable measure of municipal self-government, and in the rural districts there was a great deal of local patriotism in the various communes.

In Naples the position was somewhat different, for the Viceroy, at any rate in theory, was supposed to consult the Collateral Council, while the old Neapolitan Parliament, with its three estates, was still summoned to vote supplies. In the city itself the municipal administration was conducted by district councils, called *piazze*, five for the nobles and one for the people, and each of them chose an *eletto* to transact business with the Viceroy, though in actual fact the country was so divided against itself that this machinery never functioned properly. The memories of the old feuds between Guelf and Ghibelline, and between Aragón and Anjou, prevented any common action on the part of the aristocracy, while the mass of the people were too fickle to remain united long enough to achieve any one object. On the other hand a good deal of money was spent by the Viceroy upon public works, and the military element was not supreme in Naples as it was in Milan. The real trouble, as elsewhere in the latter part of the sixteenth century, was finance, for owing to the fall in the value of money, taxation had to be trebled between 1558 and 1620, and in this connexion the cumbrous and wasteful Spanish fiscal system was not a help.

Sicily was in a happier position, in spite of the fact that it suffered from many of the same disadvantages to which Naples was subject. It had belonged to Aragón for centuries before Spain herself had become united, and it retained its medieval constitution with a consequent independence of political life, which enabled it to resist the more bureaucratic tendencies of Spanish rule: moreover the memory of the Sicilian Vespers was sufficiently fresh to make even the most ham-handed Spanish official cautious, so Parliament continued to make laws and vote taxes, and the nobles to retain their feudal authority. The towns were specially active and independent, and the export of corn made them wealthy, but the rivalry between them, particularly between Palermo and Messina, was bitter, though this state of affairs was by no means displeasing to the authorities in Madrid.

Certainly the Spanish possessions in Italy were not a paying proposition for, far from contributing to the Spanish exchequer, the Milanese was run at a loss, and the deficit there had usually to be made up out of the surplus, if any, in Naples. What the Kings of Spain did get out of Italy was generals, such as Parma and Spinola, and soldiers, as we have already seen.

In the summer of 1571 Philip could count on as widespread support in the nominally independent states of Italy as in his own dominions, for with the Turkish fleet sweeping the Adriatic it was clear almost to the meanest intellect that the choice of master lay between Madrid and Constantinople. Genoa, where Don John had broken his journey to the seat of war, had fallen far from her proud state in the Middle Ages, but she was strongly Spanish in sympathy, and was known in the rest of Italy as *'la meretrice di Spagna'*. Spanish dress was the fashion, and the women wore the great hoop that was to be seen everywhere in Madrid, though it was liable to impede their progress in Genoa itself where the streets were so steep and narrow that coaches were almost unknown; indeed, when two ladies met with their attendants they made, as an English visitor put it, 'as great an embarras as two carts on London Bridge'. The Genoese were far from popular in the rest of Italy because of their allegedly sharp methods of business, and they acted as bankers, brokers, and tax-collectors not only in the Spanish provinces, but even in Spain itself. The city was divided into factions like all Italian cities, but at this time it was controlled by the Dorias, whose palace was one of the wonders of Genoa. It was especially notable for its large aviary, in which grew many rare trees.

The Spanish Crown and the Papacy were by no means always on good terms, and no statement is further from the truth than that Philip was the secular arm of the Counter-Reformation,[1] even if the Catholic faith was the chief link between the people he ruled. Indeed, when Sixtus V became Pope in 1585 it was widely believed in Madrid that he had sold his soul to the Devil in order to attain the office. On the present occasion, however, with Pius V the originator of the Holy League and the King of Spain its protagonist, relations between Rome and Madrid could not have been more friendly. It was the same with Savoy, whose Duke, Emmanuel Philibert, was not only a personal friend of Philip and had commanded the Spanish Army at the battle of Saint Quentin, but he owed his restoration to his throne to the King of Spain.

Lastly, there was the Serenissima. Hispano–Venetian relations have already been discussed, but adversity had brought the Republic of Saint Mark to seek the aid of the Catholic King, and however suspicious the two Powers might be of one another they were nominally allies. As the campaign in Cyprus had abundantly proved the great days of Venice were over. The discovery of the Cape route to the East and of the New World had cut at the roots

---

[1] cf. Petrie, Sir Charles, *Philip II of Spain*, pp. 183–92. London, 1963.

of her commercial prosperity; the League of Cambrai had dealt her a staggering blow; and now in the struggle with the Turk it was clear that she had an antagonist with whom she could not cope. Yet if the Republic was no longer feared, she was still respected, and her decline was not obvious to the casual visitor. She gave her subjects, at any rate in the capital, a strong, orderly, and wise government, which was in many ways a model for the age; the traditions of the public service were still alive in the governing class in spite of the undeniable growth of corruption; and in all the archives of Europe are to be found the dispatches of her ambassadors to prove the excellence of her diplomatic service. Even in the next century a Welsh traveller could say of her that she still looked fresh and flourishing without the least furrow of age in her forehead.[1]

Such was the Italy which now received Don John with open arms, in the first instance because of the mission which brought him, and before long on his own account.

Genoa certainly lived up to its Hispanophil tradition during the five days that he spent there, and the Dorias to their reputation for hospitality. He himself made a most favourable impression, as a Venetian, Savorgnano, was careful to note in his diary, when he described Don John as 'a youth of an active and well-developed frame, with light hair and a countenance very pleasing and comely'. At a ball at the Doria palace he comments that 'the Archdukes danced passably well, but that everybody was surprised and delighted by the spirit and grace of the dancing of Don John'.[2] At Genoa the young Archdukes took leave of their uncle, and continued their journey to Vienna by way of Milan. On the other hand Don John was joined by several Italian princes, including Alexander Farnese, his nephew and former fellow-student at Alcalá.

Don John did not, however, waste his time wholly in frivolities, for it was at Genoa that he began preparations for the coming campaign. Santa Cruz was sent on ahead to Naples, while Doria was ordered to Spezia to take on board some Italian and German troops. Don John himself embarked on the night of July 31st,

---

[1] cf. Collison-Morley, L., *Italy After the Renaissance*, p. 222. London, 1930.

[2] Quoted by Stirling-Maxwell, Sir William, *Don John of Austria*, vol. i, p. 356. London, 1883.

and sailed at daybreak on the following day – while the Lion of Saint Mark was being replaced by the Crescent on the ramparts of Famagusta. He touched in rapid succession at Spezia; at Porto Ercole, where he strengthened the Spanish garrison with a few troops; and at Civitá Vecchia. During this voyage he wrote flattering letters to various Italian princes, and so enhanced that reputation for charm and courtesy which has attached to him down to the present day. In particular he sent a most gracious message to Don Garcia de Toledo, who in his retirement was at the baths of Poggio in Tuscany, and whom he had succeeded in command of the Spanish Navy. Don Garcia had been with Charles V in triumph at Tunis and in disaster at Algiers; he had been with Andrea Doria at Prevesa; he had himself taken Peñon de Velez; and he had relieved Malta at a critical moment. Whether he was a great general must remain in dispute, but there can be no doubt that he was a loyal subject of the Spanish Crown, and it irked him to remain inactive at this particular moment. 'By the life of St Peter,' he wrote to Requesens, 'I swear that if I had a little better health I would ship myself as a soldier or a sailor under Don John as gladly as I would under the King himself.'[1] To him Don John wrote, 'I would you were with me here, but as this may not be, I will set great store by such prudent counsel as you may see fit to give a youth who is about to undertake such an enterprise as I now have in hand.'[2] It was by such kindly and thoughtful acts as these that Don John earned his widespread popularity.

By the time he reached Naples on August 9th he had roused the enthusiasm of his own fellow-countrymen and of the Italians to a pitch which recalled that of the earlier Crusades. On landing he was greeted by Cardinal Granvelle who had been acting as Viceroy since the death of the Duke of Alcalá in the previous April, and Don John seems to have taken care to dress the part when he made his first appearance before the Neapolitan subjects of his brother, for we are told that he was attired in a gala dress of gold and crimson tissue, with a white velvet mantle trimmed with gold, a white plume, and crimson scarf. The *ancien régime* may have been ignorant of many things, but it knew how to impress. On the 14th

[1] *Doc. Ined.*, iii, p. 10.
[2] *Doc. Ined.*, xxviii, p. 160.

a ceremony took place in the conventual church of St Clara at which Don John received the standard of the League, a gift from Pius V, at the hands of Granvelle. It was a very ornate affair, being of blue damask, and in the centre was elaborately wrought the image of the crucified Christ; beneath that were linked together the scutcheon of the Pope, displaying three blood-red bars on a silver field; the lion shield of the Republic of Saint Mark; and the shield of many quarterings of Philip II; while, lower still, the design ended in the arms of Don John himself. On the steps of the high altar Granvelle presented it to the young commander-in-chief with the words, 'Take, fortunate Prince, these emblems of the Word made flesh, these symbols of the true faith, and may they give you a glorious victory over our impious enemy, and by your hand may his pride be laid low.' 'Amen,' replied Don John, and the word was repeated by all present.

Ceremonies, however, occupied but a small part of the ten days that Don John spent in Naples, for there was much to do in drawing up a plan of campaign, especially in view of the bad news which was flooding in from Levant, and also in superintending the embarkation of troops and supplies; indeed, to prevent further delay Santa Cruz was left in charge of the latter task, and Don John himself put to sea again on August 20th, with Messina as his immediate destination.

This Sicilian port, where he arrived on the 23rd, was to be the base for the campaign against the Turks, and Don John was accorded a reception worthy of the occasion. In the harbour, in front of the landing-place, there had been erected a huge square edifice with broad steps descending to the water, while each of its sides displayed three arches, a host of heraldic devices, and a great wealth of Latin prose and verse. On coming ashore the young commander-in-chief passed up the steps and under the arches, when he found awaiting him a charger covered with silver trappings, the gift of the municipality of Messina. By this time the cannon had begun to fire salutes, and the populace to cheer itself hoarse, and Don John rode through the gaily decorated streets to the cathedral of La Nunziatella. Nothing, indeed, was omitted which might serve to fire the enthusiasm of those who were to serve under him, and at night both the city and the harbour were brilliantly illuminated. It was, indeed, a reception which might have turned the head of an older man than Don John, but he lost no time in getting down to an appraisal of the forces at his disposal.

If he had previously entertained any doubts in the matter he was not long in realizing that the Serenissima was not what she had been, in spite of the strenuous efforts which she was putting forward on the present occasion. Banished citizens were invited to return, and to earn their pardon by serving as oarsmen, seamen, or soldiers; volunteers from the mainland were attracted by a promise of exemption from all direct taxation for four years, and the cities there were called upon to supply two thousand oarsmen; while mercenaries were engaged wherever they could be found, and the Albanians were persuaded to indulge in their congenial pastime of harrying the Osmanli. All this, and the fitting out of the galleys which were in 'moth-ball' as well as the construction of new ones, cost a lot of money, and this was raised by every possible means: numerous loans were contracted, the dignity of Procurator of Saint Mark was offered to every lender of twenty thousand ducats, and much national property was sold. To improve the efficiency of the fighting forces the law which forbade the galleys of the State to be commanded by anyone who was not a member of the Venetian aristocracy was relaxed, and for the first time nobles from the mainland were declared eligible to serve as captains. Above all, the senior officers, who were held responsible for the fiasco of the previous year's campaign, were replaced.

The supreme command of the Venetian forces was conferred upon Sebastian Veniero, who was then Governor of Crete, and was in due course to become Doge. He was an outspoken and somewhat testy old gentleman of seventy-five, but he had served the Serenissima in various capacities and with great fidelity over a period of years. He was in Crete when the news of his latest appointment reached him, and on April 18th, 1571, he hoisted the flag of Captain-General: immediately under him were two *proveditori*, namely Marco Quirini and Augustin Barbarigo.

Early in May his fleet consisted of ninety-four galleys, and he not unnaturally suggested that the first step should be the relief of Famagusta, but in making this proposal he encountered the detetmined opposition of his colleagues, who declared that it was an enterprise quite beyond their strength. Veniero reluctantly gave way, but in his subsequent report he said that had it not been for this decision 'Famagusta might still have stood, and the Turks would not have ravaged Crete, Zante, Cephalonia, Corfu, and Albania, to our shame and dismay'. Possibly, but many of his galleys, especially the ones that had been in 'moth-ball', were in very bad condition; not only, however, was his squadron badly found, but it was so under-manned that he was glad to lay up three of the worst galleys, and to use the men from them to strengthen the rest. He cruised for a time round the Ionian Islands, but his relations with the various garrison commanders would not appear to have been of the happiest, for he was to write in his report that as he was leaving Corfu 'at the hour of shutting the gates there was sent to me a parcel of the most wretched fellows that ever were seen, such as I should have been ashamed to have had on board my galleys. They were short of the required number; thirty were sick and could scarcely stand, so I could do nothing but send them back.' On July 11th he put to sea, and on the 23rd he sailed into the harbour of Messina.

The month which elapsed between this date and the arrival of Don John was an extremely trying one for all concerned. Most of Veniero's troubles arose from his own commitments which he was not able to fulfil. His government had ordered him to provide a hundred soldiers for each galley, but he had proved quite unable to raise that number, so he asked Marc Antonio Colonna, who was already at Messina in command of the Papal contingent, to help him. Colonna proved willing enough, but said that his men would only serve under their own officers, who must consequently be given commissions in the Venetian service. Veniero did not like this idea at all, but he had to give way and Gaspar Toralbo and Prospero Colonna were duly commissioned as colonels: even then, however, he did not get all the men he wanted. This was bad enough, but the news from the East could hardly have been worse. Ochiali was ravaging the Ionian Islands, each in turn, and carrying fire and sword along the shore of Dalmatia, almost to within sight of Venice itself. Veniero wanted to try conclusions with him with the Venetian contingent, recently reinforced from

Crete, alone, but Colonna, who was acting as commander-in-chief pending the arrival of Don John, would not hear of it, and the impetuous old man had to restrain his ardour.

Colonna, too, was not without his difficulties, for his troops and the Spaniards were continually brawling in the streets. The Papal soldiers complained that while taking the air in the cool of the evening they would be set upon by their Spanish allies, beaten up, and robbed of their cloaks and swords, while the Spaniards, equally indignant, declared that no soldier of the King could show himself in public without being hunted like a hare. To demonstrate his impartiality and in an attempt to maintain order and discipline Colonna hanged some of both nations, and induced the Viceroy to control the movements of the Spaniards when off duty. In the middle of all these anxieties Colonna had the misfortune to lose his daughter, who had recently married the Duke of Mondragone, and as a sign of mourning he ordered his galleys to be draped in black.

In these circumstances it is hardly surprising that Don John's arrival should have come as a great relief to those in authority. To quote Veniero's report to his government:

On August 23rd Don John arrived with forty-two galleys, and was received by us with all the ceremonies that were in our power. His Highness called us together to council and said to us that we ought to see what forces we had, and that he, on his part, had eighty-four galleys including three of Savoy and those of Malta, and seven thousand Spaniards, and six thousand Italians, all good troops. Signor Marc Antonio said that he had but few galleys, but that they were in excellent order. I said that I had come from Corfu with fifty-eight light galleys, six heavy ones, and three ships; that in the channel of Corfu two light galleys and two ships laden with rations, munitions, and soldiers had been captured by the enemy's fleet, and that one ship at Cephalonia had also been taken, and that I had sent into the Gulf of Venice three galleys, that I had lost by the accidents of the sea and by fire seven, so that I remained with forty-eight galleys not very well provided with soldiers on account of sickness, the capture of the ships, and the blockade of the vessels in the Gulf by the enemy's fleet; but that the Signor

Prospero Colonna was about to bring me two thousand foot, and that I should have twelve hundred from Signor Gaspar Toralbo, and four other captains were coming with eight hundred, which would make in all five thousand, two hundred, and that they would have been ready by this time, had they not been hindered, as their rations still were, by the Viceroy of Naples; that the six heavy galleys were now in good order, and that I expected sixty galleys from Crete.

His Highness asked me how many soldiers I reckoned each galley ought to have; I replied, usually from forty to fifty, because our rowing crews all fought. He said that having a superabundance of soldiers, he would supply the rest that were wanted; as to the victuals a memorial should be given in: he then asked about the policy to be pursued. We replied that as His Highness was waiting for the remainder of his galleys from Naples and Genoa, and we for ours from Crete, we should get things in order, and then speak of the policy to be pursued: this answer was made in consultation with Signor Marc Antonio. His Highness was satisfied.

As there is never a little gladness without a great deal of sadness, I have had letters informing me of the loss of Dulcigno, Antivari, and Budua, and that part of the (Turkish?) fleet was going to Cattaro and part to Zara, towards which point the army was also moving. We said to Don John that when his galleys had come from Naples and Genoa, and ours were provided with rations and soldiers, we ought, even if those from Crete had not arrived, to sail for Taranto, to prevent the Turkish fleet, which had taken Dulcigno, Antivari, and Budua, from doing what damage it pleased, leaving orders at Messina and on the coast of Calabria for the galleys from Crete to come on to Taranto, but that this need not stand in the way of any other enterprise which it might seem desirable to undertake. His Highness seemed content and gave us orders and letters for rations, money, and soldiers, which the Viceroy did not choose that Prospero Colonna should levy, and for the money which Borizzo was to send me in specie as letters of exchange were not obtainable.[1]

[1] cf. Stirling-Maxwell, Sir William, Don John of Austria, vol. ii, pp. 391-3. London, 1883.

In view of what had gone before Don John was taking care not to lay himself open to any charge of rashness, and one of his first acts after his arrival at Messina was to send two galleys, commanded respectively by Gil de Andrade, a Spanish Knight of Malta, and Chico Pisani, a Venetian, to cruise towards the East with a view to discovering the position, strength, and probable movements of the enemy.

Everything was tending to make him cautious. His Spanish advisers were very impressed with the formidableness of the Turk and were very distrustful of their allies: in particular Don Garcia de Toledo wrote letter after letter advising the utmost circumspection, and as he had relieved Malta a great deal of attention was paid to his admonitions in spite of his manifest shortcomings. To Requesens he wrote from Pisa that the soldiers in the Spanish fleet were raw recruits who hardly knew how to fire their pieces, while the Turks had plenty of seasoned men: he, for his part, would not care to meet them without some of the veterans who were far away in Flanders. It was of course, possible that the superiority of the League at sea might do something to redress the balance, but even so, without express orders from Philip, he personally would not care to find himself in a position where he could be forced to fight. A defeat would do more harm than a victory would do good, while, as for the Venetians, they were much better at giving advice than in taking action. 'For the love of God,' he concluded, 'consider well what a great affair this is, and the damage that may be caused by a mistake; but as it will be better for various good reasons that the Venetians should not know how much or why it is for His Majesty's interest that there should not be a battle, I pray you, after having read this letter to Don John, to destroy it, or at least do not let it get into any other hands than those of the secretary, Soto.'[1]

To Don John himself the old man was equally free with his advice. In the event of an action with the Turk he advised that the fleet of the League should be divided into three squadrons, with sufficient distance between them to give room for manœuvre, but that all should sail in one line. He had learnt this, he said, at Prevesa, where the Christian fleet fell into confusion in consequence

[1] *Doc. Ined.*, iii, 8–10.

of the great length of its unbroken line, but where Barbarossa derived great advantage from the three squadron order, 'a plan,' he added, 'which I have always kept in my memory, to be used when necessity should arise.' Only in one event did he think that there should be a departure from this plan, and it was if the Venetians asked, as they well might, to be placed in the van. It was to be hoped that everybody would do their duty, but less reliance was to be placed upon the Venetians than the rest, so it might be as well to have them in front. Don John should therefore concede the point with a good grace, and say that he has done so because of all the allies they are the most deeply interested in the quarrel, though he knows it will cause some discontent in the rest of the fleet. 'This intention of yours, however, ought in my opinion to be kept secret, because if the Venetians were to learn that the foremost place was to be had for the asking perhaps they would not ask for it.'[1]

So far as Colonna was concerned, Don John's personal relations with him seem to have been more friendly than was the official attitude of his government. The Spanish ministers regarded him as little better than a Venetian at heart although he was Grand Constable of Naples. Philip would appear to have shared these suspicions, and wrote reminding him of his allegiance and obligations to the Crown, which prompted the Papal admiral to complain to his friend, the Jesuit Francisco Borja, who was then in Spain.

I have received several letters from His Majesty, always putting before me the obligations which bind me to his service. It would thus appear that my own desire to serve him, which weighs with me far more than any honours or riches, is held to be of no account. I have heard that His Majesty had intended to write to me in terms yet more extraordinary. If it should come to that, I shall throw up the business, which will be a great relief to me. At the very time when I had thought my services would have been acknowledged, having scarcely been at Rome, and having given His Majesty no offence, and, moreover, having last year saved the honour of his fleet, and this year helped to conclude the League, I find myself called upon to write a justification of my conduct.

[1] *Doc. Ined.*, iii, 13–14.

How I serve Don John, he sees and shall see; but I am distressed when I am told that they are going to make me do my duty, as though this were something new to my family and to ine. God be praised that this at least shows us the nothingness of this world. It is even publicly reported here that Don John has come with orders to keep me in fear and subjection, and that the Pope has sent hither Monsignor Odescalchi chiefly to recommend me to Don John's favour, and to transact business with him, thinking that he and his people would not listen to me. Thank God that we are all here, and that it will be seen what each of us is worth.[1]

Don John used his charm to dispel Colonna's suspicions, and on the day of his public entry into Messina he spent two hours alone with him, when he assured his colleague that nothing would be decided over his head and that of Veniero. This approach had the desired effect so far as the Papal admiral himself was concerned, but it at once endangered his popularity with his Venetian allies, and the poor man was soon found writing to the Doge, Ludovico Mocenigo, 'My ill-wishers, wearying of making me out to be so great a Venetian, are now saying that I neglect the service of Your Serenity.'[2]

Meanwhile Don John was carrying out a detailed inspection of the forces under his command. He found the Papal contingent in excellent order, but this was not the case with the Venetians, as he told Don Garcia de Toledo in a letter dated August 30th:

Yesterday I began to visit the galleys of the Venetians, and went on board the flagship. You cannot believe what bad order both the soldiers and sailors were in. Arms and artillery they certainly have, but as fighting is not to be done without men a cold shiver runs through me when I see with what materials I am expected by the world to do something of importance, knowing that my galleys will be counted by numbers and not by quality. Nevertheless, I will endeavour to lose no opportunity that I have done my share of the duty, in which I

[1] cf. Guglielmotti, P. Alberto, *Marcantonio Colonna alla battaglia di Lepanto*, p. 180. Florence, 1862.
[2] cf. *ibid.*, p. 181.

shall find your advice of great use. To the ill condition of things on board the Venetians, another thing even worse must be added, namely that no kind of order seems to prevail amongst them, and each galley appears to come and go, as its captain pleases. Fine grounds indeed for their wish to fight![1]

Don John consulted the old man on the subject of tactics, and particularly with regard to the question whether in a naval battle it was advisable to be the first to open fire. Don Garcia's opinion was that the longer a vessel's fire could be reserved the better. He wrote:

> In my judgement the troopers are right who say that you should never fire your arquebus until you are near enough to be splashed with the blood of your enemy; and I have always heard the most experienced sea-captains say that the crashing of a ship's iron beak and the first report of her guns should be heard at the same moment, and I think so too. But your people should be taught not to be considering the enemy, or who is to fire first or last, but to fire when Your Highness gives the word, and only then.[2]

All this time the forces of the Holy League were being augmented by fresh arrivals. Veniero was joined by sixty-two vessels from Crete; thirty Spanish galleys arrived under the command of the formidable Marquess of Santa Cruz; ten transports came from Spezia with German troops; and twenty-two ships from Genoa hired by the King of Spain, of which twelve belonged to Doria.

As each national contingent was complete Don John passed it in review, and when this task had been accomplished he found himself at the head of the largest Christian armament ever assembled in the Mediterranean. Contemporary accounts vary with regard to the exact numbers under his command, but there were certainly upwards of three hundred ships and eighty thousand men. The Spanish fleet was composed of ninety galleys, twenty-four large ships, and fifty frigates and brigantines; among the galleys were three each from the Knights of Saint John, the Duke

[1] cf. Doc. Ined., iii, 16.
[2] Doc. Ined., iii, 25.

of Savoy, and the Republic of Genoa. The Venetian contribution consisted of a hundred and six galleys, six galleasses, two large ships, and twenty frigates. Twelve galleys and six frigates formed the squadron of the Pope. The mariners and galley-slaves were estimated at some fifty thousand.

The land forces were about thirty thousand strong. Of these Philip provided eight thousand Spaniards, six thousand Germans, and five thousand Italians, which included the *tercios* of Naples, Sicily, and Sardinia. These were not, however, the only Italians at Messina for five thousand took the field under the Lion of Saint Mark, and another two thousand were supplied by the Pope. There were also much smaller contingents from the various Italian princes, some of whom were present in person.

Yet among all this glittering throng the one man who was to attain the greatest fame was an infantry captain of the name of Miguel de Cervantes Saavedra, who was, with Aeschylus, to be one of the two outstanding men of letters in history to take part in a great naval battle. He was of the same age as his commander-in-chief, for both men had been born in 1547, and he would seem only recently to have adopted a military career, but his movements at this period of his life are not too easy to follow. We know that as a budding poet he was in Madrid when he had just turned twenty-one, and there is his father's testimony for the fact that he was in Rome at the end of December, 1569, that is to say just a year later. What he was doing in the interval may, perhaps, be conjectured from some circumstantial evidence. There exists a warrant[1] issued from Madrid, dated September 5th, 1569, for the arrest of a Miguel de Cervantes, charged with having wounded Antonio de Sigura of that city, and for this condemned to have his left hand cut off, as well as to be exiled from the capital for ten years.

If *La Gitanilla* is to any extent autobiographical it may throw some light on the problem, for in it occurs the following passage:

It was in Madrid, in the house of a man of title to whom I was servant, not as a master, but as a relation. He had an only son

---

[1] cf. Ruis, L., *Bibliografía crítica de las obras de Miguel de Cervantes Saavedra*, vol. ii, p. 46. Madrid, 1895–1905.

and heir, who, both on account of the relationship, and because we were of the same age, and in the same circumstances, treated me with familiarity and great friendship. It chanced that this gentleman fell in love with a lady of quality, whom he would, with the utmost willingness, have chosen for his wife, if his wishes had not been, as is the duty of a good son, subservient to those of his parents, who hoped to make a more exalted match for him. Yet in spite of all this he paid her court, out of the sight of the eyes of all those whose tongues could publish his inclinations. My eyes alone were witnesses of his intentions.

One night . . . passing by the door and street of this lady, we saw close to it two men, apparently of good presence. My relative wished to reconnoitre them, but scarcely had he stepped towards them than with much agility they laid hands on their swords and their bucklers, and advanced. We did the same, and with equal weapons we engaged. The fight lasted only a short time, for the lives of our two opponents did not last long, since they lost them by two thrusts which the jealousy of my relative directed and the defence I made for him – a strange chance, and seldom witnessed.

At the end of this story the narrator of it embarks 'in one of the Genoese galleys lying in the harbour of Cartagena'. This event, if indeed it really took place, must have made a considerable impression upon Cervantes, for in *El Gallardo Español* he tells us of a character called Saavedra – the name is significant – who 'left a gentleman very badly wounded, fled, and went to Italy'.

At this point it will be well to turn to his short story, *El Licenciado Vidriera*, where Tómas Rodaja meets on the road a captain in the King's service who 'extolled the life of the army, and depicted in lively colours the beauty of the city of Naples, the pleasures of Palermo, the wealth of Milan, the festivals of Lombardy, and the splendid fare at the inns. He sketched pleasantly and exactly the "set the table, host; come here, you varlet; bring the mackerel, the fat fowls, and the macaroni".' He lauded to the skies the freedom of a soldier's life, and the liberty of Italy; but he said nothing of the cold endured by the sentries, the perils of the assaults, the terror of the battles, the hunger entailed by sieges, the devastation caused by the mines, and other things of this description which some take and consider to be but extras to the burden of a military career, whereas they form the chief constituents of it.' All the same Tómas joined the captain as his ensign, and in a few days they reached the place where his company was stationed, and from there with four others they set out for Cartagena.

Having thus decided on a military career Tómas decided to dress the part, so he discarded the costume of a student, and attired himself in the variegated colours of a parrot. The many books that he possessed he cut down to a volume of Hours of Our Lady, and a Garcilaso de la Vega without notes, which he carried in two pockets. He and his companions arrived at Cartagena sooner than they could have wished, for they found life in the billets *en route* much to their liking. The five companies, of which they formed part were embarked in four Neapolitan galleys, but Tómas did not like his experience on board them at all, what with the attentions of the bugs, the churlish propensities of the galley-slaves, the bad temper of the sailors, the depredations of the rats, and the wearying tossing of the sea. The passage to Italy was anyhow none too good, for two storms were encountered, of which the first drove them into Corsica, and the second into Toulon: at length, however, very weary, they arrived at Genoa where Tómas was most impressed by the tresses of the ladies, the gallant bearing of the men, and the great variety of wines.

There he parted with the captain, for the soldiers were going to Piedmont on their way to the Low Countries, and since service there did not apparently appeal to him he went on to Florence, and on his way he visited Lucca, *'ciudad pequeña, pero muy bien hecha, y en la que mejor que en otras partes de Italia son bien vistos y agasajados los españoles'.*[1] Florence also pleased him very much, and he specially noted its situation and its cleanliness, as well as its imposing buildings, the quietness of its streets, and the freshness of the Arno.

The real object of the Italian journey was, however, to see Rome, and here Tómas was certainly not disappointed, for he

[1] A small city, yet excellently built, in which Spaniards are better regarded and better received than in any other part of Italy.

visited her churches, adored the relics of the saints, and admired her greatness. From Rome he went on to Naples, Palermo, and Messina, and then returned to Rome where his father says Cervantes was in December, 1569. There are other references in Cervantes' writings to the march through Spain to Cartagena. In chapter twenty-four of the second part of *Don Quijote*, for examples, we have the page 'with a merry countenance' and of about nineteen years of age, bound, as he supposed, for Cartagena, where he is to embark and serve the King in his wars. Earlier, in the first part, chapter twenty-nine, the *cura* of Argamasilla says, 'You must pass through the village where I live, and from there you must take the road to Cartagena, where you may, with good fortune, embark'; while in her letter from Argamasilla, in part two, chapter fifty-two, Teresa Panza speaks of a company of mischief-making soldiers passing through the village. Again, in *El Coloquio de los Perros* we meet with a company of soldiers bound for Cartagena, of whom it is said that it 'was full of bullies and deserters who were guilty of some acts of insolence in the places we passed'. Finally, in book three, chapter twelve, of *Los Trabajos de Persiles y Sigismunda* a girl, Augustina, disguised as a page, speaking of two companies of soldiers on their way to Cartagena to embark, says, 'They got mixed up in a cruel brawl with the people of a village of La Mancha, over the matter of billets, with the result that a gentleman of the place . . . was killed.'

The cumulative effect of these various references to a march across La Mancha cannot but leave the impression that Cervantes must have taken part in one, and during the course of it he may well have participated in some incident which he did not wish to remember, for the opening words of *Don Quijote* are, 'In a village of La Mancha, whose name I do not wish to remember . . .' After his arrival in Italy he took service for a time in Rome with Cardinal Acquaviva,[1] but this cannot have lasted very long, for there is evidence[2] that before the end of 1570 Cervantes was a private soldier in a company commanded by Captain Diego de Urbina

[1] cf. The Preface to *La Galatea*.
[2] cf. Ruis, L., *Bibliografía crítica de las obras de Miguel de Cervantes Saavedra*, vol. ii, p. 20. Madrid, 1895–1905.

in the regiment of Miguel de Moncada: in this capacity he was at Messina in August of the following year.

When the allied fleets and armies were finally assembled it was discovered that the negotiations between Veniero and Colonna for the supply of personnel for the Venetian ships had not succeeded in producing the number of men required, so Don John offered the loan of two thousand Germans, fifteen hundred Italians, and fifteen hundred Spaniards. This at once aroused Veniero's suspicions that his ships were being reduced to a mere appendage of the Spanish fleet, and it was only as the result of considerable pressure on the part of his fellow-Italian, Colonna, that he consented to accept two thousand, five hundred Italians and fifteen hundred Spaniards. 'These Venetian gentlemen,' Don John wrote to Don Garcia de Toledo on September 9th, 'have now at last resolved to take into their galleys four thousand of His Majesty's troops; and these have just now been told off to them.'[1]

Don John now made his final dispositions. Ascanio de la Corgnia was appointed to command the land forces, while the three naval contingents were pooled, and like an army in three battles, they were formed into three tactical divisions – a centre, a right, and a left wing[2] – with a vanguard and a rearguard. The first consisted of sixty-four galleys under Don John himself with Veniero and Colonna to help him; the second contingent of fifty-four galleys was placed under the command of Doria; and the third of fifty-three galleys under that of Barbarigo. Don John's squadron was distinguished by blue pennants flying at the masthead (*en las calces*); Doria's by green pennants at the peak of the mainyard (*en la pena*); and Barbarigo's by yellow banderoles on the foreyard (*en las astas*). The vanguard of eight galleys was handed over to Don Juan de Cardona, and in command of the rearguard of thirty galleys, displaying white pennants from a flagstaff over the stern lamp, was Santa Cruz. Six galleasses, in pairs, were allotted to each division, and the galleons and great ships carrying supplies were formed into a separate squadron, for being dependent upon sail alone they were less mobile than the

[1] *Doc. Ined.*, iii, 20.
[2] As advised by Don Garcia de Toledo.

galleys. The frigates and brigantines were divided between these forces, and were ordered to sail astern of them.

Further instructions were issued to the effect that throughout the whole fleet the strictest discipline was to be maintained; the men were to live peaceably and religiously together; and the water was to be husbanded with special care. In the event of an action the commanders of each division were to keep their vessels sufficiently far apart to prevent the oars of one from impeding those of another, but sufficiently near to render it impossible for the enemy to pass through the line, while the spaces between each division were not to exceed four or five galleys' length. When the signal for battle was given from the flagship the galleys were to draw up in exact order, the commander of each division employing his frigates to watch over the correctness of his line. The artillery was not to open fire until it was certain that this would be effective, and the fire of at least two guns in each galley was to be reserved until she came to close quarters with an antagonist. The duty of Santa Cruz was to observe the progress of the battle, and to come to the rescue of any part of the Christian line which might appear to be in need of assistance.

The great ships under Don Gutierre de Arguello were not included in any of the divisions, but formed a separate squadron to be employed whenever their commander considered he could do most damage to the enemy. If the wind prevented his somewhat unwieldy vessels from being brought into action he was to lower and man his boats, and these, with a few musketeers in each, were to row to the engaged galleys, there to be employed as the respective captains might direct. In the same way the frigates, each armed with two *esmerils*,[1] and having on board ten musketeers under the command of a corporal, were to lie astern of the galleys to render assistance when needed, or to be sent against the smaller vessels of the enemy.

Meanwhile, Don John, Colonna, and Veniero had met privately together, and decided to take the offensive, but Don John, mindful of his instructions from his brother, insisted upon calling a council of war to confirm this decision. It was attended by about seventy officers, and was held on board the flagship on September

[1] A piece of ordnance somewhat larger than a falconet.

10th. One or two voices, notably those of Doria and La Corgnia, were raised in favour of further delay, but Don John was, he told those present, resolved to sail forthwith and bring the Turk to battle; with the help of God and the brave men round him, he was confident of obtaining a splendid victory. From that moment all opposition was at an end, and his decision was endorsed amid tumultuous applause.

On the morning of September 15th the great ships put to sea, and on the following day the whole forest of masts, which had so long filled the harbour of Messina, was in motion. As befitted what was in effect the beginning of the last crusade, the Nuncio took his stand at the end of the mole, and there bestowed his parting benediction on the vessels, as galley after galley, decked with all its flags and pennants, swept out into the straits, conspicuous among them being the flagship of Don John. That same day he wrote to Don Garcia de Toledo to inform him that he had sailed in pursuit of the enemy. 'He is stronger than we,' he wrote, 'in the numbers of his vessels, but not so, I believe, in quality either of vessels or men. So I sail, please God, to-night for Corfu, and then according to what I shall hear. I have with me two hundred and eight galleys, twenty-six thousand troops, six galeasses, and twenty-four ships. I trust our Lord that He will grant us the victory if we meet the enemy.'[1]

---

[1] *Doc. Ined.*, iii, p. 27.

Don John of Austria, *possibly by Moro Antonio*

Don John of Austria,
*portrait by an anonymous
Spanish painter, in the
Palacio de Liria, Madrid*

The Emperor Charles V, *portrait by Titian in The Prado, Madrid*

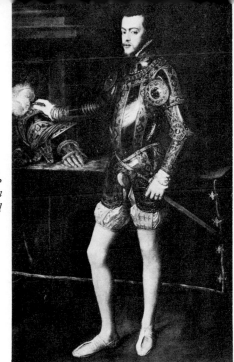

Philip II,
*portrait by Titian
in The Prado, Madrid*

The Marquess of Santa Cruz, *from a
portrait in the Museo Naval, Madrid*

Veniero, *portrait by Tintoretto
in The Prado, Madrid*

The Battle of Lepanto, *by an unknown artist in The National Maritime Museum, Greenwich*

François de Noailles,
Bishop of Dax
*from the portrait in
the Château de Maintenon,
Eure et Loire, France*

Pope Pius V:
*effigy from his monument
in the Sistine Chapel, Rome*

Sultan Selim II

Ochiali (Uluch Ali)

Mary Queen of Scots,
*portrait by
an unknown artist,
in the National
Portrait Gallery*

William of Orange,
*from a portrait
by Adriaen Key
in the Mauritshuis,
The Hague*

Elizabeth I (the Ermine Portrait), *portrait in the style of Hilliard, in Hatfield House*

7

Lepanto: The Battle

THE FIRST PROBLEM THAT CONFRONTED DON JOHN WAS
to obtain accurate information about the movements of the enemy,
and this proved to be by no means easy to acquire, save for the
fact that the enemy were apparently being directed by that most
formidable of seamen, Ochiali – as the Christians called 'Ali
El-Uluji', 'The Renegade', though to his sailors he was generally
known as *Fartas* or 'Scurvied', from the complaint from which
he suffered in common with so many seafaring men of his day.
According to Cervantes he was 'a worthy man morally, and he
treated his slaves with great humanity'.[1] He had been born in
Calabria about 1508, and was originally intended for an ecclesiastical career: he was, however, carried off in a raid by the
Barbary Corsairs with whom he then decided to throw in his lot.
Under the Crescent he rose to high office, for he played a prominent part in the siege of Malta, and not long afterwards he was
appointed Pasha of Algiers, where one of his first acts was to
recapture Tunis from the Spaniards. As recently as the previous
July he had struck a notable blow for the Sultan off Alicata, on
the southern coast of Sicily, where he surrounded four galleys
belonging to the Knights of Malta, and took three of them. The
flagship, in which was Saint-Clement, the General of the Galleys,
made no resistance at all, but the general himself managed to get
ashore. His craven conduct created such fury in Malta that the
Grand Master had great difficulty in preventing him from being
lynched, and was obliged to deliver him up to a secular court,
which at once condemned him to death; the unfortunate man
was thereupon strangled in his cell, and his body, after being put
in a sack, was thrown into the sea.[2] It certainly behoved Don

---

[1] *Don Quijote*, Part I, ch. 11.
[2] cf. Lane-Poole, Stanley, *The Barbary Corsairs*, pp. 161–2. London, 1896.

John to be careful when men like Ochiali were in command against him.

The first information which reached him was from Gil de Andrade who reported that the Turkish fleet, after doing some damage at Corfu, and blockading Cattaro for a short time, had steered south to Valona. This news seems to have decided the Christian commanders to make their base Taranto rather than Brindisi, which had been their original intention, on the ground that it was nearer, and on September 19th the fleet of the Holy League dropped anchor at La Pace. For some days after that Don John was hampered by bad weather and by the confused information which was the lot of all naval commanders before the days of wireless and radar. First of all a small boat from Gallipoli arrived with the news that Ochiali had been in the harbour of Santa Maria, near Otranto, with twenty-four galleys only two days before, and that he had gone from there apparently in the direction of the Barbary Coast, but that the Turkish admiral-in-chief, Ali Pasha, after attacking Corfu, where he did a certain amount of damage, had retired to Prevesa. This information considerably depressed Don John and his colleagues, who feared that it was to be interpreted as meaning that the Ottoman fleet had dispersed, and that there was consequently no hope of a major action before the end of the season. The weather, too, which had been squally, now became definitely rough, with strong north winds so that when the Allied armada got to Le Colonne on September 21st it was compelled to remain there for three days, in spite of repeated attempts to put to sea.

When the weather moderated Don John sent Gil de Andrade and Giovanni Battista Contarini to see if they could obtain any accurate information about the enemy's movements, and hardly had they departed on this mission than a brigantine arrived from Corfu with the news that Ali Pasha was not only still at Prevesa, but that he intended to remain there until a galley which he had sent to Constantinople returned with further orders from the Sultan.[1] This information was in fact inaccurate, but it caused Don John to change his plans; he was now more anxious than ever to get to the Adriatic as soon as possible, and he abandoned

[1] cf. Carrero Blanco, Luis, *La Victoria del Cristo de Lepanto*, p. 172. Madrid, 1948.

all idea of taking the fleet to Taranto. Instead, he ordered Santa Cruz and Paolo Canale to take twelve galleys to that port and to Brindisi, where they were to embark fifteen hundred Spanish and Italian troops who were waiting there; he himself took on board the fleet at Castello five hundred Calabrian infantry. So desirous was Don John of encountering the enemy that he even thought of sailing direct to Prevesa without touching at Corfu, but he was diverted from this by Veniero who hoped to obtain considerable reinforcements from the island.

It was not until September 24th that the fleet was able to put to sea again, and during that day Don John learned from a vessel in Gil de Andrade's squadron of observation that eight days before the enemy had sailed from Prevesa in the direction of Zante, and this was confirmed by the crew of a boat from Zante who reported that they had left Ali Pasha attacking the town. On the 27th the armada of the Holy League, save for the big ships, dropped anchor in the harbour of Corfu. Santa Cruz and Canale, it may be added, arrived there about the same time, but without the troops they were supposed to have brought with them, for these had mutinied and refused to embark, presumably because they could not get their arrears of pay.

At Corfu evidence that the Turks had been there was only too obvious. They had not been able to effect anything of importance against the fortress itself, and they had lost three galleys in the attempt, but they had sacked a number of churches and private dwellings. The spectacle of ruined altars and broken crucifixes, and of pictures of saints which had been used for target practice, incensed the soldiers and sailors of the Holy League against those who had perpetrated these enormities, and increased their desire to come to grips with the infidel as soon as possible. More important was some exact information regarding his strength. During a sally from the fortress the Venetians had captured a renegade of the name of Baffo, of whom Ali Pasha thought so highly that he was glad to ransom him at the price of ten thousand crowns and the freedom of two Venetian officers of high rank. During their period of captivity these two men had been by no means unobservant, and they told Don John that the Ottoman fleet numbered one hundred and sixty excellent galleys, and together with galliots, brigantines, and various craft probably accounted for some three hundred sail: on the other hand it was badly manned owing to illness, and its effective combatants were between four and five thousand Janissaries; also, so far as the two released prisoners had been able to gather, the Sultan's commanders were by no means agreed as to the expediency of giving battle to the fleet of the League. With regard to the movements of the enemy there was less certainty, for according to one account Ali Pasha was making for the gulf of Lepanto with his whole fleet, while another was to the effect that Ochiali with the Algerine squadron had been detached, and had sailed to Coron.

Whether Ali had his Barbary Corsairs with him or not Don John was determined to bring him to battle, but in view of his brother's instructions and of his own reputation for rashness he decided to call a council of war. It was very fully attended, for in addition to Veniero, Barbarigo, Colonna, Requesens, and Doria, there were also present Santa Cruz, Ascanio de la Corgnia, Cardona, Orsini, Priego, Miguel de Moncada, and the Princes of Parma and Urbino. With the memory of what had happened at Prevesa in 1538[1] still fresh in the minds of some who were at the council, it is not surprising that one or two voices were raised in favour of caution, but it soon became apparent that Don John had a substantial majority on his side, and that in particular he enjoyed the warm support of Barbarigo, Colonna, and Santa Cruz. The decision was therefore taken to go at once in search of the enemy; to follow him if he attempted to get away; and to spare no effort that might bring on a decisive battle.

Unfortunately Arguello and his squadron of large ships had not yet reported at Corfu, so Don John was under the necessity of sailing without them. To compensate for their absence he ordered the Venetians to take on board their vessels some additional troops and artillery from the island, and while Veniero was employed in this task he transferred himself to Gomeniza, which was a safe and spacious harbour on the Albanian shore, on September 30th. Hardly had he arrived there than he received a dispatch from Gil de Andrade to the effect that the Turkish commander-in-chief was definitely in the harbour of Lepanto,

[1] *vide supra*, p. 125.

THE BATTLE OF LEPANTO
OCTOBER 7 + 1571

MAINLAND

OXIA

Cape
Oxia

Cape
Scropha

Barbarigo   Sirocco

Amb. Bragadino

63 Galleys

56
Galleys

Ant. Bragadino

35
Galleys

Santa Cruz

Guoro

Veniero

96
Galleys

DON JOHN   ALI PASHA

63 Galleys

Colonna   Pertau Pasha

Duodo

8 Galleys   Cardona

Cesaro

64
Galleys

93
Galleys

Pisani

Doria   Ochiali

GULF OF PATRAS

CHRISTIAN
FLEET
(Don John)

TURKISH
FLEET
(Ali Pasha)

W Bromage

that his force did not exceed two hundred sail, and that illness had so ravaged his ranks that sixty galleys had been sent to Coron with the sick. This information was not wholly accurate, but it had a tonic effect upon the Christian fleet.

For Don John it was a signal for instant action. He immediately sent back a frigate with the news to Veniero and Colonna, who had stayed behind at Corfu, and instructed them to join him without delay, which they at once did. He then held a final review of the whole fleet before sailing to engage the enemy. As he passed down the lines of ships he was saluted with volleys of musketry, and several accidents occurred owing to the carelessness of the arquebusiers in firing with ball instead of blank: in fact, during the various salutes which had been fired between Messina and Gomeniza no less than twenty lives had been lost for this reason. Repeated orders had been issued against the practice but Don John realized that sterner measures were necessary, so he now declared that in future the offence would not only be capital, but that the captain of the vessel from which ball was fired on these occasions would himself be liable to a death sentence.[1]

In spite of the fact that the most critical moment of the war was clearly approaching there were still acute personal, as well as national, differences between the allied commanders, and these from time to time led to incidents which augured ill for the common cause. For example, during the last review at Gomeniza the duty of inspecting the Venetian contingent fell by some unlucky accident of routine to Doria, with whom, as we have seen, Veniero was on the worst of terms. When the Genoese admiral made his appearance the testy old Venetian refused to receive him: after some controversy, in which Don John's tact came into play, however, the duty was performed by Requesens.

Worse was to follow, though the exact particulars of what took place are somewhat in dispute. In Doria's squadron there was a Venetian galley, called *The Armed Man*, which was commanded by a Cretan gentleman of the name of Andrea Calergi, and on board were some Spanish musketeers under a Tuscan officer, Captain Muzio Tortona, who had an unsavoury reputation and

[1] cf. Caracciolo, F., Conte de Biccari, *I Commentarii della Guerra fatta coi Turchi da D. Giovanni d'Austria dopo che venne in Italia*, p. 25. Florence, 1581.

was quarrelsome at that. A dispute arose between a Spanish soldier, rudely disturbed from his slumbers, and a Venetian sailor which soon developed into a fight in which their comrades participated: as the musketeers made use of their fork-rests and the sailors of their knives it was not long before the decks were strewn with the dead and dying. Tortona, far from endeavouring to calm the storm, told Calergi to go to the Devil, drew his sword, shouted '*A mi los del tercio!*', and joined in the fray.

Calergi thereupon sent an officer to report the occurrence to Venicro, and to ask for assistance. 'Sir,' the officer said to the Venetian admiral, 'the Spanish contingent in *The Armed Man* have risen, and are killing the crew.' Veniero was not unnaturally enraged at this information, and sent his provost-marshal with four of his men to take the mutineers in custody. Hardly had they reached the ship, however, than they encountered Tortona, this time with an arquebus in his hand: with this weapon he laid the wretched provost-marshal low with a bullet in his head, while two of the latter's assistants were thrown overboard by the mutineers. By this time Veniero was in a fine fury, and ordered Francisco Dandolo to board *The Armed Man* by force, and suppress the revolt. This was none too easy, for the Spaniards threatened to open fire on him if he made any such attempt. This was the last straw so far as Veniero was concerned: he told Dandolo to clear decks for action, and treat *The Armed Man* as if she were a hostile man-of-war.

At this point a Spanish galley put in an appearance, and on its poop was Paolo Sforza, a senior officer in the *tercio* to which Tortona belonged.

'Your Excellency,' he shouted to Veniero, 'leave it to me. I am on my way to *The Armed Man*, and I will reduce these men to obedience.'

'By the blood of Christ,' retorted the infuriated Venetian, 'take no such action, unless you wish me to sink your galley and all on board. I will bring these dogs to heel without your assistance.'

'All right: I will go and ask the Captain-General of the League if he also desires me not to take any action.'

Meanwhile a platoon of Venetian musketeers soon overcame the mutineers in *The Armed Man*, and Muzio Tortona was marched in before Veniero with the introduction, 'Here is the insurgent captain, sir.' 'Hang him,' came the instant reply, and the Venetian commander-in-chief jerked his thumb in the direction of the yard-arm, from which in a few minutes the unfortunate Tuscan's body was to be seen dangling. 'Any more culprits?' asked Veniero, and a corporal and two private soldiers were produced. 'Hang them too,' the old man roared, and the order was instantly obeyed.

By this time Paolo Sforza had reached the flagship, and was explaining to Don John what had taken place, and how he had been prevented by Veniero from going on board *The Armed Man*: while he was still talking Miguel de Moncada interrupted him by exclaiming, 'Look, sir,' and pointing in the direction of Veniero's galley where the four bodies could clearly be seen hanging from the yard-arm. Don John was naturally incensed, for in lending to a Venetian vessel a company of Spanish soldiers because the Republic did not possess enough of its own, he had certainly not intended to give the Venetian admiral the right to put their captain summarily to death. 'What is that?' he burst out. 'Who has dared to authorize executions without my permission? Has the General of the Republic of Saint Mark had the audacity to commit so grave an affront to my authority? Has he received any such power from the King of Spain and His Holiness? By God I will no longer tolerate the arrogance of this old fool that Venice has placed in command of her galleys!'

At first Don John was all for passing at once from words to deeds, and placing Veniero under arrest: there was also a good deal of wild talk among the Spanish officers on his staff, and some of them even went so far as to suggest that Philip's ships should open fire on the Venetian galleys. Calmer counsels, however, soon prevailed. Colonna recalled the purpose for which the Holy League had been called into existence, and pointed out that this would be nullified if drastic action was taken against the Venetians; Barbarigo declared that Veniero had meant no disrespect to the Captain-General of the League, and that he now realized he had exceeded his authority; but the strongest plea for moderation came from Santa Cruz. He fully admitted that Veniero's behaviour was quite inexcusable and merited punishment, but in his opinion it was most inadvisable to push the matter to extremes: after all, Ali Pasha was not far away, and any division among the allies of the Holy League would be fatal.

In the face of these representations Don John gave way. 'All right,' he said, 'I will do my duty. I will forgive Veniero, but I do not wish to see him again. In future you, Augustin Barbarigo, will take his place on the Grand Council. To your ships, gentlemen, and we will put to sea.'[1]

Shortly after this episode Gil de Andrade in person reported to Don John. He had kept in the closest possible touch with the enemy until he encountered a superior Turkish squadron before which he deemed it prudent to retreat. He confirmed the information that he had previously relayed, and added that the various Greek sources with which he had been in contact assured him that Don John might offer battle with every hope of victory: what he did not know was that these same Greek sources had been in equally friendly contact with Ali, had reported to him on the movements and composition of the fleet of the Holy League, and had assured him that victory was his for the asking. As between the Pope and the Sultan, on balance they preferred the infidel.

The truth is that the proverbial 'fog of war' had enveloped both fleets alike, and counsels were as divided under the Crescent as under the Cross, though Ali did manage to get some first-hand information about his enemy from one of his officers who, disguised as a fisherman, was present when Don John reviewed his forces in the harbour of Gomeniza. Unfortunately for the Capitan Pasha it subsequently transpired that this officer had made several serious errors in his reckoning, for he had computed the vessels in the Christian fleet at fifty less than the full number, and he had greatly underrated the weight of their artillery.

Ali Pasha had greater powers than his opponent, subject, of course, to any overriding instructions he might receive from the Sultan, who was, however, his brother-in-law. He was himself a brave man with considerable experience afloat, and it may be

[1] cf. Carrero Blanco, Luis, *La Victoria del Cristo de Lepanto*, pp. 179–82. Madrid, 1948.

added that his methods of warfare were more civilized than was usual among his fellow-countrymen. Serving under him were a number of veteran officers such as Hassan Pasha, who was a son of the famous pirate, Barbarossa, and who was said to have overcome a tendency to extreme corpulence by accustoming himself to eat only once in four or five days: others of note were Mohammed Sirocco Pasha, Governor of Alexandria, and Hamet Bey, Governor of Negropont, nephew of Barbarossa and son-in-law of Dragut: the land forces were commanded by Pertau Pasha, a soldier of fortune, who had recently been promoted to that rank. Above all there was Ochiali, and the understanding between the Corsairs and the Porte was such that Ali could count upon them with considerably more reliance than Don John could place upon the Venetians.

In spite of the absolute authority which the Turkish commander-in-chief enjoyed Ali liked to hear the opinions of those who were serving under him, and when he heard that the fleet of the Holy League was sailing towards him he summoned a council of war on his flagship, the *Sultana*, over which waved a red flag with verses from the Koran picked out in yellow, the monogram of Selim II, and two crossed scimitars embroidered on it. The council consisted of some twenty senior officers, and the discussion was opened by the Governor of Alexandria, who had served for many years with Suleyman the Magnificent.

He spoke strongly in favour of caution. Cyprus had been conquered, and the Ottoman fleet had swept the sea; the season was getting late, and there was no point in running unnecessary risks. As for the fleet of the Holy League it had been assembled at great cost, and as it would be compelled to return to its bases all this money would be wasted. It was his opinion that the campaign was over, and a return to Constantinople was definitely indicated. Mohammed Sirocco was followed by Pertau Pasha, who took much the same line, though for a different reason. He spoke as a soldier, and he gave it as his opinion that the Spahis would be quite useless in the type of warfare that might be expected. They were mostly raw recruits, and although they might be all right on horseback the vast majority of them had never seen a galley before in their lives. The only troops who were first-class were the

Janissaries, and they were well-equipped, but the rest of the men under his command were very badly armed. The Sultan had, indeed, given them orders to fight, but not to commit suicide.

Hamet Bey argued in the same vein, but this was too much for Hassan Pasha, who burst in with the exclamation that neither his father nor Hamet's would have given such craven advice. 'Hassan,' replied the Governor of Negroponte in measured tones, 'your father was as good in battle as in the council-chamber: in you I recognize his bravery, but neither his ability nor his prudence.' Hamet went on to urge that enough had already been accomplished for glory; that the fleet of the Holy League was greatly superior in every respect to that of the previous year; and that it had been placed under the command of a Prince who was not likely to have been sent on a forlorn hope, or to neglect any chance of adding to the glory which he had won in the campaign against the Moriscoes. His advice therefore was that the Ottoman fleet should remain under shelter of the guns of Lepanto, ready to repel any attack upon the Sultan's dominions, or to seize any opportunity for a victory which might present itself.

As might have been expected Ochiali was in favour of taking the offensive, and he declared that they would all be dishonoured if they allowed themselves to remain shut up in Lepanto 'looking after the women and children'.

The Capitan Pasha then summed up. He began with an analysis of the two armadas, and pointed out that while there could be no denying the strength of the Christian fleet this strength was to a considerable extent nullified by the jealousy existing between the Spaniards and the Venetians. It was indeed true, as Pertau Pasha had alleged, that some of the Turkish troops were mere recruits, but they would be fighting alongside veterans, and this would serve to redress the balance. He was himself in favour of the offensive, but in any case he had no option in the matter for he had received orders from the Sultan, rendered more aggressive than ever by the conquest of Cyprus, to capture the Christian fleet, and bring it to the Golden Horn without delay. This closed the proceedings, and the officers returned to their ships to prepare for action.[1]

[1] *ibid.*, pp. 188–90.

To carry out his master's instructions Ali had at his disposal some three hundred sail, and on board were two thousand Janissaries, two thousand Spahis, and two thousand irregular volunteers. The disposition of this force, and the tactics adopted by its commander, were, as will be shown, largely dictated by the moves of the enemy.

At this point an event occurred which is eloquent of the slowness of communications in the sixteenth century – Don John received news of the capitulation of Famagusta and of the cruel fate of Bragadino: the former had taken place on August 4th, and the Venetian commander had been put to death on the 17th, but it was apparently not until October 5th that Don John became acquainted with what had occurred. It is possible that the delay may have been due to the fact that the news went to Venice in the first instance, and was transmitted from there, for Sir William Stirling-Maxwell's suggestion that the delay was a tribute to 'the efficient guard which the Turks kept over the waters of Cyprus',[1] is surely beside the point, for the Porte could have had no conceivable reason for suppressing information so favourable to the Turkish cause. However this may be the tidings could hardly have come at a more propitious moment, for they roused every Venetian in the fleet to a state of fury, and implanted a determination that the enemy should be made to pay dearly for the humiliation inflicted upon the Serenissima.

Meanwhile the weather was not proving too propitious for the Christian fleet. Don John had reached Viscardo in Cephalonia on October 4th, having sailed past Prevesa of baneful memory and the opening of the Gulf of Arta, where Octavius and Antony had once contended for the mastery of the Roman world. It was not, however, for another two days that he was able to continue on his way, but at sunrise on the 7th he was about three miles from the Curzolarian Isles. The day being a Sunday, Don John at once ordered mass to be celebrated throughout the fleet, and sent out scouts to obtain the earliest information as to the enemy's movements. In due course the watch on the maintop of the flag-ship and also on Doria's reported two strange sail to the east: in a few minutes eight more appeared over the horizon, and shortly

---

[1] *Don John of Austria*, vol. i, p. 400. London, 1883.

afterwards the whole Turkish fleet came into sight. Don John immediately ordered his foresail to be hauled to the wind, a square green ensign to be run up to the peak, a gun to be fired, and the standard of the League to be displayed from the maintop: at the sight of it a storm of cheering rang round the fleet. The long weeks of waiting were over.

It is now necessary to consider the relative positions of the two fleets. A reference to the map will show that after passing through the strait between Cephalonia and Ithaca the armada of the Holy League, in order to reach the Gulf of Lepanto, should have directed its course almost due east; instead it had sailed east by north. As a result it had become necessary for the flagship, which was to form the centre of the battle-line, to steer a southerly course in order to leave, off the Isle of Oxia and Cape Skropha, sufficient sea-room for the left of the central squadron and for the left wing.

The Gulf of Lepanto itself is a long inlet of irregular shape, extending east and west, bounded on the north by the coast of Albania and on the south by that of the Peloponnese, while it is closed at its eastern end by the Isthmus of Corinth. When the hostile fleets first sighted one another that of the Holy League was entering the Gulf near its southern shore, while that of the Sultan was about fifteen miles within its jaws, stretching in a crescent-shaped line almost from the shallows which lie beneath the Acarnanian Mountains to the Peloponnesian coast. The wind, it may be added, was at first blowing somewhat freshly from the east, and in consequence in the faces of the Christians: during the morning it fell, and what breeze there was came from the west, though in fact when the battle began the sea was perfectly smooth.

At the sound of the signal-gun each captain in the fleet of the Holy League began to prepare his ship for action. By order of Don John the *espolones*[1] of the galleys had been cut off, for he thought it expedient to sacrifice these weapons of offence to ensure the more effective working of the guns on the forecastle and gangway: the bulwarks, also, were strengthened, and in some galleys the rowers' benches were removed or planked over in order to give more freedom of action to the soldiers. The rowers

[1] Beaks, *vide supra*, p. 66.

themselves constituted a problem for reasons which have been stated on an earlier page. There was a small minority of Christians, mostly convicts, in Don John's ships; these had their fetters knocked off and were provided with arms which they were encouraged to use in the ensuing battle under promise of a pardon for their past misdeeds. Very different treatment was, not unnaturally, meted out to the Moslem slaves, and every precaution was taken to render them harmless. The chains which secured them to their places were carefully examined and their rivets secured, while they were in addition fitted with handcuffs, so that they would be unable to use their hands for any other purpose than pulling at the oar. For the rest, the arquebusier, the musketeer, and the bombardier, looked carefully to the state of their weapons; the sailor sharpened his pike or cutlass; the officer put on his stoutest casque and cuirass; the stewards placed supplies of bread and wine in convenient spots, ready to the hands of the combatants; and the surgeons prepared their instruments and bandages, and spread their tables in preparation for the service which would be required of them.

Cervantes was at this time serving on board the *Marquesa*, but he had been ill with fever, and he was advised to remain below. This advice was not at all to his liking, and he replied, 'Gentlemen, on all the occasions in His Majesty's wars that until now have offered themselves, I have served well, like a good soldier. So now I shall do no less though weak and with fever. It is better that I fight in the service of God and the King, and die for them, than keep under cover.' His wish was granted, and he was put in command of twelve men in a longboat at or near *Marquesa's* side.[1] He was to describe in *Don Quijote* what happens at such times.

Lashed and locked together they leave but two feet of beakhead for the soldier to stand upon, but, though finding as many ministers of death confronting him as there are cannon not a lance-length off on the opposing ship, and though conscious that a slight misstep will land him in Neptune's bottomless gulf, none the less, impelled by the thought of glory, he

[1] cf. Smith, R., *The Life of Cervantes*, p. 32. London, 1914.

bravely attempts to force a passage, making himself a target to that artillery all the time. But what is chiefly to be admired is that hardly has one fallen whence he cannot be raised until the end of time, than another takes his place, and should this second likewise drop into the jaws of death that await him, another succeeds and another, without a pause between – displaying a spirit and daring unrivalled in all the exigencies of war.[1]

Meanwhile both commanders-in-chief were being sounded to see if they had any second thoughts as to the advisability of coming to grips with the enemy. 'Is Your Highness going to call a council of war?' Juan de Soto, Don John's secretary, asked his master. 'This is no time for councils, but for fighting,' came the instant reply. At almost the same moment Ochiali, who happened to be on the Ottoman flagship when the Christian fleet came in sight, urged Ali Pasha to fall back under the guns of the shore-forts, so that if the enemy attacked they would be exposed to their fire. 'I will never give the impression,' the Capitan Pasha answered, 'that my fleet is in retreat before the Christians. We are definitely going to fight. Captain, give the order to form line of battle.' Like the Corsair the Turkish admiral had won a reputation for his humanity towards his galley-slaves, and he did not fail to display it on this occasion. He walked along their benches, and said to them in Spanish, 'Friends, I expect you today to do your duty by me, in return for what I have done for you. If I win the battle, I promise you your liberty; if the day is yours, God has given it to you.'[2]

Don John's order of battle was what had been decided at Messina, but to compensate for the absence of the galleons, which were still far behind, the strengths of the divisions were slightly altered. To Barbarigo, in command of the left wing, were allotted sixty-three galleys, and he was ordered to sail with his left close to the Aetolian shore in order to prevent any attempt on the part of the enemy to outflank him. To Doria, who was in command of the right wing, he gave sixty-four galleys, while sixty-three

[1] Part I, ch. 38.
[2] cf. Arroyo, M. A., Relación del progresso della Armada de la Santa Liga, folio 61. Milan, 1576.

were left for the central squadron which he kept under his own hand: he also instructed Colonna in the Papal flagship to take station on his right, and Veniero, in the Venetian one, to do likewise on his left. He increased the reserve squadron under Santa Cruz from thirty to thirty-five galleys, and instructed him to sail in rear of the central squadron and to support any part of the line that appeared to be giving way. The six galleasses were left in pairs, each pair to take station three-quarters of a mile in advance of each of the three forward squadrons in order to disorganize the Turkish before action was joined. All this gave the Holy League a line of battle between 6,500 and 7,500 yards in length.

When all this had been done Don John boarded a fast brigantine, and inspected his fleet; it is pleasing to be told that when he caught sight of Veniero on his quarter-deck he waved so friendly a greeting to him that it is said to have caused the old man to forget their former differences. The inspection completed, the Christian host knelt in prayer.

The more Ali looked at his enemy's fleet, the less he liked what he saw. In the first place he had not expected to see the galleasses as he had been informed that they had become separated from the rest of Don John's command, and he had no desire to come under the fire of their formidable artillery. Then, again, the Spanish contribution was greater than he had allowed for, and Philip's galleys were of stouter build than the Sultan's. For a brief space the spirits of the Turks were raised by a rumour which originated on Pertau's ship to the effect that the enemy right wing, commanded as we have seen by Doria, was about to fly. An old Genoese renegade was accordingly sent aloft to report, but to his practised eye it was soon apparent that his countryman was merely extending his line towards the southern shore of the Gulf in order to foil a manœuvre of Ochiali, who was endeavouring to outflank him, and take him in rear. The Genoese descended, and to those who asked his opinion he observed, 'Doria is not flying; God grant it may not turn out the other way.'

Ali had drawn out his vessels in an immense crescent stretching right across the Gulf, and like his opponent he had divided his fleet into three squadrons. On the right was Mohammed Sirocco with fifty-four galleys and two galliots[1]; in the centre was Ali himself with eighty-seven galleys and eight galliots; and on his left was Ochiali with sixty-one galleys and thirty-two galliots. His rear was not covered by anything that could be called a reserve, but merely by eight galleys and twenty-one galliots under Murad Dragut. About 9.30 a.m., as the two fleets slowly approached each other, the Turkish commander-in-chief straightened out his crescent formation since it was clear that the Christians were in greater strength than he had anticipated, and he could not afford to run any risks.

At this solemn moment before action was joined the scene must have appeared colourful indeed to the odd Greek shepherd who was watching it from the hills of Aetolia or the Peloponnese. When the Christians ended their devotions a glitter swept along their line as the sun caught the armour of the men rising to their feet, and blazed on helmet and corselet, on sword-blades, and on pikes. By contrast the Turks could show the brilliant and variegated garb of the Janissaries, their tall and fanciful crests and prodigious plumes, while the galleys displayed a multitude of flags and streamers. Furthermore, as they advanced the Osmanli rent the skies with their shouting and volleys of useless musketry, while absolute silence obtained on the Christian ships.

When the fighting actually began at 10.30 a.m. the position of the two fleets was as follows: the Christian left wing was slightly ahead, with its left at some distance from the Aetolian shore because Barbarigo, who was unacquainted with that perilous coast, was afraid that his galleys might run upon shoals. On its right the central squadron was nearly abreast, but, as has been shown, because the Ottoman left wing extended beyond the Christian right Doria was frightened of being outflanked by Ochiali, so he moved his squadron diagonally outward with the result that a gap of a mile or more developed between his extreme left and Don John's extreme right. As for the four galliasses, those of the left wing and centre were in position, as Ali had duly noted, three-quarters of a mile in front of their respective squadrons, but the two allotted to Doria were still off Point Scropha. The reserve squadron, under the extremely competent Santa Cruz,

[1] A galliot was a small galley.

was also in position, with its galleys surrounded by brigantines ready to transfer troops to the three forward squadrons as and when required.[1]

On the Turkish side the right wing under Sirocco was also slightly in advance of the centre under Ali, while Ochiali on the left moved outward diagonally in order to conform with Doria's manœuvre as soon as he understood what this implied. The general result of these movements was that the battle gradually developed into three separate actions: first between Barbarigo and Sirocco; next, about half an hour later, between Don John and Ali; and lastly, an hour later still, between Doria and Ochiali.

There was not a cloud in the sky at half-past ten that Sunday morning when the Turkish right wing came within range of the two galleasses in front of Barbarigo's squadron, and so destructive a fire was opened that Sirocco's ships were thrown into confusion, and many of them were forced towards the Aetolian shore. The Pasha determined to profit by this misfortune: his pilots were well acquainted with that coast, which was not the case with the Venetians, so he ordered them to close their galleys inshore, and to turn the enemy's flank. Barbarigo, however, saw what was afoot, and realized that where there was sufficient water for the Turkish galleys there would be enough for his own: accordingly he inclined his squadron towards the shore, and so took in flank all but six or seven of Sirocco's galleys, which succeeded in getting in rear of him. Up to this moment the Venetian right wing, under Marco Quirini, had been unengaged because Sirocco's left wing had set about to follow his right, but now Quirini seized the opportunity which presented itself, swung his galleys round, and fell upon the Governor of Alexandria's rear with the most devastating results.

So far all had gone well with the Venetians, but at this point Barbarigo was mortally wounded in the eye by an arrow, and his nephew, Marco Contarini, who at once took his place, was himself killed almost immediately. For a short time there was some confusion among the Christian ships, but order was restored by Frederigo Nani, who succeeded Contarini, and he and Quirini

---

[1] The name of the ships on both sides, and those of their captains, are given in Carrero Blanco, Luis, *La Victoria del Cristo de Lepanto*, pp. 225–30. Madrid, 1948.

before long succeeded in driving the whole of the Turkish squadron against the shore. Some of the Turks jumped overboard and escaped to land, but they were followed by the Venetians who, mindful of Famagusta, gave no quarter: it is related that one of the latter, being armed with nothing more deadly than a sharp stick, contrived with that simple weapon to pin a Turk through his mouth to the ground, where he was duly dispatched by the soldiers of the Republic.[1] Sirocco himself was severely wounded, and fell into the sea, but he was pulled out by the Venetians, who relieved him from any further suffering by cutting off his head.

In the centre the opening shots seem to have been fired about eleven o'clock, and at first events took the same course as farther north; that is to say that the two galleasses in front of Don John's squadron opened so destructive a fire upon the enemy that Ali's galleys broke formation, and rowed out of range. Meanwhile a slow stroke was maintained by Don John's ships, which advanced in a perfect line to the strain of pipes and clarions. When the two squadrons came within range the Turkish gunnery proved to be bad,[2] its shot passing over the Christian ships largely because the *espolones* of their galleys had not been removed, while as a result of Don John's forethought in that respect his gunners were able to hit the enemy vessels close to the watermark with fatal precision.

When the battle was joined the drama of the situation was at once heightened by the order given by each commander-in-chief to steer direct for the flagship of the other – *La Real* against the *Sultana*. When the prow of the *Sultana* crashed into *La Real* its beak became embedded in the rigging of the Spanish ship, and thus linked together the two vessels became a battlefield which was fiercely contested for the best part of two hours. The two sides were by no means unevenly matched. Ali had on board four hundred picked Janissaries, of whom three hundred were armed with the arquebus and one hundred with the bow. Two galliots and ten galleys, all filled with Janissaries, lay close astern, and the galliots were connected with the Pasha's flagship by ladders, up which came reinforcements as and when required.

[1] cf. Herrera, F., *Relación de la guerra de Cipre y sucesso de la batella Naval de Lepanto*, d. xviii. Seville, 1572.

[2] By contrast with what it usually was in land battles at this time.

The galley of Pertau Pasha fought alongside. On board *La Real* were three hundred arquebusiers, but Don John's forecastle artillery soon proved superior to that of the enemy, while his bulwarks, as in the case of the rest of the Christian fleet, were protected from boarders by netting and other devices with which the enemy had omitted to provide themselves. Astern lay Requesens with two galleys from which he reinforced his commander-in-chief when necessity arose.

The fight was carried on with great gallantry by both sides. At first the arquebusiers on the Ottoman forecastle did considerable execution among the Spaniards, and Don Bernardino de Cardenas among others was killed. The Turkish archers were also a nuisance for a time, and it is said that Ali himself drew a bow, which, if true, must surely be the last occasion on which a commander-in-chief has done so in a European battle. Gradually, however, the Spaniards asserted their supremacy, and twice they established a foothold on the deck of the *Sultana*, but only to be driven back by the Janissaries. The third time the boarding-party was led by Don John in person, while Ali fought at the head of the defenders. In the struggle which ensued the Pasha was struck by a bullet in the forehead, and fell forward on the gangway, whereupon, according to one story, a soldier from Malaga cut off his head, and carried it to Don John.

In actual fact there are many versions of the way in which Ali met his death, and of the subsequent fate of his head, though they all agree that he was decapitated. Arroyo says that the head was brought to Don John, 'who greatly regretted his death on account of his kindness to his Christian prisoners'.[1] Torres y Aguilera, on the other hand, wrote that 'the head was cut off by a galley-slave, who had that day been relieved of his chain; and while the man was bringing it to His Highness, it fell into the sea, and was never seen again'.[2] Caraciolo gives a different account, for according to him, 'After the Turkish warship had been taken, the Pasha was found by the soldiers lying wounded with an arquebus-shot. He said to some of them in Italian, "Go down below where there

---

[1] *Relación del progresso della Armada de la Santa Liga*, folio 64. Milan, 1576.

[2] *Chrónica v recopilación de varios sucesos de Guerra que ha acontesido en Italia v partes de Levante y Berberia desde mdlxx hasta*, mdlxxxiv, folio 70. Zaragoza, 1579.

is money." It being remarked amongst them that this must be the Pasha, a raw Spanish soldier went to kill him; upon which he, to prevent him, said, "Take this chain," holding out one of great price; but his fair words availed him nothing, for the man piti- lessly cut off his head, and leaping into the sea, swam with it to Don John, hoping for a great reward. Don John, however, answered him with displeasure, "What would you have me do with that head? Throw it into the sea." It was, nevertheless, fixed for an hour on a pike on the stern of the galley. Don John regret- ted his death, because, being a prisoner, he ought not to have been killed, and still more when he heard from the Christian slaves of his kindness and gentleness to them.'[1]

So much for the contemporary and non-contemporary accounts of the incident, which, with the lapse of time, tended to become much embroidered. In the following century, for example, Dr. Gonçalo de Ilescas wrote, 'In the Turkish flagship there were four hundred men slain, and the few that remained were giving way and jumping into the sea: whereupon Don Lope de Figueroa got to the poop and pulled down the Turkish flag, and a soldier who was with him killed the Pasha, already wounded with a musket- shot, by giving him a thrust, not knowing he was the general until a Christian rower told him who it was. Then said the soldier, "Since this is Ali I desire to try my sword upon a Pasha," and with that cut off his head, which was presently put on a pike, and they that were there began to shout "Victory! Victory!" The Turks seeing this, and also that His Highness continued the battle with the other galleys, lost all heart, and knew for certain that the day was ours.'[2]

Lastly there is Richard Knolles, who wrote in the reign of James II and gave full play to his imagination. 'The bassa, deadly wounded in the head with a shot, and all imbrued with blood, was taken, and as a joyful spectacle, brought to Don John, who, seeing him ready to breathe his last, commanded him to be de- spoiled of his armour and his head struck off. Which presently

[1] *I Commentarii della Guerra fatta coi Turchi da D. Giovanni d'Austria dopo che venne in Italia*, p. 39. Florence, 1581.

[2] *Historia Pontifical y Católica, en la qual se contienen las vidas de todos los Pontificos Romanos*, vol. ii, p. 762. Madrid, 1652.

set upon the point of a spear, he for a space held up aloft with his own hand as a trophy of his victory, as also with the sight thereof to strike a terror in the minds of the other Turks, who in the other galleys fast by fought yet right valiantly; neither was he therein deceived.'[1] The only certain fact which seems to emerge from these conflicting narratives is that the unfortunate Pasha had his head struck off, while the more contemporary the account the better Don John comes out of it.

The *Sultana* would not appear to have put up much serious opposition after the death of Ali, and she was a Spanish prize by two o'clock in the afternoon. One serious attempt was, however made to recover her, and several Turkish galleys bore down upon *La Real* with that end in view. The movement was observed in time by Santa Cruz, whose reserve squadron was still intact: he at once came to the rescue, and sank one of the enemy ships by gunfire, while another he boarded, and put its complement of Janissaries to the sword. Don John himself dealt with his remaining assailants.

Elsewhere in the centre the day went well for the Spaniards and their allies, but only after some desperate fighting in the course of which prodigies of valour were performed on both sides. Notable among them was the action of the Prince of Parma, who, followed by a single Spanish private soldier of the name of Alonso Davalos, leaped into a Turkish galley; fought his way through its defenders without receiving a wound; and in the end could boast of having, unaided, caused it to strike its flag. Juan de Cardona stormed the galley of Pertau Pasha, who only escaped in a small boat with the greatest difficulty. Another notable achievement in the central division was performed by Requesens who captured a galley in which were Ali's sons – Mohammed Bey, aged seventeen, and Said Bey, who was four years younger – who had been brought to sea by their father for the first time: their capture was of special importance because the mother of one of them was a sister of Selim himself. Among the Venetians old Veniero fought with all the vigour of youth, and fairly earned the Doge's cap, which was soon to be his.

Meanwhile on the right, things had by no means gone so well

[1] *The Turkish History*, vol. i, p. 59. London, 1687.

for the Holy League. When the battle began Doria's squadron was edging to the south to avoid being outflanked by Ochiali, with the result that an ever-widening gap was developing between it and Don John. It is true that the corsair's ships were also moving southward, but as there were ninety-three of them, galleys and galliots, to sixty-four of Doria's they could do so with the less risk.

There can be little doubt that Ochiali's original intention was to turn his opponent's right flank, but as the battle was developing elsewhere he was provided with an alternative manœuvre, and not for nothing was he reputed one of the most skilful tacticians in the Mediterranean. He now had the chance of either adhering to his original plan, or of changing his course from south to north-west, rowing through the gap in the Christian line, and falling upon Don John's rear. These were the tactics which had served Alexander the Great so well at Arbela,[1] and Ochiali decided to adopt them on the present occasion; so he suddenly changed course, and rowed all out through the gap in the direction of Don John's right. The first enemy in his path was Pietro Giustiniani, Prior of Messina, and admiral of the small fleet supplied by the Knights of Saint John. To the Algerine the white cross was anyhow like a red rag to a bull, and he fell upon the Maltese like a thunderbolt, stormed his galleys, and put their crews to the sword: next he took the Prior's galley in tow, and hoisted its banner on his own ship. At this point Juan de Cardona was sent by Santa Cruz to the rescue from the reserve with eight Sicilian galleys to restore the fortunes of the day, but he was immediately set upon by twice that number of Algerines. There then ensued some of the fiercest fighting and during the course of it Cardona was mortally wounded.

Nevertheless this was the limit of Ochiali's success. Santa Cruz had early noticed what was happening, and was coming to the rescue with the remainder of his reserve galleys, while Don John, no longer embarrassed by any enemy, was moving in the same direction; above all, Doria had now realized the mistake he had made, and was rowing all out to the fight. By this time Ochiali

---

[1] cf. Fuller, Major-General J. F. C., *The Decisive Battles of the Western World*, vol. i, pp. 99–106. London, 1954.

had come to the conclusion that the battle was lost, and as he had no desire to share the fate of Ali Pasha and Mohammed Sirocco he decided upon immediate flight: accordingly he abandoned his prizes, and with thirteen galleys rowed across the bows of Santa Cruz's advancing ships; by nightfall he had reached Prevesa, while another thirty-five of the Algerine contingent broke away eastward, and managed to get back to Lepanto. At first Don John was minded to pursue the fugitives, but the fine weather showed signs of breaking, and it was decided to seek shelter in the harbour of Petala, where the Christian fleet duly arrived by dusk.

As may be supposed, no sooner were the victors assembled together than every kind of accusation was brought against Doria, and it was alleged that such was his dislike of the Venetians that he had not wished the battle to be decisive. A simpler explanation, Major-General Fuller has suggested, 'that he was outmanœuvred would seem sufficient to account for the sorry part he played'.[1]

Of one thing there can be no question, and it is that Don John had no cause to be ashamed of the men who fought under his command, whatever their rank, for they vied with each other in deeds of the most brilliant gallantry and the most stoical endurance which was in itself a tribute to his own leadership. Mention has already been made of the exploit of the Prince of Parma, but it was equalled by Martin Muñoz, a sergeant who lay sick in the *San Juan*. When he heard the rush of a Turkish boarding-party on the deck overhead, he leaped from his bed saying that there was no need any longer to die of fever, and snatching the first weapon that came to hand he killed four of the enemy before he met his own death. Among the arquebusiers on *La Real* was a woman disguised as a man, who greatly distinguished herself, for not content with using her piece to great effect she was among those who boarded the *Sultana*, where she killed a Turk in a hand-to-hand fight. As a reward, Don John gave orders that Maria '*la Bailadora*'[2] as she was called, should be continued on the strength of the company in which she was serving.

It must also be put upon record that the Catholic clergy did

[1] *ibid.*, vol. i, p. 575.
[2] The Dancer.

their duty manfully, and they exposed themselves as freely as the combatants. A Spanish Capuchin, himself an old soldier, tied a crucifix to a halbert, and crying that Christ would fight for his faith, led the boarders of his galley over the bulwarks of her antagonist, whence, after using his weapon manfully, he returned victorious and unharmed. A Roman priest of the same Order, finding that his flock was getting the worst of it, seized a boathook, and, pulling his peaked hood over his face, rushed into the fray, where he laid about him until he had killed seven Turks, and driven the rest from the deck – an exploit which in a few weeks' time he had great pleasure in recounting to Pope Pius V[1] himself. We are told that not a single crucifix in the whole fleet was hit, and that which adorned the prow of *La Real* is now in the cathedral of Barcelona.

Cervantes was certainly no exception to this general display of valour. The *Marquesa* was one of the ships in Barbarigo's squadron, and she was early engaged with the flag-ship of Sirocco Pasha upon which she inflicted very considerable damage, but Cervantes received two gunshot wounds in the chest, and one that mutilated his left hand. Understandably, he never afterwards referred to the battle of Lepanto without a feeling of exaltation, 'More blest,' he said, 'the Christians who died there than those that lived and triumphed.'[2] Of himself he was to write:

> He lost in the naval battle of Lepanto his left hand from a shot of an arquebuss – a wound which, although it appears ugly, he holds for lovely, because he received it on the most memorable and lofty occasion that past centuries have beheld – nor do those to come hope to see the like.[3]

And again:

> If my scars shine not in strangers' eyes, at least they are respected by those knowing their origin; for better looks the soldier dead in battle than alive in flight. So firmly do I hold this that if here and now they offered me such an impossibility,

[1] cf. Guglielmotti, P. Alberto, *Marcantonio Colonna alla battaglia di Lepanto*, p. 249. Florence, 1862.

[2] *Don Quijote*, I, p. 39.

[3] Preface to *Novelas Ejemplares*.

I still would rather have taken part in that mighty action, than not be and free of wounds. The scars a soldier wears on his face and breast are stars rather, leading others to a heaven of honour and the hope of deserved praise.[1]

The casualties on both sides were exceptionally heavy, as was normal in galley battles, for once contact had been made escape was most difficult, and between Christians and Turks quarter was rare. Exact figures are quite impossible to obtain, but out of some 172,000 combatants – 84,000 Christians and 88,000 Turks – the Christians lost about 15,000 officers and men killed, wounded, and drowned, while twelve of their galleys were sunk and one was captured. The Turkish losses were estimated at 113 galleys wrecked and sunk, and 117 captured; 30,000 men killed, 8,000 taken prisoner, and an unknown number drowned, while 15,000 Christian galley slaves were set free. The plunder was immense, for such was the predatory nature of their government that the Turks who possessed wealth felt it wiser to carry it about with them, and in Ali's galley alone were found no less than 150,000 sequins.

Three men in particular distinguished themselves in this battle, namely Don John and Santa Cruz among the victors, and Ochiali among the vanquished. Don John's leadership was superb, and the high state of the morale which prevailed throughout the fleet of the Holy League was very largely due to him. His employment of the galleasses was masterly, and though they were too cumbersome to manœuvre against galleys the effect of their gunfire was deadly: had the big vessels, which did not come up in time for the battle, been present it is by no means impossible that the Turkish formation would have been broken at a very early stage. Two other advantages the Christians enjoyed thanks to their commander-in-chief, one was his removal of the *espolones* to provide a better field of fire, and the other was to mix the galleys of the squabbling members of the alliance, for had he not done this it is more than likely that the battle would never have been fought. If it be objected that in making these decisions Don John may well have been acting on the advice of others, such as Don Garcia de Toledo, then the answer must be that he is entitled to

[1] *Don Quijote*, I, p. 39.

the credit all the same, for had things gone wrong he would assuredly have received all the blame.

For the fact that Don John's tactics were so successful the praise must go to Santa Cruz, for he used his reserve squadron to the very best advantage. He supported his commander-in-chief in the centre whenever he needed help, but he was careful not to deplete his squadron unduly in the process, so that he had sufficient ships in hand with which to counter Ochiali's dangerous move in the last stages of the battle. His attitude throughout was a masterpiece of seamanship, and well might Cervantes refer to him as a 'thunderbolt of war and father to his soldiers, brave and invincible captain, Don Alvaro de Bazán, Marquess of Santa Cruz'.[1]

On the losing side Ochiali alone was first-class. All the Turks displayed the highest courage, but little else. Ali Pasha, possibly hampered by instructions from the Sultan or the Grand Vizier, seems to have had no other idea than a head-on collision with his enemy, and the same was true of Mohammed Sirocco Pasha, while Ochiali showed that he was a tactician of the highest order: had the struggle in the centre not already gone against the Turks, and had Santa Cruz not kept so watchful an eye on the course of the fighting, his move to take Doria in the rear might have altered the verdict of the day.

So ended an epoch in naval history, for Lepanto was the last of the great galley battles, which tactically remained much as they had been in classical times: henceforth sail and broadside fire were to replace oar and head-on attack.

[1] *Don Quijote*, I, p. 39.

8

Lepanto: The Aftermath

THE CHRISTIAN FLEET HAD PROCEEDED TO PETALA AS FAR as possible under sail in order to rest the oarsmen, many of whom had been given their freedom for their services in the battle. Needless to say Don John's galley was soon crowded with officers of all ranks offering him their congratulations, and when he noticed that Veniero was not among them, having been forbidden to set foot in the flagship, he sent for the old man, received him at the top of the ladder with a friendly embrace, and greeted him as '*padre mio*'. He next visited as many of the wounded as possible, and gave up part of his own quarters in *La Real* to such of them as had served in the flagship.

From Petala he sent the King a full account of the battle, which was included in a report of the proceedings of the fleet between September 30th and October 10th, and was probably written by Juan de Soto. With it went the following dispatch:

S.C.R.M.

Your Majesty ought to give and cause to be given, in all parts, infinite thanks to our Lord for the great and signal victory which He has been pleased to vouchsafe to this fleet; and that your Majesty may understand all that has passed, besides the report herewith despatched, I send also Don Lope de Figueroa, to the end that he, as a person who has served in this galley in a way justly to entitle him to reward, should relate all the particulars which your Majesty may be pleased to hear. To him therefore I refer your Majesty for all such details, that your Majesty may not be wearied by reading the same things several times over.

I desire now to follow up the good fortune which God has given us for the advantage of your Majesty, and to see whether

Lepanto can be taken, that gulf being a place of great importance; and if not, what other enterprise, time and circumstance considered, may be attempted. This I have not as yet been able to determine, on account of much which has to be done in refitting the fleet, in which we are every day discovering fresh damage, besides other things which must be supplied before we can or ought to advance; but to-morrow night or the next night we may, please God, be free to sail. Of all that happens your Majesty shall be informed, step by step; but that the good news may be no longer delayed I despatch Don Lope now, merely reminding your Majesty of the opportunity God has placed within our reach of extending your power with no greater difficulty than attends at once setting about levying troops and fitting out galleys, of which there is no lack, and providing for a supply of money and munitions in the ensuing spring. All this I believe will be much more easy than it has heretofore been, and of more advantage to your Majesty and to your greatness, of which our Lord takes so much care, and my desire to promote which prompts me to remind your Majesty of these things.

In this galley Don Bernardino de Cardenas has been slain, doing the duty imposed upon him at his birth. He leaves, as I am informed, many debts behind him, and here in the fleet a natural son; whereof it would be just and for the good of the service that your Majesty should order account to be taken. Other persons there are, about whom I am preparing a report, besides those who are mentioned in the report of which Don Lope is the bearer – persons who have in truth done good service and merited reward; and this is one of the occasions, as your Majesty well knows, when men watch what is done for those who have distinguished themselves. There are here the two Princes (of Parma and Urbino) of whom the Prince of Parma was amongst the first who boarded and took the galley with which his own was engaged, Paolo Giordana Orsini, the Duke of Mondragone, and other lords, vassals, and servants of your Majesty, to whom, if your Majesty pleases, it would be well to order letters of thanks to be written. The same may be said of the generals, who deserve it well, and the servants of

189

your Majesty here in the fleet, of whom I ask pardon for reminding you, seeing that it is for the advantage of the royal service, and that I must fulfil my duty to those about me who have served your Majesty as zealously as it is always my own desire to do.

I am, thank God, well, the cut which I received, I hardly know how, on the ankle having turned out a mere nothing. God keep and prosper your Majesty with all the things which I desire, and of which we all stand in need.

Don John of Austria[1]

The news of the victory did not reach the Escorial until Hallow'een, and it was conveyed to Philip when he was in the chapel listening to the monks singing Vespers. There was an unwonted commotion outside, and immediately afterwards an obese member of the Royal Household by the name of Pedro Manuel came waddling in and panting heavily; in a great state of excitement he told the King what had happened. Philip received the news in the same composed manner as his father had greeted that of Pavia, and merely replied, 'Keep cool. Come round into the choir so that you can tell me better.' When he had heard the whole story he went back to his seat, and prayed until Vespers were over; he then made official announcement of the victory, and the wildest rejoicings took place all over Spain.[2] In due course congratulations poured in from all quarters, both at home and abroad, even from the Queen of England.

When full details had reached the Spanish Court the King wrote to his brother:

Brother,

By a courier despatched by the Republic of Venice to their ambassador, who arrived at Madrid on the eve of All Saints, I heard of the great victory which Our Lord has been pleased to give you, which has given me such contentment as I ought

[1] cf. Aparini, José, *Colección de Documentos inéditos relativos a la celebre Batalla de Lepanto sacados del Archivo general de Simancas*, pp. 26–27. Madrid, 1847.

[2] cf. Cabrera de Córdoba, L., *Felipe II Rey de España*, vol. ii, p. 121. Madrid, 1619. Other authorities say that Philip received the news in the Royal Chapel in Madrid.

from this event to receive. Yet I was very anxious until your own advice of it arrived, to give me direct information and news of you.

By your letter of the 26th of last month, which I received before that of the 10th, and by that letter which came the day before yesterday by the hand of Don Lope de Figueroa, I have been pleased to a degree which it is impossible to exaggerate, and not less by the particulars which I have learned of the great courage and conduct you showed in the battle, by planning and ordering it all in person, as was fitting for so important an affair, and by distinguishing yourself as well as by directing others, which have without a doubt been a chief cause and part of this victory. And so to you, after God, ought to be given, as I now give, the honour and thanks for it; and some thanks are also due to me, because by a person so near and dear to me this great business has been accomplished, and so much honour and glory, in the sight of God and the world, gained for the good of Christendom and the hurt of its enemies.

As regards your coming hither this winter, you will already have been informed of the order which has been sent to you to winter at Messina, and the causes of it; and although it would exceedingly delight me to see you now, and exchange personal congratulations with you on occasion of this great victory, I postpone this pleasure, because your presence yonder was never more important, in order that you may, with vigilance, see that no time is lost in the coming year, and prosecute the great achievements which may be hoped for from the past success and your own eminent ability. And touching the affairs of importance, as to which you say you must communicate with me, you may do so in writing or by means of persons to whom such matters may be confided.

To your other letters, which I have received along with those I am now answering – Don Lope having arrived the day before yesterday – I will not reply at present, in order not to detain the courier whom I am just despatching that you may know the joy I feel, which is too great to be expressed or heightened. Don Lope brought me the standard which you committed to his charge, with which I am delighted. But as I will write again

soon in reply to your aforesaid letters, I will here say no more
but that may God have you in his keeping as I desire.
From San Lorenzo, on the 29th of November, 1571.

Your brother,

I THE KING[1]

Before resuming the account of the strategy adopted by Don
John after his victory it may not be amiss to mention an action
which redounds to his own personal credit, namely his attitude
towards the two sons of his defeated opponent who had been
taken prisoner. As soon as he knew that they were in his hands, he
sent for them, condoled with them on the loss of their father, and
gave instructions that they were to be looked after by his secretary,
de Soto. Of the two lads Mohammed would seem already to have
become a Turk of the old stoical fatalist school, for a day or two
after the battle he found the son of Cardenas in tears, and on
asking the reason was told that it was for the loss of his father,
who had just died of wounds. 'Is that all?' said Mohammed
contemptuously. 'I, too, have lost my father, and also my fortune,
country, and liberty, yet I shed no tears.'[2]

Don John followed up his kind reception of the two boys by
setting free their tutor without ransom, and allowing him to
return to Constantinople. Mohammed, however, died in Rome
during the winter which succeeded the battle of Lepanto, but his
brother, Said, remained in that city in honourable captivity until
the spring of 1573. In March of that year a Turkish vessel arrived
at Naples with the tutor on board, and a letter, as well as numerous
valuable presents, for Don John from Said's sister, Fatima:

Great Lord,

  After kissing the ground upon which your Highness treads,
that which the poor and miserable orphan desires to make
known to your Highness her lord is how grateful I am for the
favour which you have done us all, not only in giving freedom
to our servant Mohammed, but also in sending him to bring

---

[1] cf. Rosell, C., Historia de la Combate Naval de Lepanto, Appendix XV, p. 210.
Madrid, 1853.

[2] cf. Gonçalo de Yllescas, Dr, Historia Pontifical y Católica, en la qual se continuen las
vidas de todos los Pontificos Romanos, vol. ii, p. 763. Madrid, 1652.

us tidings how, after the death of my father and the rout of our fleet, my poor orphan brothers remained alive in your Highness's power, for which I still pray God to grant your Highness many years of life.

That which now remains, my lord, for me and all our family to do, is to entreat your Highness by the soul of Jesus Christ, by the life of your Highness, by the head of your mother, by the soul of your father the Emperor, by the life of His Majesty the King your brother, to do us the grace and charity of granting liberty to these poor orphans. They have no mother, and their father died in battle with your Highness. They depend solely upon the protection and pity of your Highness. As a courteous gentleman, as all men bespeak you, as a pious and generous Prince, take pity on the tears which I shed by the hour together, on the affliction of my brothers, and grant me this grace.

Of what I have been able to collect of the products of this country, I send your Highness a present which I entreat you to accept. It is far from being worthy of the greatness of your Highness, but my means are small; and may your Highness not regard the slenderness of the offering, but generously accept it in consideration of the goodwill with which it is offered.

Again, my lord, I beseech your Highness, by the spirit of Jesus Christ, do us this charity to set my brothers free, because in doing this good deed, even to those who are enemies, you will be esteemed liberal and compassionate; and since, beholding their tears, you were pleased to send Mohammed to inform us of their being alive, and of your honourable treatment of them (which the whole of this Court considers a great favour, and for which it is ever praising the goodness and magnanimity of your Highness), nothing is wanting to complete your renown but that your Highness should do us this grace and grant them their lives.

The slave of your Highness and the poor sister of the sons of Ali Pasha kisses the feet of your Highness.

FATIMA CADEM

On the receipt of this letter Don John recalled Said from Rome, and when the youth reached Naples his liberty was restored to him without ransom, while he was presented with a gold chain worth six hundred crowns, some fine horses, and various stores for his voyage to Constantinople. Don John also returned Fatima's gifts, and wrote her the following letter:

Noble and Virtuous Lady,

When Mohammed Bey and Said Bey, your brothers, were brought to my galley after the defeat of the Turkish fleet in battle, considering the misery to which human weakness is exposed, and the mutability of man's estate, and that these noble youths were in the fleet rather for the pleasure and companionship of their father than from any purpose of offence against us, I resolved not only to order that they should be treated as befitted their rank, but to give them their liberty when I should find an opportunity.

This my intention was greatly strengthened when I received your letter so full of sorrow and sisterly affection and showing so great a desire for the liberty of your brothers. While I was yet in hopes of being able to liberate both of them, to my great grief there happened to Mohammed Bey the final end of sorrows, which is death. I now restore Said Bey to liberty as well as the other prisoners for whom he has asked it, as I would also have set him free who is dead, were he still living. And believe me, Madam, that it is to me a peculiar pleasure to have it in my power to fulfil and satisfy, in part at least, your desire, holding as I do, in high esteem the noble character which you bear.

The present which you have sent me I have not accepted, but have left it in the hands of Said Bey; not, by any means, because I do not value that which has come from your hands, but because it has been the custom of my great ancestors not to receive gifts from those who apply to them for aid, but to confer favours, and as such, I hope, your brother and those who accompany him may be received. You may also be assured that, if in any other battle he or any other of those belonging to you should become my prisoner, I will, with equal cheerfulness as now, give them their liberty, and do whatever may be agreeable to you.

From Naples the 15th day of May, 1573.

DON JOHN[1]

[1] cf. Vanderhammen, Lorenzo, *Don Juan de Austria*, pp. 165–8. Madrid, 1627.

It would be interesting to know whether Fatima showed this letter to her uncle, the Sultan, and if so how he reacted to Don John's calm contemplation of another Lepanto. Anyhow, Said and his tutor daily sailed from Naples to Ragusa, whence they proceeded overland to the Turkish capital. Incidentally, in his kindness towards Ali Pasha's two sons, Don John had the full support of Philip.

Much of this, however, is to anticipate. When the fleet arrived at Petala a council of war was held to decide upon what should be attempted next, and opinions varied widely: some officers held that as the season was getting late nothing more should be attempted that year, while others were in favour of following up the victory by an attack upon Constantinople, and it is no exaggeration to say that from that day to this both Philip and his brother have been subject to criticism, chiefly civilian, for not having followed this latter course, which, according to the critics, would inevitably have been succeeded by the overthrow of the Ottoman Empire. The blame is usually placed upon the shoulders of the King either on the grounds of his habitual procrastination or of his jealousy of his brother. The matter calls for closer examination.

It is true that Philip was not of the stuff of which successful generals in the field are made, and he was thoroughly cognizant of the fact as he showed in the St Quentin campaign. Furthermore he was under no illusions as to the Turkish strength: Selim's immediate reaction to his defeat was to build a new fleet, and in any event the Osmanli on the defensive is a very formidable proposition as the British were one day to learn at Gallipoli. Nor could the Spaniards rely, like the Russians in the eighteenth and nineteenth centuries, upon the sympathy and support of the native Christians, for these were Orthodox, and much preferred the Sultan to the Catholic King. Above all, there were no Spanish possessions in the Eastern Mediterranean to serve as a base of operations, and Sicily was too far away; in these circumstances defeat would mean disaster. It is true that Crete was still in the possession of the Venetians, but the Serenissima was an uncertain ally, as the events of the next two years were abundantly to prove. It is also to be noted that the most responsible military authority of the day, namely Alba, was of the opinion that Don John's resources were far too slender to warrant an attack upon the Turkish capital.[1]

The Venetians would have liked to have followed up Lepanto by regaining some of the places in Albania and the Morea of which they had recently been deprived, whereas Don John, as he wrote to the King, favoured an attack on Lepanto, but as so often in these cases a compromise was reached, and after a good deal of discussion it was decided to attempt the reduction of the fort and island of Santa Maura, possibly with the idea of using them as a base for further operations in the Levant.

Accordingly the fleet put to sea again on October 12th, but owing to a contrary wind it was not until the next day that it reached Santa Maura. Three thousand troops under Corgnia were at once landed to reconnoitre the position, but from the beginning it was clear that the Turks were determined to put up a desperate resistance. They at once set fire to the suburbs, and laid the adjacent fields under water by opening the sluices of an aqueduct. Nor was this all, for the Greek peasants reported that the fortress was both well manned and provisioned. Such being the case it was clear that Santa Maura could only be taken after a regular siege, which might last a fortnight, and it was far too late in the season to risk an operation on such a scale: it was therefore regretfully agreed that the allied forces should go into winter quarters.

The weather, however, prevented the immediate implementation of this plan, so while the fleet lay wind-bound at Santa Maura advantage was taken of the opportunity to divide the spoils: in this division, it may be added, all ranks participated. Don John also sent Santa Cruz with a few galleys to cruise off the Curzolarian Islands in search of any stranded vessels, of which he found four. On October 24th, the fleet arrived at Corfu amid wild rejoicing, and there, on the orders of the Doge and the Senate, the Venetian contingent remained, while three days later the Spanish squadron sailed for Messina, which it reached on the last day of the month.

Meanwhile as the news of what had happened at Lepanto reached

[1] Letter to Jan de Zuñiga, Spanish ambassador in Rome, dated November 17th, 1571.

the capitals of Christian Europe it was received with enormous enthusiasm. Philip's own feelings were well expressed in his letter to his brother, while Lope de Figueroa described the attitude both of the King and the Court in a more informal epistle.

I thought I should never have arrived, but have been made into relics in Italy and France as a man sent by your Highness; and it was not until the 22nd of this month[1] that I reached the Escorial, suffering a good deal from my wound. I was as well received by His Majesty as your Highness would be by the Pope. For the first half-hour he did nothing but ask, 'Is my brother really all right?', and all sorts of conceivable questions that the case admitted. He then ordered me to tell him from the beginning everything that had happened, omitting no single detail, and while I was speaking he stopped me three times to ask for further explanations; and when I had ended he as often called me back to ask other questions about your Highness's care for the wounded, and how you gave away your share of the prize-money to the soldiers, at which he was not a little moved.

I was with him on two separate occasions, and at the second he said that he hoped God would grant your Highness health for the work which remained to be done; and that it would be necessary to build a thousand galleys to contain all who wanted to go and serve under your Highness, at whatever risk – a desire natural enough, but new since your Highness's time. The standard[2] he received with the greatest gladness that can be imagined, and he wanted to know the meaning of the inscription upon it. I answered that we could not read it, because of the letters that had been shot away, but that it was registered at the Prophet's house at Mecca, where it had been blessed by the chief priests.[3]

The Prior, and those of the Royal chamber who were there, I believe were worse than the Pope, who, the Cardinal[4] using

[1] November.

[2] The green standard of the Prophet which had been captured in the battle, the first time that it had ever fallen into Christian hands: it had been brought to Spain by Lope de Figueroa with the dispatches.

[3] The inscription was afterwards deciphered by Luis del Marmol. The standard was preserved in the Escorial until 1671 when it perished in a fire there.

[4] Cardinal de Espinosa (?)

all the influence he could, and even with the intervention of His Majesty, granted to the latter a plenary indulgence for only seven years for his chapel; and, not having given any other, he gave me a perpetual one for a monastery of my father's; and the Cardinal telling me the story, I at once placed it at his disposal, as enough for me will be those which your Highness will obtain for us by means of other victories. He said this victory was of God, such as had never before been seen, and worthy only of your Highness, whom he prayed God to allow to serve him with the affection which he knew you bore him.

In the presence of many gentlemen the Queen[1] expressed her joy, and came out with all her old women about her. The Princess[2] plied me with so many questions, more and weightier than Juan de Soto himself could have answered, that I cannot but take her for a soldier. Thus I passed an hour in the most agreeable manner possible, talking of your Highness. I do not know how it came about that your Highness did not write to the Queen, whom I told that I supposed half of the letters sent must have miscarried.

The others[3] I did not see, but I was sent to visit Doñna Luisa de Castro.

All are now minded to leave children and wives, or orders of knighthood, caring for nothing but to die in your Highness's service; and if money is wanting they would send you the Escorial, if nothing else were to be had. The Bishop of Cordova swore to me he would much rather go and be your Highness's chaplain than take possession of his bishopric. The Duke of Sesa is stouter than ever, and gayer than your Highness. A thousand men are cursing the causes why they were not with you in the battle.

The troops and other things which your Highness sent for will be sent[4] when the King comes; which will be to-morrow;

---

[1] Anna of Austria. Philip's fourth wife.

[2] The Infanta Isabella Clara Eugenia, then in her fifth year, the favourite child and companion of Philip. She married the Archduke Albert, and together they governed the Low Countries with great wisdom: she died in 1633.

[3] Of the Royal Family?

[4] As this letter was written from Madrid it would appear to establish the fact that Philip was at the Escorial when the news of the battle of Lepanto first reached him.

after which I will write more fully, when Ruy Gómez will also be here. Up to this time, your Highness has not had so many visits on board your flagship as I have had; but my entertainment has been bigger and better than that of your Highness on the night of the battle, when there was no fire, so that the rations and poor fare of that night would be more disagreeable here than they were there. Of your Highness's wound I have spoken to the King as you desired. Rejoicings are in preparation; what they will be I do not know, or whether they will be like what I saw in France. In Avignon[1] there were more processions than feasts in Andalusia, where in many places they have already had cave-plays on a great scale. I will write to Juan de Soto any other things I may hear, and shall continue to do so. Our Lord have you and the troops in his keeping.[2]

Whether Don John did or did not write to the Queen of Spain he certainly did not forget Doña Magdalena de Ulloa, for by his A.D.C., Jorge de Lima, he sent her two captured flags, one of which had been taken from the galley of Pertau Pasha, also a fragment of the Cross which had been presented to him by Pius V, and which he had worn during the battle. The two flags are no longer in existence, although they were until a comparatively recent date, but the relic is still preserved in the Jesuit college at Villagarcia founded by Doña Magdalena.[3]

It would be wearisome to describe in any detail the rejoicings that took place throughout Spain, though it may perhaps be mentioned that they were particularly marked in Seville because Don John's flagship had been built, or partly built, on the Guadalquivir. As for Philip, he showed himself as generous to the victors of Lepanto as he was later to do to the defeated of the Spanish Armada: Lope de Figueroa, for his gallantry in action and as bearer of Don John's dispatch, received the cross of Santiago and a benefice in that Order worth a thousand crowns a year. Requesens, always a favourite of the King, was made Viceroy of Milan.

In Venice there was equal joy. The Republic of Saint Mark

---

[1] Lope de Figueroa seems, however, to have forgotten that Avignon was Papal territory.

[2] The original of this letter is in the National Library in Madrid.

[3] cf. Camilo Maria, Father Abad, S.J., *Doña Magdalena de Ulloa*, p. 177. Camillas, 1959.

received the news of the victory before it reached either the Pope or Philip, for the tidings were brought by Omfredo Giustintiani who, having the wind in his favour, made the voyage in a mere ten days. We are told that his galley appeared off the lagoons on the morning of October 17th, and entered by the haven of the two Castles, in full view of the crowd in the Piazza di San Marco. The vessel's poop was covered with men dressed like Turks, and this at first caused some astonishment among the assembled multitude, but the mystery was soon resolved by the firing of cannon, the shouts of triumph, and the banners trailing astern from the galley. When it was realized exactly what had happened the citizens went mad with excitement; complete strangers embraced one another in the streets; and when the Doge and the Senate passed from the palace to the cathedral they had great difficulty in forcing their way through the crowd. The Doge, Ludovico Mocenigo, received the sacrament from the hands of the Spanish ambassador, Guzman de Silva, and the usual *Te Deum* and High Masses were followed by an order for the celebration of the victory for four days, which meant that during that period the Serenissima resounded with music and revelry.

While the city was still in a highly excited state Don Pedro Zapata arrived in a Venetian galley as the accredited envoy of Don John. He brought letters informing the Doge and Senate of the principal features of the battle; assuring them of his zeal for the safety and grandeur of the Republic; and asserting his willingness to attempt, as well as his hope of accomplishing, still greater achievements in the future for the common cause. Nor was old Veniero forgotten in the general rejoicing, for we have it on the authority of Paolo Paruta that he 'enfeebled by his great age [he was seventy-five] and many toils, having obtained leave of the Senate, returned home with the greatest glory, being met by the Bucentaur, having on board many Senators, at the Church of Sant' Antonio, which is in the outward parts of the city near the Lido, and was received with many demonstrations of honour by the nobles and populace'.[1] His real reward came on June 11th, 1577, when he was elected eighty-sixth Doge of Venice.

At Rome the news of the victory would appear to have been

[1] *Guerra di Cipro*, lib. iii, p. 214. Venice, 1605.

not wholly unexpected, for on the afternoon of the battle while the Pope was sitting at work with his treasurer he had suddenly got up, opened a window, and looked out as if he had heard some distant sound. After listening for a few moments he closed the window, and dismissed the official with the words, 'God be with you; this is no time for business, but for giving thanks to God, for at this moment our fleet is victorious', and as the man left the room he saw his master prostrate before a crucifix. Not unnaturally the treasurer was impressed by the incident, and he made a careful note of the day and hour when it took place, later to discover that it was the exact moment when Ali Pasha fell.

The Count of Priego was Don John's official messenger with the good news, and he travelled in the same galley as Zapata as far as Otranto, where he disembarked, and then proceeded overland to Rome. He was most graciously received by Pius V, who expressed the debt of Christendom to the victor of Lepanto, in the words of the Gospel, 'There was a man sent from God, whose name was John', but he would hear no good of Doria, and declared that he had behaved more like a corsair than a Christian captain: indeed so strongly did the Pope feel on the matter that the Genoese, who had been thinking of visiting Rome, decided not to do so. On the other hand Colonna in due course received as enthusiastic a welcome as Veniero had in Venice, though Pius, partly out of frugality and partly due to a desire not to give offence in any quarter, refused the Triumph which the Colonna family had planned, and pared it down to an Ovation: this meant that, instead of driving in a chariot clad in armour, the Admiral had to be content with riding a white horse, and wearing ordinary clothes, though with the Golden Fleece round his neck. All the same the procession must have been a magnificent spectacle, including, as it did, a hundred and sixty Turks, chained two and two, and wearing red and yellow liveries.

In both Spain and Italy there was a veritable spate of verses in honour of Don John, and in Messina there is a notable statue of him by Andrea Calamech, while Titian executed a picture on the subject of Lepanto for Philip – or at least there is one by him which tradition has connected with the battle. Even from faraway Scotland were to come some eleven hundred lines of doggerel by no less a poet than King James VI at the age of twelve or thirteen. More recently Lepanto inspired G. K. Chesterton to write one of the most stirring poems in the English language.

If such was the aftermath of Don John's victory in Madrid, Venice, and Rome it was very different in Constantinople, for when the news reached the Turkish capital that the whole Ottoman battle-fleet with the exception of some fifty galleys had been lost, together with forty thousand men, 'all the councillors of the Porte and all the generals were so stunned that had they seen but fifty Christian galleys approaching, they would have abandoned the town'.[1] Devout Moslems are said to have declared that when the Prophet heard Don John's guns he wept upon the knees of his houris in Paradise, and that black Azrael, the angel of death, had turned traitor upon his worshippers. All the same the Grand Vizier was very far from giving way to despair, and he even persuaded the Sultan to bestir himself. Selim was at Adrianople when the news of Lepanto was brought to him, and his first reaction to it was to order a massacre of any Spaniards and Venetians who were at the time in his dominions. Mohammed Sokolli soon succeeded in diverting his master's energies into the more profitable channel of replacing the losses incurred in the battle, and not only did Selim make a considerable donation for this purpose from his own pocket but he gave up part of the garden of his palace at Seraglio Point as a site for the construction of the new vessels. Most important of all, the Grand Vizier persuaded him to appoint Ochiali as Capitan Pasha.

Between them the creation of a new fleet went briskly forward, for the spirit of Suleyman the Magnificent was still very much to the fore in official circles in Constantinople. On receiving his appointment Ochiali pointed out to Sokolli that while it might be possible to provide a hundred and fifty galleys for the next campaign the provision of the requisite numbers of anchors might be impossible. 'Pasha,' replied the Grand Vizier, 'the wealth and power of this Empire can supply you, if necessary, with anchors of silver, cordage of silk, and sails of satin; whatever you want for your ships you have only to come and ask for it.'[2] The loss of

---

[1] Brantôme, P. de B., *Oeuvres Complètes*, vol. iii, p. 133. Paris, 1822.
[2] cf. Hammer, J. de, *Histoire de l'Empire Ottoman*, vol. vi, p. 433. Paris, 1835-43.

skilled crews at Lepanto created an even more difficult problem, and to replace them peasants from all over the Empire were conscripted, but although the desired quantity may have been recruited the quality was far below that of the men who had perished, and a realization of this fact explains Ochiali's strategy in the campaign that lay ahead. No difficulty or obstacle was, however, in this high noon of Ottoman power permitted to be insuperable, and by the spring of 1572 the Grand Vizier and the Capitan Pasha could claim that one hundred and fifty galleys and eight galleasses were constructed and ready for sea, but in no respect was this the equal of the fleet which had perished at Lepanto.

Because that battle was not followed up – largely, as we shall see, owing to the attitude of France – and in particular because it did not result in the expulsion of the Turk from Europe, it has been represented as a barren victory which yielded no fruits to those who gained it. Morally there can be no question but that it was decisive, for it lifted the pall of terror which had shrouded eastern and central Europe ever since the fall of Constantinople in 1453, and it blazoned throughout Christendom the startling fact that the Turk was no longer invincible. It is true that there were to be many ups and downs before, in 1697, Prince Eugene at Zenta drove the army of Mustapha II into the Theiss, and thereby exorcized the Turkish threat to the West, but the full prestige of Suleyman the Magnificent was never revived. His reign marked the summit of Ottoman power, and it was the day of Lepanto which broke the charm upon which it rested.[1]

[1] cf. Fuller, Major-General J. F. C., *The Decisive Battles of the Western World*, vol. i, p. 578. London, 1954.

9

The Disintegration of the
Holy League

FOR DON JOHN THE NEXT EIGHTEEN MONTHS – ONE MIGHT almost say the rest of his life – were in the nature of anticlimax. The very decisiveness of the victory of Lepanto had unloosed all the centrifugal forces in the Holy League, and all the resources of Ottoman diplomacy, ably seconded by that of France, were employed to sow dissension between Venice and Madrid, for the interests of the two chief allies pointed towards different and incompatible enterprises. The Serenissima desired above all else the recovery of Cyprus, and a general rehabilitation of her prestige in the Levant, while Philip looked to North Africa as the area where the Christian triumph could best be exploited. The Pope alone had no axe of his own to grind – his only desire was the humiliation of the Turk, and he was thus in a position to hold the balance evenly, but this imposed upon him the necessity of exercising the greatest care not to give the appearance of favouring one party for fear of alienating the other.

One weakness of the Venetian case was that the former subjects of the Republic of Saint Mark, being Greeks by race and Orthodox by religion, had no desire to come under its domination again, and particularly was this the case in Cyprus. It is true that in reality the change of régime had exercised the most profound influence upon the fortunes of the island, which only yesterday had been a kingdom renowned throughout Europe for its wealth and power, whereas now it had become an obscure province of the Ottoman Empire, and its history for the next three centuries was to be a record of maladministration and decay. Nevertheless at the outset of their rule the conquerors adopted two measures in particular which for a time rendered their rule by no means unpopular, and certainly strengthened the average Cypriot's aversion to the Serenissima.

First of all they established the Orthodox Church, and refused recognition to any other. They restored the Orthodox archbishopric, which had been in abeyance for three hundred years, and assured to the Cypriots the undisturbed possession of their churches as well as the right to worship unmolested. The Latins, on the other hand, were deprived of all their property, and their churches were either converted into mosques, or used for secular purposes. In a different field the Turks abolished the feudal system of serfdom, and the Cypriots, who had been the slaves of their feudal lords ever since the time of Richard I, now became the possessors of their own land: from being serfs they became landlords. The effect of these reforms was to convince the people of the island for some years that they had not done too badly by changing the Doge for the Sultan: certainly Cyprus was no Venetian *terra irredenta*.

While the Cypriots were thus slowly beginning to settle down under their new masters Don John was experiencing some changes at his headquarters. The appointment of Requesens to the Vice-Royalty of Milan had deprived him of his second-in-command, and he does not seem to have been consulted as to the appointment of a successor: at any rate he wrote to Don Sancho de Leyva, 'There are many pretenders, I believe, for the place which the Grand Commander lately occupied here; sometimes I expect it will be given to Don Garcia de Toledo, who is coming here from Livorno – and in truth, if you were appointed, I should be well pleased to enjoy your company – but I do not think it becoming to ask either for one or the other, having no object in thought or action beyond His Majesty's pleasure; and so I wait, in this as in other matters, to obey his orders.'[1] In the end the King appointed the Duke of Sesa, while the Marquess of Trevico, a Neapolitan, and Antonio Doria, a Genoese, were added to the war-council.

About this time an event occurred which was of far less immediate importance, but of much greater significance for the future, namely the appearance of some emissaries from Albania and the

[1] cf. Rosell, C., *Historia de la Combate Naval de Lepanto*, Appendix XXVII, p. 229. Madrid, 1853.

Morea who suggested to Don John that if he would entertain the idea of carving out for himself a kingdom in that part of the world the whole Christian population would flock to his standard. To a young man who was situated as was Don John the bait was a tempting one, and he would appear to have swallowed it hook, line, and sinker. He seems to have made no inquiries as to the numbers or resources of the people whom these emissaries claimed to represent, but he showed himself by no means unfavourable to their request, and said he would submit it to the King without whose approval he could not move in the matter. Philip's reply was that of the statesman rather than that of the crusader: he said that the alliance between Spain and the Serenissima rendered any such move inexpedient for the moment, but at the same time he instructed Don John to keep the negotiations open. What the King did get from the incident was a valuable insight into the mind of his brother, and into the direction in which his ambitions were tending.

During the winter of 1571–2 arms gave place to diplomacy. The Allies of the Holy League were active in the attempt to obtain fresh adherents among the princes of Europe and the Middle East, while the Grand Vizier was equally occupied in endeavouring not only to thwart their efforts but also to separate Spain from the Serenissima: in the end it was he, with the aid of the French, who was to be successful.

The initiative in the attempt to secure fresh recruits for the Holy League was taken by the Pope, who sent a Legate to the Emperor, and to the Kings of France, Portugal, and Poland, urging them to draw sword against the infidel. From the beginning there was little hope that Maximilian II would prove responsive: he had, as we have seen, only recently made a truce with the Sultan, and he told the Papal Legate, one Cardinal Commendon, that 'the faith of treaties ought to be considered as inviolable, and a Christian can never be justified in breaking an oath'.[1] So determined was he to preserve his neutrality that when the news of Lepanto reached him he had forbidden any public rejoicings lest he should appear to insult Selim in his distress. In any event Maximilian was the last man likely to become infected with a crusading

[1] cf. Coxe, W., *History of House of Austria*, vol. ii, p. 640. London, 1807.

spirit, and his increasing tendency to gout[1] doubtless made him more reluctant than ever to embark upon an aggressive foreign policy.

Where France was concerned the situation was exceedingly tricky, and nothing illustrates more clearly the interconnexion of events in the latter part of the sixteenth century than the happenings in the years which immediately followed the conclusion of the Third Civil War in that country by the Peace of St Germain in August, 1570. Charles IX, a young man of twenty-one, was not an attractive personality. He was far from being a nonentity like his elder brother and immediate predecessor, Francis II, and he could turn out a decent set of verses, but there was not much behind a relatively imposing façade. He was much under the influence of his mother, Catherine de Medici, who had been Regent during his minority. Years later, her son-in-law, Henry IV of France, said of her, 'What could a poor woman have done, with her husband dead, five small children upon her hands, and two families who were scheming to seize the throne – our own and the Guises? I am astonished that she did not do even worse.' This judgement is an understatement. The French Crown was left face to face with two parties, the Huguenots and the Guises, each stronger than itself, and for many years it was due to Catherine that the country did not disintegrate as was to be the case with Germany.

The Papal Legate did not arrive in Paris at a very propitious moment. For the previous ten years Catherine had alternated between two lines of conduct: at one time she had tried to act as mediator between the two religious parties, and at another she had endeavoured to preserve an equilibrium by throwing her weight into the scale of the weaker. Neither policy had succeeded, and she was beginning to incline to a foreign war against Spain with the object of dividing the Spanish Netherlands with William of Orange, who was the moving spirit in the Dutch revolt against Philip. In this Catherine was supported by Admiral Coligny, the Huguenot leader, and the King himself was seriously alarmed at the possible increase of Spanish power which it was felt might result from the victory of Lepanto.

[1] Possibly as a result of washing down the salad and prawns, mentioned on an earlier page, with excessive quantities of Hungarian wine.

William of Orange welcomed the advances which were now made to him, for he had long been of the opinion that if the Low Countries were to make head successfully against Spain they must have foreign support. Elizabeth I, in spite of her continued quarrels with Philip, was less enthusiastic: she had already burnt her fingers once by interfering in French politics[1] and in any event she had no desire to see Antwerp and the mouth of the Scheldt in the hands of the King of France. Anxious not to offend Spain openly she therefore ordered a number of Dutch privateers, who had taken refuge in English waters, to put to sea. This they did under the command of a freebooter of the name of William de la Marck. After attacking some Spanish merchant-ships, on April 1st, 1572, they seized the town of Brille at the mouth of the Meuse. The seizure of the town had not been authorized by Orange, but he soon turned it to advantage: Flushing followed the example of Brille, and before long most of the chief towns in Holland, Zeeland, Gelderland, Overyssel, Utrecht, and Friesland were lost to Philip. In May, with the connivance of Charles IX, a French force, largely Huguenot in composition, took Mons, and for a brief space it seemed as if the unity of France had been restored on the basis of hostility to Spain.

Some of this is to anticipate, but the state of feeling in Paris explains why in Rome and Madrid during the winter of 1571-2 there was great anxiety in case France should not merely stand aloof from the League but actually join the Turks. In the event what Charles did was to refuse to allow his fleet to act with that of Spain and Venice, but he held out hope of sending an army under the Duke of Anjou to co-operate with the Imperial forces if Maximilian would declare war against the Sultan. As the Most Christian King he clearly had to make a gesture of some sort, but as the Emperor remained neutral he was not required to do anything.

Sebastian of Portugal, as subsequent events were to prove, was just the man for a crusade, but he was only seventeen, and it was all he could do to defend his own territory from the attentions of the Barbary Corsairs: nevertheless, he did promise to contribute

[1] In 1563, when the French united to expel her troops from Le Havre, and she was forced to abandon her claim for the restitution of Calais.

to the Holy League a force of four thousand infantry, and to inflict what damage he could upon Turkish commerce and possessions in the Red Sea and the Persian Gulf. He further undertook to bring fresh pressure to bear on the Shah.[1] Sebastian was Philip's nephew and the son of Don John's favourite sister, the Princess of the Brazils, and this may to some extent explain his favourable reaction to the Pope's appeal: in the case of the Emperor and the King of France the ties of kinship clearly meant nothing at all for Philip was the cousin of Maximilian II and the brother-in-law of Charles IX.

In Eastern Europe the Pope had no success at all. Sigismund II of Poland, the last of the great Jagellon dynasty, was near his death, and in any case he was too concerned with events nearer home to launch out into more remote enterprises. Lithuania, in spite of its incorporation in the Polish monarchy, required constant attention, for as recently as 1569 the Russian Tsar, Ivan IV, had succeeded in wresting Smolensk and other Eastern provinces of Lithuania from Sigismund. At one time Pius V had even named a Legate to Ivan himself, 'but the stories of his cruelties perpetrated upon other envoys deterred him from exposing the nose and ears of a southern bishop to the whimsical barbarities of the Muscovite tyrant'.[2]

Thus, as the spring of 1572 wore on, it became evident that the Holy League was not likely to attract any new recruits. This was bad enough, but what was worse was that the differences between its existing members increased rather than diminished during the months of inaction and intrigue. The main subject of contention was the choice of a new Venetian commander-in-chief, for all the Spanish senior officers declared that they could tolerate Veniero no longer: his capacity was not, in their opinion, such as to compensate for his irascibility. Don John shared this view, and on December 20th, 1571, he wrote to Don Juan de Zuñiga, the Spanish ambassador in Rome, 'As to the appointment by the Venetians of another General I have already expressed my

---

[1] It was doomed to failure from the start for Tahmasp I was near the end of his life, while throughout the century hostilities with the Turks had been unfortunate for the Persians.

[2] Stirling-Maxwell, Sir William, *Don John of Austria*, p. 470. London, 1883.

opinion; but if they are determined that it shall still be Sebastian Veniero, I can assure His Holiness and the Signiory that if under my command he shall commit follies like those of last year, I will not wait for their orders to punish him; but it would be safer to remove him, as I have already said.' In a postscript to the same letter he added, 'It is with pain that I hear it is still a question whether the Venetian general remain in his command, because it is certain that he and I cannot work cordially together, for reasons which the Grand Commander will have told you. If possible, therefore, he ought to be removed, which would avoid many inconveniences, which I fear will happen if he retain his post.'[1] All the resources of Spanish diplomacy were put into effect to secure the removal of Veniero, but for a long time the Doge and Senate supported him. In the end, however, they gave way, and he was made Admiral of the Gulf of Venice, while his dignity was saved by a grant of precedence over all other Venetian commanders when their flags should happen to meet. In his place Giacomo Foscarini was appointed to command the contingent of Saint Mark in the fleet of the Holy League.

While this internal bickering was dissipating the energies of the Christian Powers an event occurred which was destined to destroy in due course the Holy League altogether, for on May 1st, 1572, Pope Pius V died. He would appear to have suffered from a series of minor strokes during the previous months, but on Easter Day, which fell that year on April 6th, he was able to give his blessing *urbi et orbi* from the balcony of St Peter's; yet he knew that the hand of death was on him. In spite of the remonstrances of his doctors he performed the pilgrimage of the seven churches of Rome, partly on foot and partly in a litter. As he came out of St Paul's the Abbot and his Benedictines assured him of their prayers for his health. 'Nay, my sons,' he replied, 'I am laying down the burden; pray that I may have a good successor, which is of importance to Christianity.' When the time came to take farewell of his ministers and attendants his thoughts were clearly focused on the affairs of the Holy League, which had been the dominant passion of his life.

[1] cf. Rosel, C., *Historia de la Combate Naval de Lepanto*, Appendix XXI, pp. 216–17. Madrid, 1853.

You will not easily find one who has a stronger desire to root out the enemies of Christ's faith and cross; but He who is able, of these stones, to raise up seed to Abraham, can give you a better and a stronger guide. The Holy League has begun a great work; my successor will have little to do but to enjoy the glory of it. I am not concerned to have lived only for the labour and to leave the fruit to another; the glory of God being my sole aim. But by the blood of Christ I entreat you, whose affair it is, to elect, as speedily as possible, a zealous man in my place, and not to choose him on mere worldly considerations. The year is already far advanced; what has to be done must be done soon; and if this year passes without some memorable action, men's spirits will fail them, and our labour and the great victory will be fruitless.

His dying words are said to have been, 'Defend us from the enemy, and receive us in the hour of death.'[1]

The dead Pontiff's wish that the Cardinals would not indulge in any unnecessary delay in the election of his successor was certainly fulfilled, for without even a ballot Cardinal Buoncampagno, a Bolognese of seventy, was elevated to St Peter's Chair under the style of Gregory XIII. He had begun his career as a lawyer, and did not take Holy Orders until he was thirty-five. The new Pope was an entire contrast to Pius V, for he was very much a man of the world, cool and self-contained. His intentions were good and he wished for reform – he certainly deserved well of posterity for his new calendar – but he liked ease and lacked energy, and his reign was to become notorious for its administrative disorders. His laws were good – was the contemporary opinion – but no one was under the necessity of keeping them, and in consequence the States of the Church, always disturbed, relapsed into a condition of positive anarchy. Nor was this all, for the coldness of his manner, and his reluctance to grant favours, rendered him unpopular; when he meant to be gracious it was said that 'the words seem to be torn out of him by force'.[2] He had a son by an early marriage who was well provided for, but he was not given any part in the

[1] cf. Fuenmayor, Antonio de, *Vida y hechos de Pio V, Pontifice Romano*, folios 142–3. Madrid, 1595.

[2] cf. Vernon, Mrs H. M., *Italy from 1494 to 1790*, p. 148. Cambridge, 1909.

government; on the other hand it was in Gregory's reign that there first appeared a Cardinal Secretary of State. Gregory XIII, it may be added, was personally acceptable to Philip, who had known him at one time when he was in Spain.

While these events were taking place, Don John remained at Messina preparing for the coming campaign against the Turk, that is to say in supervising the fitting out of galleys, the collecting of stores, and the drilling of recruits. With him was Santa Cruz, and they had both hoped to put to sea in February, but no such in-instructions reached them, though in March, 1572, Don John received orders from his brother to go to Palermo, and superintend the military and naval preparations in that part of Sicily: this he did, and was back at Messina at the beginning of April. It was now the season of the year when according to the provisions of the Holy League the Allies should have been ready to take the offensive, but as the weeks passed it became abundantly clear that something was holding Philip back, and in consequence Don John was not unnaturally suffering from what a later age would have termed frustration.

There were, however, compensations. Since Lepanto the world and his wife – not least his wife – had been at the young man's feet, and Don John soon proved no more insensitive to the charms of the Sicilian ladies than in his more unsophisticated days he had been to those of Maria de Mendoza. The Marquess of Mulhacén mentions three women in particular whose favours Don John enjoyed at this time.[1] The first was possibly Diana di Falangola who came from Sorrento where her father was a man of some condition: she was, we are told, of outstanding beauty, and she was certainly an easy conquest, since she would appear to have set her heart on having Don John for a lover from the first time she met him, and in this ambition she was encouraged by her parents. On September 11th, 1573, she gave birth to a girl who was christened Juana, but after that event she seems to have ceased to be Don John's mistress, though, according to the pleasant custom of the time, he arranged a suitable marriage for her, and he continued to take an interest in their daughter. Juana was brought up by her aunt, Margaret of Parma, and in due course at the age of

[1] *Don Juan de Austria*, pp. 219–25. Madrid, 1944.

sixteen she entered a convent in Naples. Like her sister, Ana, she later owed much to the good offices of her cousin, Philip III, who tried to bring about a marriage for her with the Duke of Urbino, but in the end nothing came of the project. However, Philip was more successful with the Prince of Pietrapersia, the eldest son of the Prince of Butera, and they were married in 1603, when the bride was thirty. Juana finally died in Naples at the age of fifty-seven, leaving an only daughter, Margaret, who became the wife of Frederick Colonna, Duke of Paliano.

Another lady who had an *affaire* with Don John at this time was Zenobia Sarotosia, a Neapolitan, also renowned for her good looks: she bore him a son, who, however, died a few days after his birth – a calamity which so weighed upon the sorrowing mother that she entered a convent.

A very different, and far more dangerous, type of woman was Ana de Toledo, wife of the Lord Warden of Naples, with whom Don John also became entangled. She was domineering and ambitious, and her lover's staff were for a time seriously worried at the influence she was exercising over their chief. For a space she certainly had him in her toils, and she persuaded him to give her forty slaves, picked from the whole of the Spanish Navy, to crew a galliot in which she proposed to go on a cruise.[1]

It was inactivity that provided Don John with the time to engage in these amours, and this inactivity was due to doubts about the policy which France was likely to pursue. We have already seen that the spring of 1572 was marked by a triumph of the centripetal forces in that country which boded ill for Philip, and it was certainly not the moment to commit large Spanish forces to the Levant until the intentions of Charles IX and his mother were more obvious. In effect, Philip was prevented from following up the victory of Lepanto for precisely the same reason that he had to delay so long in coming to the relief of Malta, namely uncertainty about the line which France was likely to take. Fortunately the clouds showed signs of lifting as spring passed into summer. Catherine de Medici began to fear the influence of Coligny over her son, for rumours reached her ears that the

[1] cf. Porreño, B., *Historia del serenisimo Señor Don Juan de Austria*, Appendix, p. 365. Madrid, 1899.

Admiral was telling Charles that he would never really be King until he had freed himself from his mother's control. Even so she might have held her hand had the new foreign policy showed signs of proving successful, but such was not the case, and she began to doubt the result of an appeal to arms as reports came in of the superiority of the Spanish troops over anything that could be brought against them: de la Noue was driven out of Valenciennes, and in July a French force which was endeavouring to relieve Mons was cut to pieces by Alba's son, Fadrique de Toledo. Then the Serenissima sent a special envoy to Charles beseeching him not to break with Philip, as this would only play into the hands of the Sultan, and Catherine was always susceptible to any argument in favour of Italian interests. Furthermore, the attitude of Elizabeth of England was far from reassuring, and it was widely believed in France that she was preparing to betray Flushing to the Spaniards.[1]

While Philip and his brother were thus compelled to mark time the Grand Vizier had by no means been idle. A few days after he received the news of the battle of Lepanto he sent for the Venetian envoy who, according to Turkish custom, had been incarcerated on the outbreak of war, and said to him: 'You come to see how we bear our misfortune, but I would have you know the difference between your loss and ours. In wresting Cyprus from you, we have deprived you of an arm; in defeating our fleet, you have only shaved our beard. An arm, when cut off, cannot grow again; but a shorn beard grows all the better for the razor.'[2] Mohammed Sokolli, however, went on to insinuate that his master was not unprepared to negotiate, and he continued to talk in this vein for some time while Ochiali was rebuilding the Ottoman fleet. Meanwhile the representative of the French King, the Bishop of Dax, was industriously fishing in these troubled waters with the ultimate object of the disintegration of the Holy League, though without committing Charles to any definite action which indeed, he was in no position to take.

The repercussions of this uncertainty continued to make them-

[1] cf. Erlanger, P., *Le Massacre de la Saint-Barthélemy*, p. 107. Paris, 1960.

[2] cf. Hammer, J. de, *Histoire de l'Empire Ottoman*, vol. vi, p. 434. Paris, 1835–43.

selves felt at Messina. Don John had, for example, counted upon reinforcements from the Milanese, but Requesens wrote that in view of the possibility of a French invasion he could not spare a single man. The Venetians were not slow to take advantage of the opportunity to say that they were ready to fight, and that their forces were suffering from desertion and sickness in consequence of the delay, but the only reply which Don John could make was to express his regret. Then the new Pope gave evidence that where the Holy League was concerned he held the views of his predecessor, and he instructed his nuncio in Madrid to remind Philip that the proceeds of the bull of the crusade and some other ecclesiastical revenues had been granted to him to assist his preparations against the Sultan, and that if he did not take the offensive these concessions could not be continued. Until he received favourable news from Paris all that the King could do was to procrastinate, and put the best face he could upon his inaction. Even Don John, who must have guessed why his brother was marking time, at last sent de Soto to Madrid with a letter warning him that the continued delay might endanger the very existence of the Holy League, and asking him for permission either to sail or to send a portion of his fleet to act in conjunction with the Venetians whose territories were being threatened by Ochiali.

The Ottoman fleet had in fact put to sea in two portions. First of all early in the spring Carack Ali sailed from Constantinople with seventy galleys, and in June he was followed by Ochiali with a hundred more: this armament was impressive, but the vessels were mostly new and built of green timber; the guns had been hastily cast of worthless metal; the officers and men were raw; few of the oarsmen had previously handled an oar; and the soldiers, with the memory of Lepanto fresh in their minds, had to be driven on board with sticks: nevertheless, Ochiali had improved on the weapons of the previous year, for he had persuaded his people to leave their bows at home, and had provided them with twenty thousand firelocks. All the same, the Bishop of Dax thought the whole armament contemptible, and declared that it was 'sur le poinct de souffrir une merveilleuse bastonnade'. Inadequate it may have been, but with it Ochiali made an impressive showing in Greek waters in June and July, and was even able to threaten

Crete. Never had the Turkish power of resilience after a defeat been displayed to greater advantage.

The truth is that although the Venetians never tired of complaining of the inactivity of their Spanish allies they effected singularly little themselves; indeed, when Foscarini took up his command he received positive orders from the Council of Ten not to attempt anything until he had been joined by the Spaniards. In these circumstances it is hardly surprising that the only Venetian achievement during the winter and spring had been the capture of Margariti, on the coast of Albania, when the Turkish morale proved so low that it became obvious that had more energetic measures been put into operation the results might well have been far-reaching. In July, Don John so far met the wishes of Foscarini as to allow a few of his galleys to sail with Colonna and Soranzo to Corfu. Colonna had under his command on this occasion twenty-six galleys, that is to say thirteen belonging to the Pope, eleven to the Grand Duke of Tuscany, and two to Michael Bonelo, while Soranzo had twenty-four: to these were now added eighteen Spanish galleys commanded by Gil de Andrade, with five thousand infantry aboard under the orders of the Count of Sarno. Colonna thereupon hoisted the standard of the Holy League, but Don John, mindful of his restraining orders from his brother, only accompanied the squadron as far as Punta del Faro, and from there he went to Palermo.

Colonna touched at Otranto and reached Corfu on July 15th, where he was met by Foscarini with a not inconsiderable armament and much rejoicing. Shortly afterwards he put to sea at the head of 126 galleys and twenty-six larger vessels. As in the previous year the Christian fleet was divided into three squadrons. Colonna himself, with Foscarini and Gil de Andrade, commanded the centre, with Soranzo in command on the right and Canale on the left. This force reached Gomeniza on July 28th, and between that date and the end of the following month Colonna vainly sailed the seas in an effort to bring Ochiali to battle. Twice he nearly succeeded, but the Algerine was too well aware of the insufficiency of the men and ships under his command to run any risks, and on August 31st, Colonna was back in Corfu, where he found Don John who had at last been let off the lead. What had happened?

As the weeks went by Catherine de Medici had become increasingly jealous of the influence of Coligny over her eldest son. She saw that power which she coveted above all things slipping from her, and she feared a return to the obscurity which had been her lot while her husband was on the throne. Had the attempt upon Coligny's life on August 22nd proved fatal it is possible that his death would have sufficed, but he had stooped to adjust his stirrup, and the wound he received was unlikely to prove fatal. The outspoken threats of the Huguenots, the indignation of King Charles, his determination to run the perpetrators of the crime to earth, and the fear of her own complicity being discovered, may well have driven Catherine into a panic which caused her to drown her guilt in the blood of the whole Huguenot party.

Of one thing there can be no doubt, and it is that so far as she was concerned the Massacre of Saint Bartholomew went too far, and got thoroughly out of hand. She did not intend that it should be taken to imply any change in French foreign policy; all she aimed at was to recover the reins, and though she might moderate the pace she had no intention of altering the direction. Fate willed it otherwise, and any prospects of success which might have been expected for her foreign policy were nullified by the loss of French unity which was attendant upon the Massacre. Once more Catholics and Huguenots were at each other's throats, and France ceased to be an object of hope or of fear to her neighbours: twenty years were to elapse before the promise of the spring of 1572 was fulfilled.

The Massacre only occurred on August 24th, and it is not suggested that within a week Philip had heard the news and that his order to take the offensive had reached his brother. What happened was surely that the King, who had a first-class information service, early in the month foresaw the course which events in Paris were likely to take, and on this intuition he told his brother to go ahead. However this may be, the Turks owed it to their French friends that they had been given nine months to repair their losses at Lepanto.

Don John received his colleagues with his customary courtesy in public, but in private conclave he expressed dissatisfaction with their conduct, chiefly because he considered that they should have awaited his arrival before putting to sea. Colonna and Foscarini justified themselves, and the former said that if his explanation was not accepted he was prepared to resign his command, to go to Madrid, and to explain his behaviour to the King in person: Gil de Andrade, though he was only acting under the orders of a superior officer, also appears to have incurred Don John's displeasure. In the end, after a good deal of discussion, Don John decided to forgive and forget, but the general opinion in the fleet seems to have been that though Colonna's excuses were plausible his chief had good grounds for reprimanding him, because the real motives of his conduct had been either an erroneous estimate of the Turkish strength or an eagerness to achieve some independent success.[1]

The past being thus disposed of Don John proceeded to a review of the forces under his command. He had brought with him from Sicily fifty-six galleys and thirty large vessels, so that his total armament amounted to one hundred and ninety-four galleys, forty large sailing-ships, and eight galleasses. There were a num- of newcomers, among them a galley, a galliot, and a brigantine, flying the Lilies of France and the Cross of Lorraine, under the command of the Duke of Mayenne, brother of the Duke of Guise, for he and a number of his fellow-countrymen were determined to prove that the Catholic subjects of Charles IX did not share the Turcophil sentiments of the Most Christian King. The Venetians, as before, were found deficient in their complement of soldiers, and Foscarini flatly refused to allow any Spaniards on his ships. Colonna, however, interposed as mediator, and lent the Venetian thirteen hundred Papal infantry, receiving a like number of Spanish troops to replace them.

Before he put to sea Don John drew up his order of battle which was based on that which proved so successful the previous year. The right wing, commanded by Santa Cruz, consisted of fifty-two galleys distinguished by green pennants on the foremast; the left wing of the same number, but with blue pennants at the brace of the yard, was given to Soranzo; and the centre, comprising seventy galleys, was under the command of Don John, with whom

[1] cf. Caraciolo, F., Conte de Biccari, *I Commentarii della Guerra fatta coi Turchi da D. Giovanni d'Austria dopo venne in Italia*, pp. 78–89. Florence, 1581.

were Foscarini, Colonna, and Gil de Andrade. The vanguard, which formed part of the centre, was confided to Giustiniani, who had in the end escaped from Lepanto with his life when Ochiali abandoned his prizes, while two galleasses sailed in front of each of the wings. The rear was covered by a reserve of twenty-six galleys, with white streamers on their poops, commanded by Nicolas Donato and Juan de Cardona. The heavy ships, under Rodrigo de Mendoza, were left in the safe, but accessible, harbour of Zante.

The fleet of the Holy League sailed from Gomeniza on September 8th, and it spent the next six weeks in fruitlessly attempting to bring Ochiali to battle. The first news that reached Don John was to the effect that the enemy had divided his armament, and that part was at Modon and part at Navarino. On receiving this information he decided to proceed at once to the island of Sapienza, which lies to the south and in front of the harbour of Modon, for from there it would be easy to cut off all communication by sea between that port and Navarino. The strategy was eminently sound, but the pilots made a mistake in their reckoning, and laid the fleet abreast of the island of Prodano, which is eight miles to the north of Navarino. This error rendered surprise out of the question, and the Turks in the bay of Navarino withdrew in good order to Modon, where their fleet was reunited. Don John reconnoitred Modon, but soon came to the conclusion that a sudden attack was out of the question, and withdrew towards Sapienza: as he did so Ochiali sallied out from the harbour with fifty galleys, but as soon as he saw that the Christians were only too eager to accept the challenge the Corsair withdrew.

The next day, however, did see some fighting, for Don John doubled Cape Gallo, and put into the Gulf of Corone for water: it was then found that water could only be obtained several miles inland, so it became necessary to land troops to protect the watering-parties which consisted of galley-slaves. This operation did not escape the vigilant eye of Ochiali, who led sixteen hundred Janissaries and two hundred cavalry over the hills from Modon in an attempt to frustrate it. In this he was unsuccessful for the bold front and steady fire of the Spanish arquebusiers forced his men to retire. Prominent in this action was the Prince of Parma, whose

extreme daring was such that Don John remonstrated with him
for it – an excellent example of Satan rebuking sin. All the same it
was decided by the Council of War that it was too dangerous to
attempt any decisive blow against the Turk in that area, but that it
would be wiser to retire to Navarino, where there was plenty of
water and a safe anchorage: accordingly, the fleet assembled there
on September 27th, and Don Martin de Padilla was sent with a
squadron of eighteen galleys to Zante, whence he was to bring
back the heavy ships, or, if bad weather made that impossible,
as many of the troops, and as much of their stores and munitions,
as he could get on board his galleys.

The bay of Navarino has twice made history.[1] It is a semicircular
basin, two and a half miles in length, stretching from the north-
east to the south-west, and enclosed on the land side by a range of
bare limestone hills. On the side of the Mediterranean there lies
the long island of Sphagia, the ancient Sphacteria, where the
Athenians won so signal a victory over the Spartans,[2] and between
this island and the mainland there are two channels. That on the
north is half a mile wide, but so shallow as to be quite useless for
shipping: the one on the south is a very different proposition, for
although it is only five hundred feet wide the water is deep. In
1572 there arose above this entrance to the harbour the town and
castle of Navarino, built by the Venetians and now garrisoned by
the Turks. Had the rock on the other side been fortified the passage of a hostile fleet into the bay would have been rendered
impossible, but this precaution had been neglected alike by the
engineers of the Serenissima and by those of the Sultan, with the
result that the guns of the castle could neither sweep the channel
nor molest the anchorage: consequently Don John could sail in
and out as if it were a port in Spain itself.

His position had the further advantage that to all intents and
purposes it enabled him to blockade the Turkish fleet at Modon
which was a mere six miles distant. On the other hand the campaigning season was almost at an end, so greatly indebted was the
Sultan to the King of France for rendering it impossible for Don
John to commence it earlier. There was a certain amount of

[1] In 425 B.C., and in A.D. 1827.
[2] cf. Thucydides, *Peloponnesian War*, Bk. IV, pp. 33–40.

skirmishing in which, on balance, the Turks had the worst of it, but the allies of the Holy League decided that the capture either of Navarino castle or of Modon was beyond their capabilities, while Ochiali carefully avoided a fleet action. The monotony of this inactivity was to some extent mitigated, especially for the Duke of Mayenne and his compatriots, by the arrival of the news of the Massacre of Saint Bartholomew. There was, however, one minor action in which Santa Cruz managed to cut off from the main Turkish fleet a galley commanded by Hamet Bey: during it Hamet was knocked down by one of his own oarsmen. The Governor of Negroponte fell among the rowing-benches, where he was immediately torn to pieces by the rowers who fell upon his body with their teeth like a pack of hounds:[1] deprived of her commander the galley soon struck her flag.

It was now clear that nothing would be done that year, and on October 8th the fleet set sail from Corfu. Don John seems to have made little effort to disguise his dissatisfaction, and he derived no great pleasure from being told that Ochiali's refusal to meet him was in itself a tribute to his reputation. The truth is that the Holy League was beginning to disintegrate, and before the end of the month Don John was writing to the Spanish ambassador in Venice deploring the suspicions of the good faith of his brother entertained by the Serenissima, and hoping that there was no truth in the rumour that the Doge and Senate were negotiating a separate treaty with the Sultan.[2]

On October 25th he returned to Messina, distributed his troops in winter quarters, and then himself went on to Naples. About the same time Colonna reported to the Pope in Rome, and after a brief interval Gregory sent him on to Madrid to concert with Philip on the preparation for the following year's campaign. The King received him with his habitual courtesy, and apparently expressed himself as satisfied with his services. As for the Pope he was eulogistic in the extreme where Don John was concerned. 'That young chief,' he said in full consistory, 'has proved himself a Scipio in valour, a Pompey in heroic grace, an Augustus in good

[1] cf. Arroyo, M. A., *Relación del progreso della Armada de la Santa Liga*, folio 98. Milan, 1576. The story is also told in *Don Quijote*, Part I, ch. 39, where Hamet is described as 'the bravest and most cruel of all the Moors'.

[2] The original of this letter is in the National Library in Madrid.

fortune, a new Moses, a new Gideon, a new Samson, a new Saul, a new David, without any of the faults of these famous men; and I hope in God to live long enough to reward him with a royal crown.'[1]

At the other end of the Mediterranean the Capitan Pasha returned to Constantinople as soon as he was assured that the Christians would not attempt anything against him that year. He was well satisfied with himself, as he had every reason to be, for, without abandoning the shores which it was his duty to defend he had for many weeks foiled all the efforts of a superior force to bring him to action: the Sultan and the Grand Vizier were equally satisfied with his conduct, so Ochiali alone of the commanders on either side may be said to have emerged from the campaign of 1572 with an enhanced reputation.

The winter was spent by the allies of the Holy League in different ways. Gregory was as enthusiastic as his predecessor had been in the matter of the war against the Turk, and he saw to it that his galleys were put in good order against the coming campaign. Don John was equally active in this respect, but, as we have seen, he also found time for more than one *liaison*. In addition, he made the acquaintance of his sister, Margaret of Parma, whom he had not previously met. Since she left the Netherlands in 1567 she had been living in the kingdom of Naples, and from the moment that brother and sister came together a close friendship was established between them, though this is in no way surprising seeing that Margaret's son, Alexander, had been the trusted companion of Don John since Alcalá days. She was at this time almost twice the age of her brother. He seems to have stayed with her at Aquila for about a fortnight at the beginning of February, 1573, and again at the end of 1575. They corresponded frequently, and their correspondence in the Archivo Farnesiano at Naples amounts to some two hundred letters: the last, from Don John to his sister, is dated August 12th, 1578, six weeks before he died. The utmost confidence existed between the two, and Margaret was fully informed regarding her brother's love affairs – and their material consequences.[2]

[1] cf. Vanderhammen, Lorenzo, *Don Juan de Austria*, folio 165. Madrid, 1627.
[2] cf. Mulhacén, Marqués de, *Don Juan de Austria*, pp. 21-2. Madrid, 1944.

While the Pope was getting ready to fight the Turk, and Don John was dividing his time between Venus and Mars, the Republic of Saint Mark was concentrating its activities upon stabbing its allies in the back by concluding a separate peace with the Sultan: it is true that there was a great show of levying mercenaries and reinforcing overseas garrisons, but these preparations were made as much with a view to allaying the suspicions of Philip and the Pope as to meeting the armies and navies of Selim. It would appear that the protagonist of a separate peace was the Doge, Ludovico Mocenigo, but he had no great difficulty in securing support in the Council of Ten: he was able to point to the reluctance of the Spaniards to regain Cyprus and the other places recently lost to Venice in the Levant, and he naturally put this down to bad faith on the part of Philip rather than to his caution in the light of French policy. The truth was that the Serenissima was on the decline, and war – even a victorious war – was for her a losing game: she was more exhausted than the defeated Turk.

In this policy of appeasement the Republic of Saint Mark could rely upon that right competent diplomatist, François de Noailles,[1] Bishop of Dax, the French ambassador to the Sublime Porte. This worldly prelate had been frequenting the *coulisses* of Constantinople for some months, and, presumably on the instructions of his master, had been very much all things to all men. He assured Sokolli that the Sultan had no firmer friend than the King of France, but at the same time he endeavoured to stand well with the Holy League by treating for the liberation of some Venetian and Spanish prisoners, and he is even said to have smuggled out of the Ottoman Empire some escaped Christian captives. He kept the French ambassador in Venice fully informed regarding anything in the Turkish capital which might strengthen the hands of the peace party, and in the same way he supplied the Grand Vizier with all the information at his disposal about such movements and preparations of the Holy League as would make it desirable for the Sultan to detach Venice from her allies.

During the greater part of the year 1572 the Bishop made very little progress. Sokolli told him roundly that Charles should give proof of his friendship for Selim by declaring war on Spain, or by

[1] 1519–85.

preparing a fleet for such a contingency: at the very least he should prevent his subjects serving under Don John in large numbers. The Bishop, however, was in no way put out by these arguments, and he carried the war into the Turkish camp by saying that it was unreasonable to blame his master for not breaking with Philip when the Sultan himself had neglected the opportunity of striking an effective blow against Spain by not coming to the aid of the Moriscoes. The Grand Vizier neatly parried this attack by saying that he had himself always favoured assisting them, but that he had been overruled by his colleagues in the Divan, who had been bribed by Spain. The next point made by the Bishop was to admit that the French fleet was in poor shape, but that this would speedily be remedied if the Turks would grant a loan for the purpose. This request the Divan refused on the ground that the lending of money to Christians was forbidden by the Koran – a reply which the Bishop transmitted to Paris with the comment that this convenient precept was the only injunction of the Prophet which was obeyed at the Porte. With regard to the presence of French volunteers in the forces of the League the Grand Vizier was assured that this was entirely contrary to the wishes of the French King who had, moreover, ordered Mayenne to return to France.

The Bishop was, indeed, rarely at a loss for an answer. He arrived for an audience of the Sultan without bringing the usual presents, and when he was taxed with this omission he said that it must not be taken as meanness on the part of his master, but that as the King of France was the greatest monarch in Christendom he could not run the risk of Selim treating any gifts as tribute. Furthermore, he refused to follow the normal custom of being escorted into the Sultan's presence with a *kapidji* on either side of him on the ground that it gave the impression that he was a slave, and when he got there he contented himself with kissing the monarch's hand instead of throwing himself at his feet.[1] Considering the weak and divided state of contemporary France the behaviour of her representative surely calls for the highest commendation.

All the same it was some time before his mission produced any

[1] cf. Jonquière, Vicomte de la, *Histoire de l'Empire Ottoman*, vol. i, p. 213. Paris, 1914.

result, and in whatever esteem the Grand Vizier may have held him personally he would not appear to have entertained any very high opinion of the French King or his country. At any rate when, acting on instructions from Paris, the Bishop suggested that the Duke of Anjou would be willing to hold Algiers as a vassal of the Porte, he was curtly informed that if the Duke would take an army there for the service of the Sultan he would be suitably rewarded. By this time the Bishop was weary of the whole business, and without asking for permission he decided to return to France. Another reason for his desire to leave Constantinople seems to have been that he expected a repetition of Lepanto, and he did not wish to be in the Turkish capital when this took place. However, on his arrival at Ragusa he received letters to the effect that Charles did not approve of his action, and that he was to return to his post at once.

When he was back in Constantinople he found a completely changed situation, for the peace party had carried the day, and in an extremely able minute the Bishop persuaded the Sultan to adopt their point of view. Accordingly on March 7th, 1573, the preliminaries of peace were concluded between the Serenissima and the Porte, and they were such as to cause Voltaire later to remark that they raised doubts as to who had won the battle of Lepanto. The Sultan was to retain Cyprus; the Ottoman and Venetian boundaries on the Adriatic were to remain as they had been when war broke out, which meant that the Turks were to retain all the territory of which Suleyman had deprived Venice; merchantships taken on both sides were so far as possible to be restored; the Republic of St Mark was to restore the fortress of Sopoto in Albania which had been captured; and she was to pay an indemnity of three hundred thousand ducats in three equal instalments annually. On the same day the Venetian ambassador in Rome swore in the presence of the Pope to carry out the military commitments of the Holy League.[1]

The Bishop of Dax lost no time in taking the credit to himself. 'You will observe,' he wrote to the Duke of Anjou, 'what has happened about peace with Venice; how the Venetian envoy and the

[1] cf. Charrière, E., *Negotiations de la France dans le Levant*, vol. iii, p. 377. Paris, 1848–53.

Pasha have been brooding over it in secret for three months, and I have hatched it in three days.' As the representative of the Most Christian King, however, he did not want to be too closely associated with the humiliating terms imposed upon the Serenissima, so he continued, 'As to the terms I did not meddle with them; I did what the King ordered me, and nothing more. Venice did not ask me to interpose; and, indeed, I received more than one hint that my interference was not required.'

The Pope was staying with one of the Cardinals at a villa at Frascati when he heard the news. The Venetian ambassador, having asked for an audience, had duly made the announcement when Gregory started from his chair, rushed upon the luckless envoy as if to do him personal violence, and, on the poor man taking flight, chased him through the adjoining apartments, and finally drove him out of the building altogether.[1] When Philip was informed of the defection of his ally he retained his usual composure, and his first comment hardly went beyond the sarcastic. 'If Venice,' he said, 'thinks that she consults her own interests by such a proceeding, I can truly say that in what I have done I have endeavoured to consult both her interests and those of Christendom.' Later, however, he was a good deal more outspoken. Finally, when Don John was told he ordered the banner of the Holy League to be lowered on all the ships under his command, and replaced by the Lions and Castles of León and Castille.

[1] cf. Hübner, J. A. von, *Sixte-Quint*, vol. i, pp. 101–2. Paris, 1870.

10

A Prince in Search of a Throne

DON JOHN WAS NOW TWENTY-SIX, AND FEW MEN IN THE history of the world have risen at so early an age to the heights which he had reached. What is more he deserved his success, for if he owed his earlier commands to his birth he had subsequently fully justified the confidence which his brother had reposed in him, and he was unquestionably one of the greatest captains of his age. Hitherto he had always obeyed to the letter the instructions which he received from Philip, even though he had on occasion disagreed with them. From the disintegration of the Holy League, however, a change came over his attitude, and he began to play for his own hand. This is not surprising for he was young and ambitious; he was essentially a man of action rather than one of the council-chamber, and many of the intricacies of the international situation were hidden from him; and, last but by no means least, he was surrounded by a crowd of flatterers and place-hunters who never ceased to tell him that there need be no limit to his ambition. The offer of the throne in Greece, which had already been made to him, was undoubtedly still at the back of his mind.

From now onwards he seems to have forgotten that he was primarily a Spanish soldier, and that his duty was to advance, not his own interests, but those of Spain – Philip, it may be added, was never under any illusions on this score, and his patience with his errant brother in the circumstances has never received the tribute from historians that it deserves. As we have seen, a kingdom for Don John in Greece or North Africa would have to be established and sustained by Spanish arms and Spanish money, and it would not serve any specific Spanish purpose. This was certainly not the way that the proposition appeared to Don John, but that was how it was regarded by Philip and his ministers.

About this time it would seem that the King came to the

conclusion that his brother's secretary, Juan de Soto, who had been with him for three years, was encouraging him in these undesirable ambitions,[1] so he adopted the time-honoured practice of getting rid of de Soto by promoting him, and he was accordingly made Commissary-General of the Spanish Navy: de Soto, however had no illusions about the reason for his new appointment, and he would much rather have stayed with Don John, but there was nothing he could do about it. In his place there was sent out the ill-fated Juan de Escobedo, who, it was hoped, would take a more detached view of his new master, though before long he fell as completely under Don John's spell as his predecessor had done, with the most unfortunate consequences to himself. There can be little doubt that Escobedo largely owed his appointment to Ruy Gómez de Silva, but there is no reason whatever for supposing that he was imposed upon Don John against his will or without his consent.

In July, 1573, Ruy Gómez, possibly the ablest of all the able men who served Philip died, and lesser figures, notably Antonio Pérez, took his place. The death of Gómez could hardly fail to weaken to some extent the link between the King and his brother, for he and Don John had always worked closely together, while later events were to prove that Antonio Pérez was an arrant rogue.

Meanwhile the defection of Venice had left the plans for the campaign of 1573 very much in the air, and there was considerable difference of opinion among Don John's counsellors regarding the next move. Some of them took the view that the Spanish, Papal, and Maltese squadrons should mount an immediate offensive against Ochiali who was hovering in Ionian waters, for they considered it to be of the first importance to prove that Spain, even without the assistance of the Serenissima, was still a match for the Turk. Doria opposed this suggestion on the ground that the chief beneficiary would be Venice, and that Philip would merely be doing for the Republic what she had refused to do for herself. Santa Cruz, with an eye to the Mediterranean situation as a whole, advised a direct attack on Algiers, in spite of the discouraging

---

[1] Juan de Soto had been in Spain on a mission in the previous year, and it may well have been then that the King's suspicions were aroused.

precedents in the days of Cardinal Ximenes and Charles V: this, he argued, would not only deprive the Sultan of one of his most important naval bases, but would also strike a telling blow at the Corsairs who were continually raiding the Spanish coast and interfering with shipping in the Western Mediterranean. Don John favoured the less ambitious course of the capture of Tunis, his argument being that his present resources were not sufficient to justify an attack on Algiers, while in the case of Tunis its port of Goletta was already in Spanish hands, and this would greatly facilitate the operation. This was no new idea on his part, however, for in the previous year he had sent Don Jaime de Losada to Tunis, nominally to see what could be done in the way of an exchange of prisoners, but in actual fact to spy out the land.[1]

In view of these differences of opinion the matter was referred to the King who found the Council of State just as divided as were Don John's advisers, but after a long discussion instructions were given to capture Tunis, and then to dismantle it:[2] at the same time the expedition was not to sail until it was likely to be safe from molestation by Ochiali.

When these orders reached Don John he lost no time in carrying them out. He set sail from Naples on August 5th, reached Messina on the morning of the 8th, and stayed there for a month taking on board munitions and provisions. At this point, however, the weather turned unfavourable, and it was only after trying several harbours that he found a bay near Marsala which suited his purpose. It is true that its entrance, facing the south, was rather narrow, and was rendered difficult by shallows, but the basin inside was so large and well protected that it could accommodate two hundred galleys with perfect safety. Don John named the place the port of Austria, after himself, and then proceeded to take stock of the forces at his disposal, which were not inconsiderable. His naval armament consisted of 104 galleys, 44 large ships, 12 barges of one hundred to two hundred tons, 25 frigates, and 22 feluccas. As for the land forces there were nearly 20,000 infantry, of whom about a third were Spaniards, and the

[1] cf. Mulhacén, Marqués de, *Don Juan de Austria*, p. 235. Madrid, 1944.
[2] cf. Pérez, Antonio, *Memorial, Obras*, p. 296. Geneva, 1654.

rest Italians and Germans: in addition there were light horse, pioneers, and an adequate park of artillery.

At the head of this force Don John put to sea on October 7th, the second anniversary of Lepanto, and the crossing to Africa went off without a hitch. No sail appears to have been sighted except a French merchantman who reported that there was not a single enemy vessel off the coast. On the evening of the 8th, the Spanish fleet anchored off the Goletta. This fortress, which commands the sea approach to Tunis, had belonged to Spain since the Turks had been driven out by Charles V in 1535, and the last of the Hafsids, Muley Hamida, was living there under Spanish protection.

What ensued is best expressed in the words of Don John himself in a dispatch to Philip dated October 11th:

S.C.R.M.

At the Goletta I found the King, Muley Hamida, who told me how greatly he had suffered in the service of Your Majesty. I replied that Your Majesty was a most just Prince, and would take care that he should be rewarded according to his deserts.

Yesterday morning, Saturday, the 10th October, news was still coming in that the Turks were in great alarm, and retiring from the city. Thinking that success depended on despatch, I therefore set forward with the army, leaving orders that the troops who were still in the act of disembarking should muster at the Goletta, and come on thence by lake, so that the Moors should not be able to molest them. I also directed the fleet to be posted near the Goletta, so that if the enemy were to come he should not be able to attack it; and I entrusted the command of it to Don Juan de Cardona, thinking that Antonio Doria and the Marquess of Santa Cruz might be of use to me, as indeed they have been, in my expedition.

I marched until the hour of vespers, and as night fell pitched my camp near the village of Diana, four miles from Tunis. then I sent on the Marquess of Santa Cruz, Major Don Diego Enriquez, and the warden Andres de Salazar, with two thousand five hundred foot, taken from the garrison of the Goletta, in order that, if there were no difficulties in the way, they might take possession of the Alcazaba or fortress and secure the town, and advise me of the state of affairs therein. They arrived with their troops before it was dark, and found the place deserted, except by old men and old women too old to fly, and in this Alcazaba about two Moors with an alcalde, who said he was keeping the place for the King, Muley Hamida, but caused the gates to be opened for the Marquess and his people, who entered without hindrance.

Very early this morning, having put the troops in order, I marched to the city gate, where I left them, with orders that not a man was to enter it until the word of command was given. I myself then went in with such persons as I thought fit to take with me, and immediately inspected the ground with a view to the erection of fortifications which should form a connexion with the Goletta. I also directed that quarters should be prepared in the city for the troops.

Having come into this Alcazaba, I gave orders for the troops to take possession of their quarters. Being advised that the Duke of Sesa had this morning come in with four galleys from Palermo, I sent word to him to come on here by the lake without loss of time. The Turkish governor and his soldiers who held this fortress have gone, I understand, to Kerouan, Bizerta, and other places adjacent.

Such has been the issue of the expedition to Tunis, in accordance with the Christian zeal and good fortune of Your Majesty, an issue achieved in little more than two days, for which infinite thanks to our Lord, and for which I myself can never be sufficiently thankful.

I shall continue to advise Your Majesty of whatever may happen. May Our Lord endow your sacred, Catholic, and Royal person with such increase of kingdoms and lordships as I desire.

Don John of Austria.

This dispatch closed with a postscript in Don John's own handwriting:

These Turks have behaved like very sorry soldiers, seeing that not a man of them has stopped to look at us, as they might well have done, and perhaps might have defended themselves for some days more than some of us imagine. However, I am well pleased that they have done as they have done: and Your Majesty may be of the same mind, giving, as I on my part do, many thanks to Our Lord for what we have gained, which is of greater importance and value, than without seeing it, can be estimated. I will report to Your Majesty whatever steps it may be needful to take for your Royal service; and I may now remind you that I am in sore need of money, and how necessary it is that so great a want should be supplied. May God keep Your Majesty and make you victorious.[1]

Don John's next task was to consolidate his position, and to make arrangements for the administration of his conquest. A puppet of Hafsid descent was deemed advisable in order to reconcile the Moors to the new régime, but Muley Hamida was not considered suitable for the purpose: he was not only unpopular on his own account, but his disposition to severity was more likely to alienate friends than to conciliate enemies. He was accordingly exiled to Italy, and replaced on the Tunisian throne by a brother, Muley Mohammed, who was duly invested by Don John with his new dignities, and exhorted to rule with justice and moderation.

The Turks had withdrawn into the interior, where the Spanish High Command felt that they could safely be left to their own devices, but Don John was about to march against Bizerta when circumstances handed it over to him. A Spanish Fifth Column in the town rose against the Turkish garrison, and put it to the sword, after which the insurgents added to their strength by releasing and arming the slaves of an Ottoman war-galley which was in the port. A deputation of Moors then proceeded to Tunis where they offered Bizerta to Don John as the representative of the King of Spain. Don Francisco de Avila was sent to garrison the town with three hundred men, and he received strict orders to the effect that moderation must be the keynote of his policy. Indeed, so absolute did the calm appear that Don John and his staff found time for a little hunting, and Don John acquired a lion cub, which, we

[1] Arch. Gen. de Simancas, Estado, Legajo 487.

are told, became so tame that it lived and slept in his room. In due course he took the animal back to Europe with him.

It was now the middle of October, and the situation in Tunisia seemed such that Don John could safely return to Italy; before doing so, however, he wrote a dispatch to Philip telling him of his decision to fortify Tunis, and of his reasons for doing this. The weather was breaking, and he had a rough passage to Sicily, but he arrived safely at Palermo on November 2nd. About this time Don John also received permission from his brother to visit Spain, should he so desire, but he displayed no great eagerness to do so: the charms of the Sicilian and Neapolitan ladies may have been one reason why he preferred to tarry in the Kingdom of the Two Sicilies rather than face the rigours of winter in Castille, but he may also not have been too desirous of meeting Philip in person at that particular moment, for his preoccupation was rapidly becoming a kingdom for himself.

Escobedo who had soon fallen under the spell of his master, was now as enthusiastic a supporter of his plans for acquiring an independent sovereignty as de Soto had been. Soon after the return from Tunis he was sent on a secret mission to Rome to ask the Pope to intercede with Philip to give permission to his brother to assume the crown of Tunis. Gregory was highly flattered that he should have been asked to intervene in a matter of such importance, and he readily agreed to do what he had been asked.

Accordingly on January 16th, 1574, the Papal Nuncio in Spain presented the King with a memorandum containing Gregory's views on a number of subjects relating to Don John. Nicholas Ormanetti was, it is on record, a man of learning and virtue, and four years earlier he had been made Bishop of Padua by Pius V, but on the present occasion he found himself in the unhappy position of one who tenders unwelcome advice. His Holiness had heard with great concern, wrote the Bishop, that the Spanish fleet was about to be reduced, and Don John recalled from the command of it: in view of the continued Turkish threat he doubted the prudence of either step. Surely the fleet should be increased rather than diminished, and Don John encouraged to take the offensive, while 'it might be well to consider whether it would not add to his power and authority were he invested with the title of

King of Tunis, so that Your Majesty might evince your gratitude to God for the conquest, after the manner of your ancestors, by founding a new Christian realm'.

The Pope went on to suggest a revival of the Holy League in view of the Venetian dissatisfaction with their peace with the Sultan. Turning to the unhappy state of the Low Countries he advised Philip to go there in person, or at any rate to send Don John – surely advice which was incompatible with his desire that the victor of Lepanto should remain in the Mediterranean. It might even be advantageous if Don John were to 'undertake the enterprise of England, it being much desired, as has already been shown, by the English Catholics that he should become their King by marriage with the Queen of Scots'. Finally, it would do no harm if Philip would pay a visit to his kingdom of the Two Sicilies, have a meeting with the European and Italian princes, and above all with the Pope himself. Personal diplomacy of this nature could not fail to be of benefit to Christendom as a whole.[1]

Philip had by now a sufficiently long experience of the Holy See to be able to rebuff its incursions into what he regarded as his own affairs in a manner that was at once decorous and respectful, and this was what he did on the present occasion. With regard to Gregory's suggestion of a Christian kingdom in Tunis the Pope was assured that he need not concern himself lest Don John's services should go unrewarded for his advancement was very close to his brother's heart, but the reward proposed was neither adequate to these services nor as yet sufficiently in the power of the King to grant; and, lastly, the matter certainly would, at a fitting opportunity, receive the careful consideration which it deserved.

It was thus at this point that the affairs of the British Isles first began to attract Don John's attention, for if there was no kingdom to be had in the Mediterranean there might be one to be acquired in North-West Europe, more particularly in view of the peculiar situation of Mary, Queen of Scots. As early as the spring of 1570 Zuñiga had written from Rome to Philip to the effect that the Pope, then Pius V, had suggested a marriage between Mary and Don John, and that this had the approval of the Cardinal of

[1] Arch. Gen. de Simancas, Estado, Legajo 924.

Lorraine, who was Mary's uncle.[1] To what extent Pius was acting on his own initiative, and to what the proposition had been suggested to him by Don John, is not easy to determine.[2] At that time Philip displayed no enthusiasm for the idea, which is not surprising in view of the fact that he had many more pressing matters on hand much nearer home.

Spanish relations with Scotland had not previously been very close, save for a short period at the end of the previous century, when an intervention of Spain in the affairs of the northern kingdom had been dictated by a desire to frustrate the designs of France. Ever since Edward I had endeavoured to subjugate Scotland it had been the policy of the Edinburgh Government under successive monarchs to ally with France, so that for England a war with one Power nearly always led to hostilities with the other. From the French point of view this state of affairs had everything to recommend it, and the rôle played by the Turks, the Poles, and the Swedes in relation to the Empire was enacted by the Scots where England was concerned, that is to say they were the allies of France, and could be relied upon to attack her enemies in the rear. From time to time the English tried to put an end to this nuisance once and for all, but for many years their action was paralysed by the continuance of the Wars of the Roses.

When, in 1485, the House of Tudor ascended the English throne in the person of Henry VII a change came over the international scene, for England soon became the ally of Spain, and it did not suit the policy of Ferdinand V that she should be embarrassed on her Scottish frontier by intrigues which could only benefit their common enemy, France, so Don Pedro de Ayala was sent to Edinburgh with the task of improving Anglo-Scottish relations. It was not an easy mission, for in addition to the long-standing suspicion which existed between the two countries James IV was supporting a Pretender to the English throne in Perkin Warbeck, who claimed to be Richard, Duke of York, the younger of the two princes supposed to have been murdered in the Tower, and consequently Richard IV: to bind the Scottish

---

[1] cf. Mulhacén, Marqués de, *Don Juan de Austria*, pp. 265–6. Madrid, 1944.

[2] cf. Törne, P. O. von, *Don Juan d'Autriche et les projets de conquête de L'Angleterre, 1568–1578*, vol. i, p. 235. Helsingfors, 1915.

King more closely to him Warbeck had promised to cede to Scotland the town of Berwick-on-Tweed as soon as he was in a position to do so. Nevertheless in spite of the difficulties with which he was thus confronted Pedro de Ayala succeeded in his task, for he not only persuaded James to withdraw his support from Perkin Warbeck but he induced him to marry the daughter of the King of England. Admittedly this new orientation was not of long duration, for the Scots soon reverted to their old alliance with the French, which, incidentally, led to one of the greatest disasters in their history at the battle of Flodden.

For many years after this Spain and Scotland had few dealings with one another, and it is now necessary to pass on to a consideration of John's suggested bride, Mary, Queen of Scots, one of the most controversial figures in history. She had the irascibility of the Stuarts, but as was the case with most of them her anger soon cooled, and she was perhaps too ready to pardon insults and to forgive affronts when she would have done better to have stayed her hand and punished. She was headstrong, courageous, full of life and animal spirits. Candid and open, often to a fault, in her dealings with others, it was not unnatural that she should expect to receive like treatment from them, but unfortunately those with whom she was brought in contact rarely shared her characterstics in that respect. Mary was naturally of a religious turn of mind, but it would be a mistake to regard her as particularly devout in the days of her youth, though there can be no doubt that religion was a great source of consolation to her in her later misfortunes. She clearly possessed to the full all the charm of her family, though both as Dauphine and Queen of France some of the Court ladies seem to have found her a little too haughty for their liking.

The powers of her mind were considerable. She was always quick to act with judgement in a crisis, as is proved by the success of her efforts to detach her husband, Darnley, from the conspirators who murdered Rizzio, and by her escape from Edinburgh in his company; there were other instances, too, which attest very plainly her daring and resource on a critical occasion. What she lacked was concentration, and that determination to pursue a settled policy to its conclusion which marks the great women of history, such as Isabella the Catholic. Mary was apt to allow her personal likes and dislikes to influence her attitude towards individuals and the advice they gave her, when from the point of view of her own ends and of the public interest she would have done better, temporarily at any rate, to have suppressed her feelings. It is true that by fits and starts she had a good deal of application, though not nearly enough of it considering the troubled times in which she lived. In effect, in spite of all her talents, it is difficult to resist the conclusion that she was temperamentally unfitted for the part which she was called upon to play.

For many years Mary's French connexions placed her in the opposite camp to Philip. When, in 1559, her husband, Francis, became King of France, all power in that country passed into the hands of the Guises, who were her uncles. Their policy was to place their niece and Francis upon the English throne, and then to constitute a close alliance between, France, England, and Scotland. This scheme, though for different reasons, was equally objectionable to Philip and Elizabeth, and it might have produced an Anglo-Spanish understanding but for the fact that it was not destined to proceed very far. The tumult of Amboise in March, 1560, proved to the Guises how strong was the opposition to them in France, while four months later the death of their sister, Mary's mother and Regent of Scotland, led to the Treaty of Leith between Mary and Elizabeth, of which one of the clauses stipulated for the withdrawal of the French troops who were at the time in Scotland.

In these circumstances there was no material change in the situation when Francis II died of a cerebral abscess at the end of 1560, and Mary returned to Edinburgh in the following year. The immediate beneficiary was Elizabeth, whose position was greatly strengthened. It may have been irritating to Philip that the English Queen would not continue the Hispanophil policy of her sister, yet if she were dethroned her heir was Mary Stuart, who would clearly further French, rather than Spanish, interests from London. Thus for several years Elizabeth was in the happy position of knowing that Philip dared not attack her for fear that Mary would take her place, and she was thus able to play France and Spain off against one another in the way that her father had tried, but failed, to do. As for Mary herself, some idea of her feelings can be gathered from the fact that in 1582 she was to say that for twelve years she had been trying to get a plain statement of Philip's intentions out of him. It was an effort which many other people had made without success, but where she was concerned the fact was that with him the interests of Spain came first, and the substitution of her for Elizabeth was not in accordance with those interests.

Absolute, however, as Philip might be at home he was subject to many pressures from the outside world, not least by the Holy See. To represent him as the secular arm of the Counter-Reformation is the veriest nonsense, and Sixtus V was much nearer the truth when he wrote, 'The King of Spain, as a temporal sovereign, is anxious above all to safeguard and increase his dominions. . . . The preservation of the Catholic religion, which is the principal aim of the Pope, is only a pretext for His Majesty, whose principal aim is the security and aggrandisement of his dominions.' Such being the case the Papacy was naturally more sympathetic towards Mary than was the King of Spain, and this was particularly so after 1566 when the Scottish Queen became the prisoner of her English cousin.

On May 15th of that year Mary had been decisively defeated by the Scottish rebels at Langside, and on the following day she fled into England. Magnanimity was not Elizabeth's strong point, and she could not bring herself to exercise it towards the dangerous rival whom fate had thus delivered into her hands, so Mary, who had thought to be a Royal guest, found herself a prisoner. She was still only twenty-five, but to all intents and purposes her career was finished: for seventeen dreary years more she was to drag out a captive life, first at the residences and in the care of the courteous, kindly Earl of Shrewsbury, and lastly under the severe tutelage and close surveillance of the grim Sir Amyas Paulet.

The earliest relations between Philip and the Queen of Scots would seem to date from 1565 just before she married Darnley, and until the death of Don Carlos in July, 1568, if a Spanish husband was to be found for Mary it would have been he, not his uncle. In the following year, 1569, there was also no proposal for marriage between Don John and the Scottish Queen.[1] What seems

---

[1] cf. Törne, P. O. von, *Don Juan d'Autriche et les projets de conquête de l'Angleterre*, vol. i, pp. 6 and 90. Helsingfors, 1915.

to have given the scheme a new lease of life, that is to say if it had any before, was the capture of Tunis, for during the winter of 1573–4 advices from the Spanish ambassador in London informed Philip that Charles IX was pressing Elizabeth to enter into a closer alliance with him on the ground that the Spanish position in the Mediterranean had now been strengthened to such an extent that Don John was free to come to the Netherlands, and also take the necessary steps to liberate and marry Mary. With what local backing cannot be determined the Spanish ambassador went on to suggest a double marriage, namely Don John with Mary and James VI with the Infanta Isabella, and he asserted that the Scottish Queen was well disposed to the idea. At this point Dr Nicholas Sanders, a Jesuit and one of the ablest as well as one of the most active of the English Catholic exiles, assured Philip that he had the authority of Mary's most confidential advisers, that is to say Sir Francis Eaglefield and the Countess of Northumberland, for saying that she was extremely well affected towards Don John.[1]

The situation was complicated by the fact that in February, 1570, Pius V had excommunicated Elizabeth, a move of which Philip by no means approved. Twice he had used his influence at the Holy See to prevent this step being taken; the first time was in 1561 after she had refused to receive the Pope's nuncio, and again two years later when he stopped the matter being debated in the Council of Trent. When the Bull was finally issued it was without any previous communication with Spain, and not only did the King forbid its publication in his own dominions, but he did all he could to prevent it reaching England. He protested to the Papal nuncio in Madrid, and he wrote to his ambassador in London that the Bull 'will embitter feelings in England, and drive the Queen and her friends to oppress and persecute the few good Catholics who still remain there,' while he told Elizabeth herself that no act of the Pope had caused him so much displeasure.

Then there was the kingdom of Ireland which the Papacy was continually dangling before his nose with the suggestion that if he did not want it for himself it would do very well for Don John, who was by no means averse to the idea. Until the reign of Henry

[1] Arch. Gen. de Simancas, Estado, Legajo 828, folios 2, 29, 50 and 79.

VIII the King of England had been styled *Dominus Hiberniae*, but Henry persuaded the Irish Parliament to declare him King of Ireland. He was the first English monarch to bear the title of 'Majesty', as all his predecessors had been content with that of 'Sovereign Lord Highness': Henry also described himself as the 'supreme head on earth of the Church of Ireland', and this style was also adopted by his son. Mary I, of course, abandoned any such ecclesiastical pretensions, but Pope Julius III created a kingdom of Ireland for her benefit and that of her husband, Philip. What a Pope could grant, a Pope could clearly take away, so on the excommunication of Elizabeth this somewhat shadowy Irish throne became vacant. In these circumstances it is in no way surprising to find the Spanish ambassador in London writing to Philip, under date of February 12th, 1571, that he had received news through France that the Pope had ceded the kingdom of Ireland to him, and it was rumoured that Philip was going to send Thomas Stucley – of whom more anon – there with fourteen or fifteen companies of Spanish infantry.[1] In any event feeling in Ireland against an excommunicated Queen was very strong, and when it was combined with religious persecution, not to mention the proselytizing activities of such men as Adam Loftus, Archbishop of Dublin, and Thomas Jones, Bishop of Meath, it gave the Irish cause all the aspects of a crusade.

Another reason for increased Spanish interest in Ireland at this time was the accentuated intriguing of Elizabeth against Philip in the Low Countries. Naunton summed up the position admirably when he wrote, 'for as the Queen by way of division had at her coming to the crown supported the revolted states of Holland, so did the King of Spain turn the trick upon herself towards her going out by cherishing the Irish rebellion.'[2]

In March, 1575, the nuncio at Madrid on behalf of his master presented to Philip a memorandum in which were recapitulated the advantages of an invasion of England, and the advisability of such an attempt was strongly urged. The King was clearly not impressed, and he allowed several months to elapse before he returned a non-commital answer. Towards the end of June the

[1] cf. Montesa, Marqués de, *Julián Romero*, p. 216. Madrid, 1952.
[2] *Fragmenta Regalia*, pp. 101-2. London, 1641.

Spanish ambassador at the Vatican announced the arrival in Rome of a Friar Patrick O'Healy with a letter from Philip, and this incident is eloquent of the difficulty of arriving at the truth of what was taking place – especially of the credence to be attached to the statements made by the parties concerned. The worthy friar announced that his presence in Rome was to obtain the Pope's sanction for a certain Irish Catholic gentleman, whose name he did not disclose, to rise in revolt against Elizabeth, and also to request for assistance to enable him to do this. He went on, with all the assurance of an exile, to tell the ambassador that if the Irish Catholics could once be certain that their leader was acting under the authority of the Holy Father they would in a few days overthrow English rule in Ireland, and then gladly accept Don John for their monarch. Finally, he asserted that he had discussed the proposition with Philip, who had given it his blessing.

Juan de Zuñiga was far too cautious to take Father O'Healy's statement at its face value, and he temporized until he had communicated with Madrid. He advised the friar to get in touch with Cardinal Alciato,[1] the vice-protector of Ireland, and through him to find out what were the Pope's real views in the matter, but to make no mention of Don John's name. In a letter to the King, the ambassador said that he had advised the suppression of his brother's name because he had noticed that whenever the Pope discussed English politics he never failed to stress the fact that no French or Spanish claimant to the Crown must be put forward, but that the candidature of some native-born Catholic must be supported, and Zuñiga believed that he took this line because 'he was very much resolved that Your Majesty should not acquire more territory than you now have; and it might be that if Don John were to obtain the kingdom of Ireland His Holiness would think it as much the property of Your Majesty as any of the realms God had already given you'. All of which goes to show how uneasy were the relations upon which Philip and Gregory stood with one another.[2]

That the King did not attach much importance to the affair

[1] A Milanese, born in 1522, and created a Cardinal in 1560; he died in Rome in 1580. A man of considerable learning.

[2] Arch. Gen. de Simancas, Estado, Legajo 925.

would appear to be evident from the fact that although he received his ambassador's letter on July 14th, he did not reply to it until September 8th. He began by saying that urgent business had prevented him from giving due attention to the matter, but so far as Father O'Healy was concerned the letter which he had given that worthy was merely one of introduction, and that the Irishman had no authority whatever to enter upon the discussion of any public business. He then went on to point out that the Pope's apprehension regarding an increase in Spanish strength, and his prospective opposition to a scheme for placing Don John on the throne of Ireland, were completely at variance with the memorandum which the nuncio had presented to him in the previous March.

All the same he was prepared to guarantee the pay of two thousand men for six months, as well as to defray the cost of their transport to England, on condition that the enterprise was conducted wholly in the Pope's name: after all, at the worst it would give Elizabeth employment at home, and compel her to cut off the aid she was giving to the rebels in the Low Countries. If any concessions, such as the prolongation of the bull of the *cruzada*, could be extracted from Gregory so much the better, but Zuñiga was to impress upon him the necessity for the greatest secrecy. Next he was to find out the Pope's views regarding the time and place of the invasion, the choice of troops and the person of their commander, and the sum of money expected from himself. Lastly, the ambassador was to ask whether any attempt was to be made against Elizabeth personally, because it was obvious that if she was out of the way there would be the greater confusion among the heretics, and the greater confidence among the Catholics.

The ambassador did what he was told, and on October 17th he reported to his master in a dispatch that would seem to indicate that Gregory's enthusiasm had somewhat diminished for the project which he had so eagerly embraced in the spring. As for the points upon which Philip wanted further information the Pope said that he had not yet considered them, and that he had forgotten what had been told him by the English Catholics. The best thing that he, Zuñiga, could do would be to discuss the matter with the Cardinal Secretary of State. This ecclesiastic was Tolomeo Galli, of Como, Bishop first of Rieti and later of Ostia, who had been raised to the purple in 1560 by Pius IV: at this time he was a man of fifty, and was usually known in Vatican circles as the Cardinal of Como.

To him the Spanish ambassador accordingly applied, but without any very satisfactory result. The scheme upon which the Pope's memorandum of the spring had been based had originally been put forward by two or three 'persons of zeal', but unfortunately they were now at some distance from Rome, though the Cardinal would recall them by the beginning of November for consultation. In their opinion the force required would be five thousand strong, and it should be landed at some point on the English coast near where Mary was imprisoned:[1] it might, however, be better if the troops disembarked in Ireland, but that was a point which it would be well discussed when these two or three mysterious individuals had returned to Rome.

Of the respective parts to be played by the Pope and the King in this enterprise the Cardinal of Como was somewhat more explicit. Gregory believed that Mary was the rightful Queen of England, and he wished to act in her interests, the more so since she had placed herself unreservedly in his hands: according to him she had promised to marry whomsoever he should suggest, and he would be perfectly agreeable for this to be Don John. The Pope was quite willing that the expedition should sail from Civita Vecchia under the Papal flag, and under a commander approved by Philip,[2] but as the King would reap all the benefits of success it was only fair that he should defray the entire cost of the expedition, and this he put at a hundred thousand crowns. At this point Zuñiga interrupted to suggest that if all went well it would tend so much to the glory of God and the Church that he felt the Pope should make some contribution towards the expenses. This line of argument made no appeal to the Cardinal of Como, but he replied that Gregory might contribute something if he could see his way to some more material advantage: it was, of course, impossible for the Holy See to hold territory in the British Isles, but compensation in Italy would not come amiss. On this Zuñiga merely

[1] Liverpool was much favoured, but cf. Törne, P. O. von, *Don Juan d'Autriche et les projets de conquête de l'Angleterre, 1568–1578*, vol. ii, pp. 65 and 82. Helsingfors, 1915.
[2] The name of Julián Romero had been canvassed.

observed that the proposition might form the subject of future negotiation.

In his report to the King he excused himself for the line he had taken on this last point, but said that unless some such hopes were encouraged in Gregory he did not feel that there was anything to be got out of him. In any event the whole project seemed to him to be still very much in the air, and he felt that the cost would greatly exceed the figure mentioned by the Cardinal of Como; yet the attempt might be worth trying if the Pope could be persuaded to contribute half the expense. Elizabeth had neither competent generals nor first-class troops, and in any event her attention would be distracted from the Netherlands which would be a definite advantage: even if the English Queen were to suspect Philip's complicity, there was nothing she could do to injure him more than she was at present doing. What was of the first importance was to ensure that Mary, when liberated, married the right person, and therefore it was essential that the commander of the expeditionary force should be a married man, for with the captive Queen in his power there was no knowing what an ambitious and victorious general might not do. In this respect the Pope was not to be trusted, for if it suited his policy he would not hesitate to connive at her marriage with a Valois prince.[1]

While this correspondence was following its somewhat desultory course there appeared upon the scene that most colourful of adventurers, Thomas Stucley, who, more than likely, was one of the exiles with whom the Cardinal of Como was in touch. Stucley was not, incidentally, an Irishman himself, but a cadet of the well-known Devonshire family of that name. His early life is wrapped in some obscurity. His father is said to have been a clothier of substance, though it has been claimed that he was an illegitimate son of Henry VIII: young Thomas would appear early to have obtained a post in the household of the Bishop of Exeter, but his mode of life was unsuited to an episcopal palace, and he is next heard of in London where he married the daughter of a wealthy alderman, for he was clearly a plausible scoundrel; yet a scoundrel he undoubtedly was, for when he had spent all his wife's money he deserted her, so Camden had good reason for describing him as 'a

[1] Arch. Gen. de Simancas, Estado, Legajo 925, folio 212.

ruffian, a spendthrift, and a notable vapourer'. The latter part of the sixteenth century was the heyday of the unprincipled adventurer, and so, like many of his contemporaries, he decided to retrieve his broken fortunes abroad; so he joined a party of pioneers who were going to found a colony in America, and he actually contrived to get himself presented to Elizabeth before he sailed. His cheek was colossal, and was worthy of a better cause, for he is said to have told the Queen on this occasion that he would prefer to be sovereign of a molehill than the subject of the greatest King in Christendom, and that he had a presentiment that he would be a prince before he died. Elizabeth remarked, 'I hope I shall hear from you when you are installed in your principality,' to which Stucley replied that he would certainly write to her. 'In what language?' the Queen asked. 'In the style of princes – to our dearest sister,' came the instant retort.[1]

Boldness of this nature was generally appreciated by Elizabeth, so it is not surprising to find her writing to the Earl of Sussex, then Lord-Lieutenant of Ireland, on June 30th, 1563, instructing him to give a friendly reception to Stucley if he arrived in Ireland. The expedition to America was a failure, and in due course Stucley made his appearance in Dublin; thereafter he displayed a marked reluctance to return to England, possibly because he realized that too much was known about him there. Anyhow, he managed to recommend himself to the authorities at Dublin Castle, though as he was not averse to a little piracy when the opportunity arose he soon incurred the suspicion of Elizabeth, who, in 1567, rebuked Sir Henry Sidney with some asperity for employing him in negotiations with Shane O'Neill. Indeed, Stucley's continued employment in Ireland may be regarded as proof of the low morality of only too many of the English officials to whom the destinies of that country were then entrusted.

As the years passed it would seem as if Stucley was becoming somewhat dubious about his exact position in the eyes of Dublin Castle, so in 1570 he decided to put his fortune to the test by asking for the post of Steward of Wexford. This was refused, so he renounced his allegiance to the English Crown, and went to Spain, where he received a warm welcome from Philip, who did not

[1] cf. Wright, T., *The History of Ireland*, vol. ii, pp. 461, et seq. London, 1853.

know much about him – to the astonishment of the English ambassador, who must have known a good deal.[1] In the Spanish capital he was the cause of some alarm to Elizabeth and her ministers, for in March, 1573, one of Burghley's correspondents wrote to him:

> Lastly, I have to advertise your lordship of a new conspiracye that is intended by certain decayed men, to go over into Spayne, and to joyne with Stukeley in his practices for the invading of Ireland, and the subversion of this state, as far as in them lyes. The matter is handled in Saint Liger's house, and there concluded upon. The chief parties be Sir Warham Seint Liger hymself, and Jerem Brett, having allured to them Martin Furbisher,[2] with the promise of £20 land by the year, or with the vallew of hit in ready money, to transport them over to their cosin Stukeley. They have joyned to them one Haseley, a seaman, and John Poole my friend, for whom I am most sorry, but I prefere loyalty to any friendship. They also intend to bring in some more decayed gentlemen, and some others, and among those they would have younge Brune with them, a base brother to the lord Montacute.
>
> Their pretence will be to ship corn over to Ireland, and therein to passe into Spayne, to which end, if John Brett have not bene already to your lordship to obtayne a lycense for the sayd corne, he meanes to be.

Whether Stucley outstayed his welcome in Madrid, or whether his past came to Philip's ears, is uncertain, but in due course he moved on to Rome: in June, 1575, he visited Naples, where he had an interview with Don John, who, as we shall see, had recently returned from Spain. On the 28th Don John reported the meeting to his brother.

> Thomas Stucley has come here from Rome, and in great confidence and secrecy has informed me that, while at that court, he had found means to make the Pope aware of the great service to God, and benefit to Christendom, that would

---

[1] Alba, however, had no high opinion of him, cf. *Epistolario*, vol. ii, p. 469.
[2] The celebrated navigator.

be rendered if a resolution were taken to assist the Catholics of England, seeing that they are so many and of such quality that, with proper means and industry, there was reason to hope an affair which appeared difficult might obtain all the success that could be desired. The Pope replied that this affair concerned Your Majesty and the King of France, as the princes most nearly interested, and as possessing the power necessary for so important an undertaking; and after many questions, answers, and rejoinders, referred him to the Cardinal of Como.

After various other conferences on the business with His Holiness and the Cardinal, they resolved to enter into it by giving one thousand five hundred Italian soldiers, paid for six months, and providing them with food and means of transport; and with these troops, and one thousand five hundred more which Stucley expected to be able to raise, he looked forward to sailing for England early in the month of October, passing through the Strait, and landing in a convenient place which he named; and that having raised in arms some persons in whom he had great confidence, he would then be able to deliver the Queen of Scotland from prison, and she being free, he hoped in a very few days to be in possession of the whole kingdom, and to send to call me for the purpose which has been on other occasions treated of. But it was first of all necessary that I should assist him in raising the one thousand five hundred foot soldiers whom he had offered to His Holiness, and that it must be done in such a way as would insure the secrecy on which depended the whole advantage of the business.

I asked if any account of the affair had been given to Your Majesty; he said no, but that he had written something of it to Dr Sanders. I then represented to him certain obvious difficulties: the first being that so grave a matter should not be entered upon except at the pleasure and by order of Your Majesty, upon whom at present depended the support and safety of Christendom. To this he answered that he much feared the weighty affairs in which Your Majesty was usually engaged would defer the taking of any resolution as had happened in time past, and that such delay would prevent the desired end being attained. I then observed that three thousand men appeared to me a very small number for so important an enterprise, and I could give him no assistance, great or small, without the express order of Your Majesty. His reliance, he said, was not on his foreign auxiliaries, but on the native force of the kingdom; and a small number was sufficient to form a rallying-point for those who he was sure would come to his aid.

I then placed before him other difficulties; such as, that it would be easy for the Queen of England to move the Queen of Scotland to some place further inland, where her rescue could not be effected with the facility which he expected; that levying and embarking troops in Italy could not be done without a good deal of noise, and that secrets of this kind were hard to keep; to all which objections he answered by making light of them, as is the way of men driven from home and longing to return to it; and he finally said that if the enterprise were conducted as he would plan it, and in the Pope's name, it would have a better issue than if it were to be undertaken in the name of Your Majesty.

I ended our long conversation by telling Stucley that, as there was time between now and October to look about us carefully, he ought to go back to Rome and continue the negotiation, while I would advise him of anything that should occur to me on the subject. On this understanding he will set out in two or three days for Rome, I having made him promise, and having promised on my own part, to keep the matter secret, which was the point, he says, on which His Holiness and the Cardinal were most urgent, and which is of equal import-ance to the affair and to his own personal safety. I humbly beg Your Majesty will order due consideration to be given as to what ought to be done in this business for your service. To me it appears that if the Pope shall resolve to take up the enterprise in earnest, and defray the cost of it, it may open a way by which the affairs of Flanders may be helped, and Your Majesty may be considerably served.[1]

Philip took his time in answering this letter, and when he did so his reply was non-commital. He told his brother that he had

[1] Arch. Gen. de Simancas, Estado, Legajo 1067.

done well to inform him of his interview with Stucley, and he commended him for the judicious line he had taken. At the same time he must be careful not to encourage any such overtures, though it was just as well to hear what these English exiles had to say.[1]

Meanwhile, events had been taking place in North Africa which had ruined any hopes that Don John may have entertained of finding a throne there: these were nothing less than the recapture of Tunis by the Turks, and the fall of the Goletta into their hands.

For this disaster Don John has been blamed by many historians, and a modern biographer of Philip II, W. T. Walsh, has gone so far as to say that 'nearly ten thousand of the best fighting men in Christendom had gone to untimely death because a vain ambitious youth had failed to follow the orders of his far-sighted King'.[2] In other words, Don John had clung on to the two places for reasons of his own when his brother had told him to evacuate them. It is not, however, quite as simple as that, though the well of truth has been so muddied by Antonio Pérez that it is by no means easy to discover exactly what did happen. However it is not impossible that, as so often in war, divided counsels must bear no inconsiderable part of the responsibility.

Don John's original instructions, at any rate according to Antonio Pérez, were to dismantle Tunis after he had captured the place,[3] but before he returned to Italy in October, 1573, he had ordered the engineer, Gabriel Serbellone, to construct a new fortress there, and had informed Philip of what he had done. In view of the King's earlier decision in the opposite sense it might have been supposed that he would either have approved of this change of plan, or given orders for the work to be stopped, but it was not until the following April that he replied to Don John's letter. There would seem to be two possible reasons for the delay: one is that he had so many matters on hand of what appeared to him to be of greater importance that he put the problem on one side, and the other is that he expected to see his brother in Madrid

[1] Arch. Gen. de Simancas, Estado, Legajo 1144.
[2] *Philip II*, p. 545. New York, 1937.
[3] *vide supra*, p. 229.

in the autumn of 1573 when he could talk it over with him – indeed both considerations probably played their part.

However this may be it was not until April 5th, 1574, that Philip put pen to paper. He began by saying that he had hoped that he and his brother might have come to a decision when they met, but as Don John had decided to remain in Italy for the present longer delay was out of the question. The arguments in favour of the retention of Tunis were that this was desired by the Pope; to give it up for fear that it might be attacked would result in a serious loss of prestige; and, if it remained in Spanish hands, even during the current year, it would prevent the Turks from concentrating against the Goletta or raiding the coasts of Italy and Sicily. On the other hand, it would be better to evacuate the place than to be driven out by force, while in these circumstances its recovery by the Turks would encourage them to attack the Goletta, and the influx of fugitives from Tunis would demoralize the garrison there. In effect, there was a good deal to be said on both sides.

Passing from the general to the particular Philip raised doubts about the new fortifications which Serbellone was erecting. Were they not overlooked by two neighbouring hills and was there an adequate supply of water? The question of cost was extremely important: on this the King had formed no opinion, and would be grateful for his brother's advice. If it was decided to hold the place this must be done with Italian troops only as the possible loss of any large number of Spaniards could not be contemplated: if abandonment were to be decided upon it must take place in good time, so that the Turkish fleet should not attack the troops while they were in process of embarkation. Anyhow, the final decision was left to Don John after consultation with Serbellone.

This was bad enough, but a postscript in Philip's own handwriting made the matter worse:

In this letter you have what occurs to me about this affair; and although both on one side and the other difficulties offer and present themselves, it appears to me that by far the greatest will be found in holding the fort; and therefore my opinion is, that it will be better to abandon it, supposing this can be done in good time; and so I earnestly entreat you to look at the matter as one of great importance, and without regard to anything except what is most suitable for the success of the business itself.[1]

In these circumstances Mr Walsh's strictures upon Don John would appear to be somewhat excessive. No doubt it would have been better if he had gone to Madrid and talked things over with his brother, instead of devoting himself to the flesh-pots of Italy; on this score he was certainly to blame, but when he did not come Philip should surely either have sent him a peremptory order to do so, or at once given him definite instructions with regard to Tunis. The truth probably was that neither man realized the seriousness of the situation while there was still time to take effective action. Sokolli was still Grand Vizier, and so long as he was at the helm Ottoman resilience after defeat continued to be remarkable. Equally, of course, Don John might have refreshed his brother's memory, but as things seemed to be going his way he probably did not see the necessity. That the King was right in what he said in his postscript events were soon to prove, but by then it was too late. The real sting of his letter, however, lay in the tail, which was clearly meant as a reminder to Don John not to be influenced by any aspirations in the direction of a North African crown.

A less satisfactory document can rarely have reached a commander in the field, and Don John's immediate reaction was to send his former secretary, Juan de Soto, now Commissary-General of the Navy, to Madrid to report to the King in person, which he did on June 20th. His statement began with a recapitulation of the circumstances of the conquest of Tunis, and the reasons for the siting of the new fortress. Dealing then with the question of finance he went on to say that the ordinary land revenue of the Hafsids had been 375,935 ducats, but that there was also other property at the disposal of the State, besides the produce of fines, while valuable taxes were levied on the gold imported from the South and on the trade with Europe.

All that was required to develop these extensive resources was a

[1] Arch. Gen. de Simancas, Estado, Legajo 1142.

good and stable government, but de Soto doubted if this could be provided by any Hafsid. Therefore he was of the opinion that Muley Mohammed, who was proving unsatisfactory, should be deposed, and in his place there should be appointed a Spanish governor, with special instructions to favour the Moorish population. Passing from the general to the particular de Soto, or rather Don John, suggested that local government should be entrusted to twelve Moors chosen by the local inhabitants, while Moslems should not only be allowed full and free exercise of their religion, but Christians should continue to be forbidden to enter the mosques or to interfere in any way with the rites of Islam. The Turks had made themselves so unpopular during their occupation of Tunis that by measures such as these a wedge might be driven in between them and the Moors.

The economic advantages of retaining Tunis were also stressed. The country abounded in natural wealth of all kinds, which would be extremely useful to the economy of the Spanish Empire, while the wines of Spain and Italy would find a ready market among the Moors, from which one may gather that the Tunisians did not enjoy any very high reputation as orthodox Mohammedans. The quartering of Spanish troops there would not cost as much as elsewhere, and as the Pope was so desirous that the Lions and Castles should continue to float over Tunis perhaps he might be induced to contribute to the expense. Finally, it would be suicide to withdraw the Spanish contingent, for without a stiffening of Spaniards the Italians could never hold Tunis against the Turks, while as for dismantling the fortifications it was now far too late.[1]

At this point it may be well to note that Philip was very far from being what a later age would have described as an Imperialist, for a few years later the Governor of the Philippines, one Don Francisco Sande, offered to undertake the conquest of China with an army of about five thousand men, and the project seems to have had considerable backing in the more jingoistic circles in Manila. 'The Chinese', the Governor wrote to the King, 'are so cowardly that no one rides on horseback,' and he thought he could obtain assistance from the Japanese and the Filipinos 'who are much braver than the Chinese are.' All, however, that he got

[1] Arch. Gen. de Simancas, Estado, Legajo 1142.

from Philip was a snub, for he was told that 'as regards the conquest of China which you think should be undertaken forthwith,
it has seemed to us here that this matter should be dropped, and
that on the contrary good friendship should be sought with the
Chinese'.[1] On the present occasion, however, Philip gave way, and
ceased to advocate the evacuation of Tunis.

A further difficulty by which Don John found himself confronted at this time was the unco-operative attitude adopted by
the Viceroys of Naples and Sicily, Cardinal Granvelle and the
Duke of Terranova, who took the line that Tunis was very
definitely his affair, not theirs. To some extent it is possible to see
their point of view, for with the Netherlands in rebellion, and
England and France to a greater or lesser extent aiding the rebels;
with Genoa, as will be seen, in a state of unrest; and with a war on
hand with the Sultan, quite apart from the necessity of defending
their own vice-royalties, they may well have felt that this was no
time for adventures in North Africa. Where they erred was in not
realizing that the die was cast, and the forward policy could not be
put into reverse. At first, indeed, it did seem as if there was no
immediate danger, and Serbellone reported that he hoped by May
20th his new fortress would be capable of holding out against any
force that was likely to be brought against it. As the days passed,
however, the situation deteriorated, and on June 4th Don John
wrote to Escobedo, who was in Madrid: 'I am well aware, God
knows, how necessary it is to look after affairs at Court; and that,
although affairs may be forgotten for a while, the time will come
when a remedy must be applied, perhaps at double cost of cash
and credit. "Of that dust has come this mud", as the saying goes;
and for want of foresight one is driven to much greater outlay,
which after all sometimes proves useless.'[2]

As the summer advanced it became clear that unless some
drastic action were taken time was not on the side of the Spaniards. Arab hordes from the desert were beginning to threaten
Tunis, and the Turkish fleet put to sea. Don John mobilized what
reinforcements he could, but it was not until August was well
advanced that this relief force was assembled at Naples. Either

[1] cf. Schurz, W. L., *The Manila Galleon*, p. 68. New York, 1959.
[2] Arch. Gen. de Simancas, Hacienda, Legajo 136.

there or at Messina he received a lengthy dispatch from his brother dated July 30th. This told him, what he must have suspected if he did not already know, that the Ottoman fleet was off the Barbary coast, and was apparently about to attack Tunis. The King hoped that he had received a hundred thousand ducats from the Marquess of Ayamonte, and he approved of his brother's move to Sicily because his presence there would be good for morale, and would 'supply much that was apt to be wanting'. Don John's 'hand and diligence must make amends for many faults', including, apparently, shortage of money, for the hundred thousand ducats would have to last as long as possible. The Viceroys of Naples and Sicily had received repeated orders to give all the assistance in their power, but Don John must use his discretion in insisting on compliance with his demands 'having regard to his own needs and to theirs'.

Of the military situation Philip took a gloomy view. He estimated the naval force at his brother's disposal at no more than a hundred and twenty galleys, which was a great deal less than the armament which the Sultan could command: he must therefore avoid anything in the nature of a fleet action, which meant that he must go no farther than Sicily. Such being the case the best the Spanish ships could do was to hang on the rear of the enemy, cut off stragglers, and take evasive action. The King continued:

> In such work it comports neither with your authority and reputation nor with mine, nor my service, that you should be engaged in person; and you must therefore direct such operations as may be possible from some point that may be convenient: and so one of the things which I most expressly charge and order you is that in no manner and for no cause you go on board the fleet while the enemy remains in those seas, for this is what is proper; and I insist upon this order the more because I know how necessary it is, seeing that your courage and your desire to be active in my service are not slight, and may make you endanger your person and the fleet, whose safety is of much more importance than those places which you might desire to relieve, or indeed anything else; wherefore I charge if it be needful to employ any part of the fleet, or the whole, in relief of

the Goletta or Tunis, you should be very careful before exposing it to such risk.

Once more Philip's fears of his brother's rashness had been aroused, possibly now stimulated by Antonio Pérez, and once more he showed himself so little of a leader of men as to imagine that an army or a fleet could be satisfactorily commanded from a remote base – a mistake which his father would never have made.

If Garcia de Toledo were well enough to go with the fleet, that would, the King thought, be an ideal solution; failing him recourse might be had to Giovanni[1] Andrea Doria. Finally, 'one thing has here seemed convenient, and it is this, that although you are not to go on board the fleet, the fact is to be kept secret, because by doing so more people of importance will desire to join you in the enterprise, and afterwards it will be easy to provide that they shall continue in it and share its fortunes, seeing that there will be no help for them; and so on this point you are advised'.[2] This line of conduct, however advisable, was not calculated to inspire confidence in troops either.

At this point the weather took a hand in the game, and so adverse was it to the Spaniards that for several weeks Don John was cut off from North Africa; even Gil de Andrade, who had been so successful on previous occasions in obtaining information regarding the enemy's movements, failed to do so this time: when the storms abated the first news that reached Don John was that the Goletta had fallen on August 23rd after a siege of five weeks, and that Tunis was in great danger. 'I have received this intelligence,' he wrote to his brother, 'with the great regret which the case demands, seeing the poor means I have of affording relief, and of doing what is required, and that this might have been otherwise had we all in concert provided for the most pressing needs.'[3]

A combination of circumstances had produced this disaster, of which a divided command was by no means the least important. Serbellone was active enough, but his writ did not run beyond Tunis, where he was Captain-General, for the Goletta was under the command of one Don Pedro Portocarrero, member of a family

[1] Also known as Gian.
[2] Arch. Gen. de Simancas, Estado, Legajo 451.   [3] ibid., Legajo 450.

well-known in Spanish history, but himself apparently lethargic and with little experience of active service conditions. The reluctance of the Viceroys of Naples and Sicily, fearful of a Turkish attack upon their own territories, to send reinforcements to Africa has already been mentioned, and to this must be added the vacillation of the home government. The result was that the Spanish garrisons at the Goletta and Tunis were quite inadequate in view of the forces which were being mustered against them. Never, too, was the *damnosa hereditas* of the Low Countries more clearly demonstrated, for had Philip not had his hands tied in the north he would in all probability have been able to forestall by three centuries the work of France on the African littoral of the Mediterranean.

Yet when all is said and done probably the decisive factor in the Spanish defeat was Ochiali, who had a personal interest in regaining Tunis for the Crescent, since he had originally captured the town in the name of the Sultan four years earlier. He was now one of the most powerful men in the Ottoman Empire, and he was determined to avenge at one and the same time the defeat of Lepanto and the loss of Tunis. He had rebuilt the Turkish Navy, and he was to be favoured by fortune in that the plans of the Spanish defensive system were unexpectedly revealed to him. This was due to a certain Giacomo Zitolomini, an Italian engineer, who had served in these fortifications long enough to be thoroughly acquainted with them. For some purpose he paid a visit to Spain, where he fell foul of the police at Aranjuez, and was soundly beaten by an *alguacil*: this was not at all to his liking, so he shook the dust of the Peninsula off his feet, passed on to Constantinople, and took service under the Sultan in the name of Mustafa. His inside information was of the greatest value to Ochiali.

The rest of the story is soon told. Towards the end of June large forces of Arabs began to make their appearance from the neighbouring vilayets, and in the second week of the following month Ochiali brought his fleet to anchor in the Bay of Tunis. He was in command of three hundred sail, while on their decks were forty thousand soldiers, of whom seven thousand were Janissaries, under the orders of Sinan Pasha, the Sultan's brother-in-law. In face of this armament the Tunisians showed no disposition to adhere to their Spanish allegiance, and although the Spaniards and Italians fought bravely it was to no purpose against such tremendous odds; the Goletta surrendered on August 23rd and Tunis did the same on September 3rd. It is pleasant to read that while Sinan Pasha treated his captives with great severity Ochiali lived up to the reputation which Cervantes gave him, and his behaviour was very different: Portocarrero died at sea off the Peloponnese, but Serbellone was exchanged in the following year for a Turk who had been captured at Lepanto.

News of the loss of Tunis did not reach Don John, at Trápani, until October 3rd, and in a letter to his sister, Margaret of Parma, he puts much of the blame on the short-sightedness of the Viceroys of Naples and Sicily. He might have added that overseas possessions cannot, or could not in those days, be held without naval forces sufficiently strong to keep open the lines of communication with them,[1] as the Venetians had discovered in the case of Cyprus.

On the same day he wrote to Philip.

The Goletta and the fort of Tunis are lost, as Your Majesty will see by the enclosed account. No grief can be more sincere than mine, seeing that so short a time has brought so great a loss. I determined to send Juan de Soto to Your Majesty because I dreaded such a disaster, as the papers of which he was the bearer will show; and I ordered him specially to urge that provision should be made for the safety of the two places, because we had been so often advised of the approach of the enemy; and my fears even led me to put all other business aside, and hasten here to see if matters might in any way be mended. But nothing could be done; the Goletta was lost on the day on which I sailed from Naples, and the fort of Tunis before I had been able to assemble half the fleet at Palermo; and there was no opportunity of attempting anything, and no time for any of the plans I had devised for their relief. Moreover, the supply of money which Your Majesty was pleased to order to be sent by Don Juan de Soto had not come to hand.

[1] cf. Porreño, B., *Historia del Señor D. Juan de Austria*, p. 340. Madrid, 1899.

Don John went on to say that he proposed to come to Spain as soon as possible, as the only way of preventing further disaster, 'the difficulties in the business being so many, and the distance between Italy and Madrid so great, that time, however precious, was always being wasted'. He had not sent any squadron after the enemy fleet (which had now returned to Constantinople) as he did not wish to incur any unnecessary risks. Next he turned to the Royal instructions with regard to himself contained in his brother's letter of July 30th.

Your Majesty does me great honour in stating the reasons for which you forbid me to go in person against the enemy. I must nevertheless take leave to observe, that knowing what the safety of this fleet requires, and keeping in view my duty to please and serve Your Majesty, no personal object or interest shall ever deter me from undertaking that which I deem most for the advantage of your service; and I therefore venture once more to entreat Your Majesty to be pleased sometimes to refer such questions as these to us who are on the spot where they arise, for it may be that things will be better done in the absence of orders so very precise.

The letter concluded with an earnest appeal on behalf of the prisoners captured by the Turks.

I remind Your Majesty of these gentlemen, thus urgently although, I know, unnecessarily, to discharge the duty I owe both to them and to your Royal service; and I entreat that negotiations for their rescue may at once be opened. Meanwhile I will use all diligence here to learn with certainty the names of the prisoners, and by what means they may be ransomed.[1]

How right Don John was in his comment on the slowness of communications between Madrid and Italy is proved by the fact that it was not until November 21st that Philip was in a position to reply, though some of the delay was due to the necessity of deciphering and enciphering. The King accepted the disaster with his habitual composure on such occasions, and it is important to note that he showed no disposition to place the blame on his

[1] Arch. Gen. de Simancas, Estado, Legajo 451.

brother. 'Yours of the 3rd and 4th of last month,' he wrote, 'reached me on the 12th of this month with the information of the loss of the fort of Tunis, which I regret as much as is reasonable.' The proposed visit of Don John to Madrid was forbidden. The fleet would require looking after; plans must be made for the following year; 'and so, although I should be exceedingly glad to see you here, I have determined to postpone my private gratification to the benefit and security of public affairs, and you must be content to do the same'.[1]

The reaction of the outside world was, save in London, what might have been expected. The Pope did not mince matters, and wrote to Philip, 'These unhappy events in Africa have filled us with grief and confusion. Never could we have believed that the ministers of Your Majesty would have been so negligent in not giving aid of all kinds to these poor people. We do not blame one more than another; but we say in general that Your Majesty is very ill-served, and that if you do not provide some remedy in time to come, and let it be seen that it is so, we fear that, old as we are, we shall ourselves witness the ruin of Christendom, which God forbid.'[2] In France there was general satisfaction at the Spanish discomfiture, for the Guises were not yet in the pocket of Madrid to such an extent as to forget that they were Frenchmen: the same attitude was, needless to say, adopted by the rebels of Holland and Zeeland, who looked on every enemy of Philip as their ally. Only in England, curiously enough, was a more realistic view taken, for the Spanish ambassador in London reported that Burghley had assured him that the Queen and her Council were much grieved, and that Elizabeth had offered her mediation between the Governor of the Netherlands, Requesens, and William of Orange as a step towards a general union, for which she thought the time had come, of the Christian Powers against the dangerous aggrandizement of the Sultan.[3]

[1] Arch. Gen. de Simancas, Estado, Legajo 451.
[2] Arch. Gen. de Simancas, Estado, Legajo 926.
[3] Arch. Gen. de Simancas, Estado, Legajo 828.

II

Italy and the Netherlands

WHILE THESE EVENTS WERE TAKING PLACE TWO OF DON John's most important contemporaries had been removed by death, namely Charles IX of France and Sultan Selim II. The French King died on May 30th, 1574, and was succeeded by his brother, the Duke of Anjou, who was at the time King of Poland, to which throne he had been elected in the previous year. Henry III, as he now became, at once laid down the Polish crown, and Don John seems to have had thoughts of letting his name go forward for the vacancy; at any rate he exchanged letters with Don Garcia de Toledo on the subject, but he must have thought better of the project, for he took no action in the matter, and in due course Stephen Bathori became the successor of Henry of Valois.

Henry III proved to be the last of his line, and for many years he enjoyed a very bad reputation among historians. Armstrong described him as 'at once pathetic and contemptible',[1] and not at all the sort of man who would have been acceptable company in an Oxford Common Room at the turn of the century. Yet there was more to him than that in spite of his earrings, frizzled head, puppy-dogs, and *mignons*. He fought with notable bravery at Jarnac and Moncontour; when Clément stabbed him he tore the dagger from the wound, and plunged it in the assassin's jaw; and he never faltered when Guise had to be struck down: also, when there was business to be done he displayed more than ordinary intelligence, for twice he thwarted the States-General, and twice he outmanœuvred Guise. More recently Henry's stock has risen, and Jacques Bainville went so far as to say that 'Henry died for an idea – that of the State, of the monarchy, and of national unity'.[2] In the present generation Philippe Erlanger has been equally

[1] *Wars of Religion in France*, pp. 90–91. Oxford, 1904.
[2] *Histoire de France*, p. 179. Paris, 1924.

laudatory, and has left it on record that 'the last Valois gave his life for France'.[1] However this may be, it will hardly be denied that the most Catholic of French monarchs was murdered while leading a combined army of Catholics and Huguenots in the cause of toleration and the legitimate succession.

If Henry III was a considerable improvement upon his predecessor the same could hardly be said of Sultan Murad III, who succeeded his father, Selim the Sot, on December 12th, 1574. He was twenty-eight at the time, and the Vicomte de la Jonquière says that he was 'brave and the friend of culture', and that his accession was greeted with high hopes among his subjects.[2] This may well have been the case, but the hopes were soon doomed to disappointment. Murad was certainly a traditionalist, for his first act on arriving in Constantinople from Magnesia, where he had been living as heir to the throne, was to order the execution of his five brothers. In the morning after his arrival, in the capital, the high officers of State assembled to greet him, and they anxiously awaited the first words of their new master to provide a clue to the policy of the coming reign, but the Sultan's opening words, addressed to the Aga of the Eunuchs, were, 'I am hungry; bring me something to eat.'[3]

Murad's weakness was women, and they played the same part in his life that the bottle had done in that of his father. His procreative capacity was such that he sired no less than a hundred and three children, and such was the demand for beautiful girls for the Imperial harem during his reign that it is said to have raised the price of this commodity in the slave-market of Constantinople. Not unnaturally his activities in this direction left him little time or energy for the government of his Empire, but this was of no great importance so long as Sokolli, the last of the statesmen trained in the school of Suleyman the Magnificent, remained Grand Vizier, which he did until his murder four years later.

Another casualty, though fortunately not a fatal one, during these years was Cervantes himself. 'Liberty, Sancho, my friend,' Don Quixote told his faithful squire, 'is one of the most precious

[1] *Le Massacre de la Saint-Barthélemy*, p. 227. Paris, 1960.
[2] *Histoire de l'Empire Ottoman*, vol. i, p. 215. Paris, 1914.
[3] cf. Creasy, Sir Edward, *History of the Ottoman Turks*, p. 225. London, 1878.

gifts that Heaven has bestowed on mankind; all the treasures the earth contains within its bosom or the ocean within its depths cannot be compared with it. For liberty, as well as for honour, man ought to risk even his life, and he should reckon captivity the greatest evil life can bring.'[1] Cervantes ought to have known. After Lepanto he had served in Lope de Figueroa's regiment in the expedition against Tunis, and had then returned to Italy: he also served in the force which Don John raised for the relief of that place and the Goletta. The rest of the time he spent in Sardinia and Naples, and, as readers of *Don Quijote* will appreciate, he neglected no opportunity of extending his acquaintance with Italian literature.

In the summer of 1575 Don John gave Cervantes leave to return to Spain to seek promotion, and he also provided him with a letter to Philip in which he spoke highly of his merits and asked that he should be given command of one of the companies which was being raised in Spain for service in Italy. Cervantes sailed from Naples in the galley *Sol*, but on September 26th she was attacked by corsairs off Marseilles, and after a fierce fight captured. Among the prisoners was Cervantes, and as Don John's letter was found on him, as well as one from the Viceroy of Naples, he was regarded by his captors as someone of importance, and was accordingly reserved for ransom. He was taken to Algiers, in those days a polite name for Hell, and there he was destined to remain for five unhappy years.

Philip's letter telling his brother that the moment was not opportune for him to come to Spain did not deter Don John from making the journey, though he was clearly in some apprehension with regard to the consequences of so flagrantly disobeying the King's orders, for on December 30th, 1574, he wrote from Palamos, in Catalonia, to Antonio Pérez, saying it no doubt appeared strange that he had acted in violation of the instructions he had received.

Yet God is my witness that I know, believe, and can affirm, that that which I do is that which ought to be done, and that up to this time no one has chosen to understand how dangerous

[1] *Don Quijote*, II, 58. (Professor Walter Starkie's translation). New York, 1964.

is the state of His Majesty's affairs in Italy, and how entirely the treatment of them must be changed if it is ever to be better. I may also add that not to see myself any longer a minister of mischief from which there is no honourable escape – mischief long foreseen and denounced – I have left my post, and incurred the guilt of disobedience rather than the certainty of dishonour.

Now I wish very much to know how my coming to Barcelona is taken, and what kind of welcome I have to expect; for welcome I do not look for, however my zeal may deserve it.[1]

Don John need have had no fears, for his brother was as gracious as ever, and as obviously pleased to see him: there were no recriminations with regard either to the reverse in North Africa or to his visit to Spain. Two points in particular Don John raised with the King – one was the danger of divided command in Italy, and the other was a personal request to be given the rank of Infante. He seems to have had little difficulty in persuading Philip that so far as the first of these points was concerned matters could not be allowed to continue as they were, and the problem was referred to the Council of Italy for its consideration, but on the subject of the rank of Infante the King would give no definite answer, and merely postponed it until a more suitable moment.

In all Don John spent the best part of six months in Spain, and in March, 1575, he visited Doña Magdalena de Ulloa at Abrojo. On his way he looked in at the Escorial to see how it was progressing, and he arrived there in such a storm of wind and rain that he refused to allow the Prior and his monks to cross the threshold, saying that it was weather fit only for soldiers like himself to be out. He sailed from Cartagena on May 9th, and after calling at Spezia and Genoa he reached Naples in the middle of June.

Among those whom he found waiting for him there was Girolamo Lippomano, who had been sent by the Serenissima to report on the existing situation in the kingdom of the Two Sicilies, and who had naturally a good deal to say about Don John himself. First of all he describes his appearance and habits.

He is of middle stature, well made, of a most beautiful countenance, and of admirable grace. He has little beard, but a large

[1] Arch. Gen. de Simancas, Estado, Legajo 335.

moustache of a pale colour; he wears his hair long and turned up, which becomes him greatly; he dresses sumptuously, and with such neatness that it is a pleasure to see him. . . . Some say that he is much given to women, which may well be true, seeing that he is so young, but nevertheless he has never given any cause for scandal by which disquiet or dissatisfaction has arisen among the nobility of Naples; because he is careful to seek his pleasure with those women who are in the habit of intriguing with princes, and does not employ in this way any time which should be otherwise spent.

It would appear that Don John must have exercised his charms to the full upon the Venetian diplomatist for he is credited with rather surprising intellectual gifts, and we are told that 'besides the Spanish tongue, he has spoken French with me excellently well; he understands Flemish and German, and he can also speak Italian, but not with much confidence'. His six chief advisers were the Viceroy of Naples, Don Garcia de Toledo, Giovanni Antonio Doria, the Duke of Sesa, the Marquess of Santa Cruz, and Don Juan de Cardona.

With the chief princes of Italy he does not, to say the truth, stand well. The Pope is dissatisfied with his conduct in the affairs of Genoa, about which many unpleasant words have passed on both sides; although His Highness endeavours to conciliate His Holiness by showing him every respect. With Savoy he is not well-pleased, and although they write letters to one another, calling each other 'Most Serene' and 'Highness', in truth there is bad blood between them. Of Florence and Genoa I will say nothing, the reciprocal displeasure and ill-will between these States and Don John being clear and public.

With the Emperor he is not at heart very well pleased, perhaps because he thinks His Majesty does not give him due consideration, and perhaps because the Emperor would have been glad to obtain for one of his own sons the employments held by His Highness, who, nevertheless, behaves to His Majesty with all befitting respect, and is especially fond of the most Serene Prince Ernest, the second son of His Caesarian Majesty.

With the King of France he is on the worst terms, which may

be accounted for by the feeling which exists between the French and the Spaniards, and by the envy with which each looks upon the victories of the other. The Duke of Mayenne told me that, conversing one day on board ship, Don John said to him 'that he would have given a great deal had Monsieur d'Anjou (who was not then King) been present at the victory over the Turks'; to which he himself replied, 'Then Your Highness, as a brave soldier, would also have given a good deal to have been present at the victories which my Lord of Anjou gained over the rebels at home.'

With respect to this Most Serene Republic, although after the rupture of the League, an event so hurtful to his aggrandisement and glory, he was inwardly displeased, yet he esteems as a great honour the sending of an ambassador to him, and those other favours which he receives from your Serenity, with whom, in the hope of another League, he seeks to maintain the best understanding. I think, therefore, that it will be judicious for your Serenity to continue your good offices towards him, always mentioning him with honour to the resident ambassador, who will give him an account of everything; and this will be sufficient to keep him well disposed to our affairs.[1]

This analysis of Don John's relations with the Italian states is the more interesting in view of the fact that he had been concerned with the politics of Genoa in particular more or less continuously for two years from the spring of 1574.

Genoa had declined even more rapidly than Venice, and in the fifties and sixties of the sixteenth century she was further weakened by an insurrection in Corsica led by one Sampiero, who held out for something like ten years, until the commander of the Genoese forces opposed to him managed to secure his assassination. This rising demonstrated not only the weakness of Genoa but also its vulnerability from the Spanish point of view, for the Corsicans had received underhand encouragement from Paris, while the French government could never forget that it had once controlled the republic, or that it still had many sympathizers

[1] *Relazione di Napoli del Senatore Girolamo Lippomano ritornante ambasciatore del serenissimo D. Giovanni d'Austria, l'anno 1575*, printed by Eugenio Alberi, in his *Relazioni delli Ambasciatori Veneti al Senato*, Firenze 1841, Serie II, vol. ii, pp. 265–311.

among its citizens. However, when the war in Corsica came to an end in 1569 the Genoese showed themselves merciful and even magnanimous.

Hardly had Corsica been pacified than civil war broke out in Genoa itself, and in the troubled waters the Powers of continental Europe set themselves industriously to fish. The rival parties consisted of the older families, the *Portico Vecchio*, among whom were the Dorias, who looked to Spain for support, and a younger group, the *Portico Nuovo*, who appealed for help to France, and to a lesser extent to Tuscany, where Francesco I, who succeeded to the throne in 1572, wavered between a desire to divide the territory of Genoa with Philip, and to revive certain old claims of Florence on the frontier towns of Sarzana and Sarzanella. The succeeding contest did not result in any material change in the status of Genoa which continued to be a satellite of Spain with the Dorias very much in control. At the same time Don John's skilful handling of a difficult situation seems to have made a very favourable impression upon his brother, and may well have contributed to his appointment as Governor of the Netherlands.

Requesens had died there suddenly on March 5th, 1576, at a very critical stage of the struggle with the rebels, and Philip was under no illusion but that the sooner his successor was appointed the better. He seems to have favoured Don John for the vacancy from the beginning,[1] but the Council was at first divided, though there was a small party that supported his brother.[2] The King thought the matter over, and discussed it with his ministers, for a fortnight, and then, on April 8th, he wrote to Don John announcing his decision to appoint him to the vacant post. He made no attempt either to disguise the seriousness of the situation in the Low Countries or his own anxiety concerning it. To pacify Flanders and to maintain religion there required new measures, and the first step was to put a member of the Royal Family at the head of the government. In consequence Don John was at once to set out for Lombardy, where the necessary instructions would be sent him.

[1] His name had been considered on previous occasions, cf. Mulhacén, Marqués de, *Don Juan de Austria*, p. 267. Madrid, 1944.
[2] cf. Gachard, L. P., *Correspondance de Philippe II*, vol. iii, pp. 429–32. Brussels, 1848–51.

I would myself go if my presence were not indispensable to these kingdoms, to raise the money here which is needed to sustain all the others: otherwise, surely I would have devoted my person and my life, as I have often wished to do, to an affair of such high importance and so close to the service of God. It is necessary for me, therefore, to avail myself of you, not only for what you are and the good qualities God has given you, but for the experience and knowledge of affairs that you have gained. . . . I am trusting to you, my brother, that since you are informed of the state of affairs of the Low Countries . . . and that no one else is available. . . . I am confident, I say, that you will dedicate your strength and your life and all that you hold most dear to an affair so important, and so much concerned with the honour of God as well as the welfare of His religion: for on the conservation of that of the Low Countries depends the conservation of all the rest, and since they are in peril, there is no sacrifice one ought to avoid to save them.

Thank God, matters are now in good state . . . but the sooner you arrive, the better. By all means see that you arrive while the present favourable state of affairs endures, and before any change is caused by delay, from which grave inconveniences could result; and the remedy then would be vain. This is why it must be administered before such an eventuality occurs; and I wish that the bearer of this dispatch had wings to fly to you, and that you had them yourself to get there sooner.

Characteristically, the King sent detailed instructions for his brother's journey. He was to travel with as small a suite as possible – twelve was suggested as a reasonable number – and no one except Escobedo was to be informed of the object of his journey. The fleet was to be left under the command of the Duke of Sesa, but the impression was to be created that this was a purely temporary measure. Don John was only to take with him Escobedo and his personal servants, because in view of the existing situation in the Netherlands the less pomp with which he arrived the better the impression he would create there.[1]

[1] cf. Gachard, L. P., *Correspondance de Philippe II*, vol. iv, pp. 38–52. Brussels, 1848–51.

The King's letter reached his brother in Naples on May 3rd, and it was by no means to his liking, nor was there any reason why it should be: quite apart from the fact that he was called upon to succeed such experienced statesmen as the Duke of Alba and the Grand Commander, all his experience of war and diplomacy had been in the Mediterranean, not to mention the more sentimental bonds which he had forged for himself in Italy. He was certainly left in no doubt with regard to his brother's anxiety that he should go to the Netherlands for the courier who brought the Royal letter also arrived with no less than three more on the same subject from Pérez to Escobedo, clearly intended for him to see. In these the minister used every argument which he could devise to induce Don John to hasten north: he reminded him of his duty to God and the King, and he emphasized the glory which would accrue to him if he was able to pacify the rebels – a glory which would exceed even that which he had won at Lepanto. The need for secrecy was again stressed, and not even the Pope was to be informed until Don John was actually on his way to Flanders: above all, he was on no account to waste time by visiting Madrid before going to Brussels.

That these letters from Pérez to Escobedo were not his own unaided work is proved by the drafts of them which are to be found in the archives at Simancas. In one, for instance, Pérez writes, 'Thus, Sir, I am of opinion that Don John should obey His Majesty with much love and eagerness, setting off at once, imitating his father, who on a like occasion ventured himself into the midst of his enemies in order to bring the single city of Ghent to reason, and who by that means obtained his end. And I hope that the result of a like determination will, in this case, be as much the greater as the necessity is the more urgent.' Philip apparently thought that the more historical precedents that could be cited the better, so he added in his own handwriting another incident taken from the life of the Emperor.

Who afterwards, being in Germany – I believe at Innsbruck – and learning that the French were marching to attack the Low Countries, old and sick as he was, having dyed his beard and otherwise disguised himself, set off with only two or three attendants, in order to reach the Provinces with the greater secrecy, which he would have done, for he had already made two or three days' journey, had he not been seized with so violent a fit of the gout that he could go no further, and was forced to turn back to the bed in which he had left Adrian,[1] to whom mass had been said and meals brought, in order that the world might think the Emperor still there, until his journey had been nearly accomplished.[2]

Don John seems to have regarded his brother's letter not so much as an order to be obeyed as the basis for a discussion, for although it reached him on May 3rd, it was not until twenty-four days later that he vouchsafed a reply. On the 27th he wrote to Philip saying that of course he would do as he was told – he could hardly have said anything else – but making it quite clear that in consenting to govern the Low Countries he was conferring a favour. He recalled that his name had been already mentioned in this connexion, and how pleased he had been when the King had abandoned the idea of sending him there. Since that time the state of affairs had become much more alarming: the King's enemies were much more powerful; disaffection and heresy had made great progress; there was good reason to expect an invasion from England and France; the country was wasted by the Royal troops whom the low state of the King's credit prevented him from either paying or disbanding; the Spanish name was abhorred by the people; and many of the King's ministers were implicated in the rebellious policy of the Estates. Before he undertook the task which had been assigned to him he would like to have had a personal interview with his brother, but since this had been denied to him he was sending Escobedo to Madrid in his place.

He then proceeded to lay down the policy which he considered should be pursued in the Low Countries.

All ordinances contrary to the laws and customs of the Provinces, which have been issued by recent governors, and which give so much offence, ought to be annulled.

---

[1] Adrian de Bues, vide supra, p. 30.
[2] cf. Gachard, L. P., Correspondance de Philippe II, vol. iv, pp. 43–44. Brussels, 1848–51.

All possible means of bringing back to the Royal service the vassals of Your Majesty, who may repent of their faults, should be adopted.

In appointing to places of trust, and in the general administration, the ancient customs of the country ought to be observed.

No person ought to be attached to my service who can give offence, and no foreign lawyers, who are so unpopular, should be employed.

As affairs are to be conducted without the employment of force, and solely by the authority of Your Majesty and myself, I must have a household well appointed and respectable, and composed of persons of all nations.

To meet the unavoidable expense of even such an establishment as I have at present, I can assure Your Majesty that neither the ordinary allowance nor the extraordinary subvention is sufficient, and that I am in debt to the amount of several thousand ducats. As I have no means of meeting these liabilities, I must entreat Your Majesty, in this as in all things else, to supply my needs, with due regard to the part which Your Majesty desires that I should sustain in the world.

One of the things which will most contribute to the success of my mission is, that I should be held in high esteem at home, and that all men should know and believe that Your Majesty, being unable to go in person to the Low Countries, has invested me with all the powers I could desire. Your Majesty will see that I will use them for the re-establishment of your authority, now so fallen, in its due place. And if my conduct shall not satisfy Your Majesty, you can resume these powers without fear of murmur on my part, or of opposition founded on my private interests.

The true remedy for the evil condition of the Netherlands, in the judgement of all men, is that England should be in the power of a person devoted and well-affected to Your Majesty's service; and it is the general opinion that the ruin of these countries, and the impossibility of preserving them to Your Majesty's crown, will result from the contrary position of English affairs. At Rome and elsewhere the rumour prevails that in this belief Your Majesty and His Holiness have thought of me as the best instrument you could choose for the execution of your designs, offended as you both are by the evil proceedings of the Queen of England, and by the wrongs which she has done to the Queen of Scotland, especially in sustaining, against her will, heresy in that kingdom.

Although neither for that nor for aught else do I believe myself to be fitted except in so far as it is Your Majesty's pleasure; yet, as in the world's opinion that task is incumbent on me, and as Your Majesty, ever ready to show your kindness to me, lends a willing ear to the project, and gives such evident marks of your desire that it should succeed, I cannot but long to kiss your hands for this favour; for although I esteem it at its just value, my own sentiments considered, it is of still great value in my eyes, because it is conformable with my fixed purpose to desire nothing from your Crown, even should Your Majesty offer it, beyond that which as your creature I can and ought to have, and beyond those things which by your grace and favour, when your arms are at liberty, may dispose me to manifest my zeal for your service and aggrandisement. That this zeal cannot be greater either in vassal, servant, or son, I hope Your Majesty will believe; and I hope God will grant me his grace to make it good.

Don John concluded with the promise that he would set off for Lombardy as soon as possible, but he made two definite requests, one was that he should be empowered to draw on the Fugger Bank in Antwerp, and the other that Lorenzo Spinola, presumably a financier, should be attached to his staff as financial adviser, or that he should send someone else to act in that capacity.[1]

Together with this letter Escobedo was sent to Madrid with further instructions of various kinds, for there were a number of points upon which Don John required enlightenment: to what extent he was genuine in this professed desire, and to what he was merely postponing his departure to the Low Countries in the hope that if he kept the negotiation going long enough Philip would send someone in his place, it is impossible to say, but in either case it is clear that he did not appreciate the seriousness of the

[1] cf. Gachard, L. P., *Correspondance de Philippe II*, vol. iv, pp. 161–6. Brussels, 1848–51.

situation there. At the same time there were a number of knotty problems to be solved, one of which was extremely personal, namely the treatment to be accorded to Don John's mother, and her son took the line that it would be advisable for her to live a very retired life. Nevertheless, the real object of Escobedo's mission was clearly to impress upon the King the necessity of keeping Don John well supplied with funds, not only for the future, but to enable him to pay his debts before he left Italy for the north.

The secretary reached Madrid in July, and he was soon extremely active there both in his master's interest and in his own, for he was hoping to get his son into the Royal secretariat, as well as to obtain an increase in his own salary and a bonus for some extra work he had done in Rome in bringing the Pope round to the Spanish way of thinking in the matter of Genoa. Philip was not long in answering his brother's letter: he thanked him for his acceptance of the post, but again stressed the fact that as the situation in the Netherlands was going from bad to worse the presence of the Governor was extremely urgent. Escobedo was therefore being sent back to Naples with the necessary papers, and Don John must be prepared to start the day after his secretary's arrival. He was to take the road through Savoy, for which journey the Viceroy of Milan, the Marquess of Ayamonte, was to provide horses and an escort, and in Burgundy this latter would be replaced by Belgian cavalry. The King made no comment on his brother's political arguments.[1]

Two further letters from Philip reached Don John at this time, one of them obviously in reply to some communication now lost. The first of these was confided to Escobedo, and concerned such matters as Don John's household, which should not be too large, and should largely be composed of natives of the Netherlands. The way for him to obtain the confidence and goodwill of the Provinces was to trust and employ the local people, using their language and adopting their manners and customs, so that in due course he might himself come to be regarded as a native. As for his mother, the suggestion that she should live in retirement was fully approved by the King, while if necessary her son could be pen-

[1] cf. Gachard, L. P., *Correspondance de Philippe II*, vol. iv, p. 260. Brussels, 1848–51.

sioned off in Italy. In a second letter, which was presumably in reply to one from Don John asking for a personal interview, he was told that he must abandon the idea. 'Although,' Philip wrote, 'I am well aware that as to time and everything else it is enough for you once to be informed of my wishes, I have thought it proper again to charge you in no wise and for no cause whatsoever to think of coming here, for, when your coming is permissible, no one would more desire or invite it than I should, on account of the delight I take in seeing you.'[1]

At this point Don John made the greatest blunder of his career, and in making it allowed the seething cauldron of the Netherlands to boil over – he again deliberately disobeyed his brother's order not to come to Spain. The consequences of his delay in proceeding to the seat of his governorship were to prove catastrophic, but what is most remarkable was Philip's attitude towards this act of the most flagrant disobedience. He knew that so far as the Low Countries were concerned time was all important, and ever since the death of Requesens he had been pressing this fact upon Don John, yet he now proceeded not only to overlook his brother's refusal to obey orders, but he acted as if time were a matter of no particular importance. The mental processes of Philip II are never easy to follow, but his behaviour in this particular instance defies analysis.

Don John duly sailed for Spain with a squadron of three vessels, and as soon as he was in Barcelona roads he wrote on August 22nd to Philip asking him not to take his arrival amiss, as it was a step to which he had been impelled 'not only by his desire to kiss His Majesty's hands, but by the interests of His Majesty's service, which were the guide of his conduct at all times, as Escobedo would more fully explain, until he could himself reach Court'. The King was then at the Escorial, and he replied in kindly vein, accepted his brother's excuses, and said that although the state of affairs prevented him from looking forward to their meeting with his usual satisfaction, he was sure that Don John had come not to raise but to smooth difficulties with regard to his mission to Flanders. Don John arrived at the

[1] cf. Gachard, L. P., *Correspondance de Philippe II*, vol. iv, pp. 260 and 276. Brussels, 1848–51.

Escorial early in September, and met with the favourable reception which by now he had come to expect.[1]

Sir William Stirling-Maxwell records, by no means on the best authority, an incident which he dramatically describes as 'ominous of evil' with regard to Don John's appearance at the Escorial. According to this story having received the embrace of the King, and having made his bow to the Queen, he was in the act of turning to kiss the hand of the young Infante Ferdinand when he stumbled backwards against him, and dealt the child such a blow in the face with the chape of his scabbard as to throw him on his back and bruise his head. Don John was profuse in his apologies, but although the King told him not to worry as there was no harm done his brother exclaimed, 'Is there no window to throw me out of?' Whereupon Philip told him in so many words not to make a fool of himself over what was a pure accident. What was 'ominous' about the episode is difficult to see.[2]

The King and Don John remained at the Escorial until September 22nd when they went to Madrid. At both places they discussed the situation in the Low Countries in all its aspects, apparently as if time had suddenly become of no account. Philip was not the man to leave any representative abroad without the most detailed instructions, and in view of his brother's known desire to establish himself on a throne somewhere he was probably wise to take this opportunity of discussing with him his position in respect of Mary, Queen of Scots, once he had established himself in Flanders. At any rate it is difficult to believe that the instructions forwarded to Don John soon after his departure were not the result of discussions held before he left.

The memorandum began with the injunction that England was not to be invaded until the Low Countries were pacified, and until it was certain that no opposition would be offered by France. 'You are to consider,' Philip reminded his brother, 'what a mistake it would be to leave our own dominions in danger while we are trying to take possession of those of other people.' The assistance that might be provided by the English Catholics was to be

---

[1] cf. Gachard, L. P., *Correspondance de Philippe II*, vol. iv, pp. 321–2. Brussels, 1848–51.

[2] *Don John of Austria*, vol. ii, p. 123. London, 1883.

carefully examined and weighed, 'for no kingdom is so weak that it can be conquered without aid from within'. Don John was to get on the most amiable terms with Elizabeth that he could, to acquire the most detailed possible knowledge of English naval and military resources, and to take every means of suborning the English ministers. With regard to the Queen herself Philip proved a shrewd judge of the character of his erstwhile sister-in-law. 'And as you are aware of the nature of that Queen, and how she usually gets into correspondence and relations with the persons whom she thinks she might perhaps marry, it may be that, by some roundabout way, she may entertain the same notions about you, and draw you into correspondence. If this should happen, you must not be by any means backward, but let her run on as she pleases, as it will afford a good occasion of furthering the aforesaid design.'

The actual invasion of England was to be effected with troops withdrawn from the Low Countries under pretext that they were needed for service in North Africa. The expeditionary force must take with it a sufficient supply of provisions, and also arms for the English Catholics, but in the first instance nothing should be said about the Queen of Scots for fear that Elizabeth might have her put to death. Plymouth, Falmouth, Southampton, or Liverpool were suggested as possible ports for disembarkation, but the one nearest to Mary's place of imprisonment was to be preferred, and once she had been freed she was to be placed at the head of the expedition. As for Don John himself, he was not to land in England until a substantial bridgehead had been established. The whole enterprise was to be carried out in a spirit of 'liberality, kindness, and forgiveness' and the less said about rebellion and heresy the better.

The great brotherly love with which I regard and always have regarded you makes me desire the success of this affair, because I consider in it, next to the service of God, the means it may afford me of showing how much I love you; in token whereof I now assure you that, if all goes well with this enterprise of England, it will please me to see you settled there and married to the Queen of Scots – a marriage which I understand she desires, and which indeed will be due to the man who shall deliver her from so great misery, and set her free and in possession of her realms, even to one whose quality and valour might not, as yours do, of themselves deserve it.

In case of success there will be some things to fix and determine; but upon these it is not expedient to enter till the time shall come. Meanwhile, it is sufficient to advise you that your settlement in the aforesaid kingdom will have to be in such form and on such conditions as shall appear to me expedient, for my service and for the good of our affairs and States.[1]

In effect, Philip saw that a Spanish interest could be served by the establishment of his brother on a throne in London or Dublin, which would not be the case were his kingdom to be in the Levant.

It was officially announced that Don John would travel to Flanders by way of Barcelona and the north of Italy, but in reality it had been decided that he should proceed by a more direct route. So, towards the middle of October, he left Madrid, and for what proved to be the last time went to pay a visit to Doña Magdalena de Ulloa at Abrojo. Whether she had some premonition that they would not meet again in this world is impossible to say, but their parting seems to have upset her considerably.[2] The better to conceal Don John's movements it had been put about that he would return from Abrojo to Madrid to take farewell of the Royal Family, while in actual fact he went direct to the Low Countries, though whether disguised as a Moorish servant or not would appear to be in some doubt. He was accompanied by Ottavio Gonzaga, and two or three servants, among whom was a French postilion, whose knowledge of travelling in France is said to have been encyclopedic.

On October 24th he was at Irun, and from there he wrote to the King.

I have just arrived here at Irun, never in my life having experienced so much fatigue as in this single journey, for, the

---

[1] Arch. Gen. de Simancas, Legajo 570.

[2] cf. Camilo Maria, Father Abad, S.J., *Doña Magdalena de Ulloa*, p. 179. Comillas, 1959.

horses being few, we have been obliged to ride the same often for twelve leagues,[1] and sometimes for sixteen, and in addition to consider ourselves lucky if we could get away from the post-houses within two hours, or a little less, after our coming hither. So Your Majesty will believe we have undergone much fatigue and had little sleep, although our pace has been slow, in spite of which I have been troubled by a return of some old ailments. Yet, God willing, they shall not stop me, seeing it is so important to the service of God and Your Majesty that I should surmount all complaints and difficulties. I am therefore only waiting for Ottavio who, in order to save time, went to Fuenterrabia, while I came on here to have all things ready to proceed. A French merchant has just arrived. He does not speak favourably, they tell me, of the safety of the roads; but I am neither doubtful nor apprehensive of pushing on, since there are so many reasons and obligations to do so.

Now, Sir, the pressing matter is that you should conclude the arrangements for money, and along with that send me Escobedo; for without these two things I do not know how to make a beginning, and it is at first that I specially wish to be provided with means, which afterwards may be supplied to me with little advantage. And as cases may arise in which you would be glad to aid me with your own blood, if it would avail anything, I once more entreat that Your Majesty will now assist with what I require which is money, money, and more money, for without this it would have been better not to have hazarded so great a stake.

I know not that I have anything further to tell or to ask of Your Majesty. Ottavio has just arrived with Garcia de Arce; and I therefore end my letter in order to proceed on our journey, praying Our Lord to keep Your Majesty in health and happiness.[2]

Another six or seven days took Don John to Paris, where, according to Brantôme, never a witness whose evidence should be

[1] One league approximates to three and a half miles.

[2] cf. Gachard, L. P., *Correspondance de Philippe II*, vol. iv, p. 446. Brussels, 1848–51. It is to be noted that during the sixteenth century the general price level rose by one hundred per cent, and in the case of some commodities, such as wheat, by two hundred per cent.

accepted unchecked, he was present at a Court ball at the Louvre. On all grounds, especially in view of the need for secrecy, this seems highly improbable, and there is no hint of it in a letter which he wrote to his brother from the Spanish embassy in the French capital on October 31st at six o'clock in the morning.

After having suffered much fatigue on the way on account of the bad state of the roads and the constant rain, and having been detained half a day at Bordeaux, not being allowed to pass, and having fallen in with a Frenchman, in whose company I travelled two days, we acting as his servants, and I having carried his portmanteau for three posts; in short, having suffered much fatigue and little rest, it has pleased God that we should arrive here last night. I should have been here before, but for these delays, about which, if I can, I will write more at large to Antonio Pérez, though it will not be now, for I am in haste to depart, because in coming to this house of the ambassador, as he will write, I have been seen and recognized by his servants, and the houses of ambassadors are closely watched. I believe, therefore, that it will not be long before some report of my arrival gets wind, seeing that everyone is expecting it; and since a reasonable suspicion and a few whispers may coincide with each other, Your Majesty will perceive that it is better to avoid the danger which may thus arise.

Don John's immediate problem was to decide at what point he should enter the Netherlands. He had originally thought of Gravelines or Cambrai, but there was always the possibility that the inhabitants of these towns might refuse to receive him, or that he might get shut up in them: in any event, if he failed there he could only fall back on Paris, which would be inconvenient from many points of view, not least because that city was itself in a very unsettled condition. After anxious deliberation, therefore, it was decided that the best course would be for him to begin his work at Luxembourg. All this he explained in his letter to the King, and he concluded it with a further appeal for money and for the return of Escobedo.

Accordingly he left Paris as soon as he had finished writing to Philip, and went first to Joinville where he met the Duke of

Guise – *le balafré* – who was the cousin of Mary, Queen of Scots, and brother of that Duke of Mayenne who had served under his command in the Mediterranean. From there he passed on by way of Metz to Luxembourg, where he arrived on November 3rd, to be greeted by news which was to render his task almost insuperable, and which must have made him bitterly regret the time he had wasted since his appointment – the news was of the massacre at Antwerp which has gone down to history as the 'Spanish Fury'.

12

Don John and William of Orange

IT WOULD BE IMPOSSIBLE TO EXAGGERATE THE IMPORT-
ance of the Revolt of the Netherlands in the history of Europe
during the second half of the sixteenth century, for it produced an
international situation which might otherwise never have arisen.
Had Charles V not made the fatal mistake of burdening Philip
with what remained of the Duchy of Burgundy the decline of
Spain might well have been delayed for many years; she would
have been able to concentrate upon what were her real interests
in southern Europe, the Mediterranean, and the Americas, and
this task would in all probability not have overtaxed her resources.
Equally, the clash with England would in all probability have been
postponed, if not altogether avoided, for during the reign of
Elizabeth I the real cause of dispute between London and Madrid
was neither religion nor rivalry in the New World, but English
dislike of the control of the Low Countries by a Great Power, and to
prevent this England had fought on many a previous occasion just
as she was to fight many times in the future. The Netherlands were
no concern of Spain, and in her effort to retain them she ruined her
self, with consequences which were felt throughout Christendom.

At the same time it would, perhaps, be unfair to blame Charles
overmuch for developments which it would have been difficult for
him to have foreseen. He had himself been born in Ghent, and as a
Fleming he had never lost his personal popularity in the seventeen
provinces which constituted his inheritance in the Low Countries.
His strength and weakness lay in the differences which existed
between his subjects there. In Flanders, Brabant, and Hainault
there was a powerful landed aristocracy; Ghent and Bruges
enjoyed a civic independence comparable with that of the cities of
northern Italy in the earlier Middle Ages; and in Holland and
Friesland there was a seafaring population with very decided views

The
NETHERLANDS
during
DON JOHN'S
GOVERNORSHIP

NORTH

SEA

FRIES-
LAND

DRENTHE

OVERYSSEL

GELDER-
LAND

Utrecht

CLEVES

UPPER
GELDERLD

Bruges

Antwerp

Ghent

FLANDERS

BRABANT

LIÈGE

LIMBURG

Cologne

Brussels

Gembloux
X

Liège

ARTOIS

HAINAULT

Namur

LUXEM-
BURG

THE EMPIRE

FRANCE

LORRAINE

HOLLAND		HAINAULT	
UTRECHT		LUXEMBG	
ZEELAND		LIÈGE	

0   Miles   100

WBromage

as to its own rights, and by no means amenable to any control by the central government. More recently, religious differences had added to the general lack of cohesion, for on the whole the north tended to be Calvinist, while the south remained true to Rome. The Netherlands, it may further be added, had traditional ties with France, England, and the Empire, but none at all with Spain. Charles knew his own fellow-countrymen, and although he had to crack the whip over them from time to time, his administration was tactful and moderate; furthermore, throughout his reign he was aided by the fact that England was no serious danger, and on many occasions was his ally.

Of the seventeen provinces which formed the Netherlands at the accession of Philip II, the greater number had been gradually collected together by successive Dukes of Burgundy in the previous century either by marriage, or cession, or conquest. The tie which bound these provinces together was purely personal, and they were held by different titles. Four were duchies, five were lordships, six were countships, and two were margravates. Each province had its own peculiar government; some had special privileges guaranteed to them by charter; while no native of one province could constitutionally hold office in another.

During the early years of the Revolt of the Netherlands the international repercussions were, it may be noted, unimportant: the neighbouring Powers were largely occupied with their own problems, and in any case it was by no means clear exactly what was at stake. The hostility to Spain was at this stage on national grounds, and there was unquestionably a desire to get rid of the Spanish troops, whose presence seemed to serve no useful purpose, after the war with France came to an end in 1559. What changed the nature of the struggle as the sixties passed into the seventies was the appearance of the Prince of Orange at the head of the malcontents, and with the full support of the moneyed interests to whom allusion has been made on an earlier page. His career is an excellent illustration of the cosmopolitanism of the age in which he lived, for the man whose name was for all time to be associated with the cause of Dutch independence was a German by birth, had commanded the armies of Charles V, and took his title from a principality on the Rhône.

William was not a particularly good general, but as a propagandist he has had few equals, and no superior, in history. He realized that a legend of Spanish cruelty and barbarism had to be created if Europe were to be induced to sympathize with the revolted Netherlanders, and the Inquisition was the most natural choice of weapons. In actual fact the Low Countries already possessed an Inquisition which Philip himself declared was 'more merciless than the one here'[1] and the rumour that the Spanish variety was to be introduced into the Low Countries as a means of subduing them was little more than propaganda to discredit Spain and to incite rebellion.[2] The truth on this very disputed subject has recently been very well stated by Dr Kamen:

Apart from his Italian states Philip had little serious intention of exporting the Spanish Inquisition. Even in England, where he exercised some influence as husband of the Queen, no steps were ever taken to introduce the tribunal. The truth was that most European countries had their own machinery for dealing with heretics, and had no need for outside help. Besides this, the Spanish tribunal was not by nature a primarily anti-Protestant body, and would have needed substantial modification if introduced into some European states. Finally, the foreign policy of Philip II was by no means consistently anti-Protestant, so that the picture of Spain as a rabidly Catholic Power distorts the reality of sixteenth century international politics.[3]

William had never forgiven Philip for not appointing him Governor of the Netherlands when he returned to Spain in the summer of 1559, and thereafter he was a man with a grievance. Granvelle had fully realized this, and early wrote to the King, 'The Prince is a dangerous man, subtle, politic, professing to stand by the people, and to champion their interests, even against your edicts, but seeking only the favour of the mob, giving himself out sometimes as a Catholic sometimes as a Calvinist or Lutheran. He is a man to undertake any enterprise in secret which his own

[1] cf. Diericke, M., La Politique religieuse de Philippe II dans les anciens Pays-Bas, Hispania, vol. xvi (1956), p. 137.
[2] cf. Rolland, P., Histoire de Tournai, p. 197. Tournai, 1964.
[3] The Spanish Inquisition, p. 290. London, 1965.

vast ambition and inordinate suspicion may suggest.'[1] As for William's immediate followers they have been described by a modern historian as 'a parasitic group of riotous and profligate aristocrats, much given to eating, drinking, loud talking, and brawling. Nearly all of them, in spite of their great holdings of land, were deeply in debt'.[2] On the score of their morals there may be differences of opinion, but there can be none in respect of their indebtedness.

Philip sent various representatives from Madrid to govern the Netherlands, and the most famous was the Duke of Alba, who was there from 1567 to 1573, but they all experienced the same difficulty. They never had enough money to pay their troops, whose discipline in consequence became extremely lax, and on more than one occasion the *tercios* lived on the country. This did nothing to endear them to the inhabitants, who displayed an increasing reluctance to vote the money out of which the soldiers might have been paid, and thus more easily controlled by their officers. In this way the vicious circle was complete, and none of Philip's representatives succeeded in breaking it.

All the same from the Spanish point of view the situation improved under Requesens, who proved a very competent Governor. The state of France precluded any intervention by that country, and in the last resort Elizabeth was not prepared to do a great deal for people whom she really regarded as rebels against constituted authority. Furthermore, the Spaniards began winning a series of victories in the field, so Philip was fully justified in the optimistic note he struck in his letter of April 8th, 1576, to his brother, and the Grand Commander's policy did seem to be beginning to achieve definite results when he died. What brought about a complete reversal of the situation was the delay in Don John's arrival in Flanders for which he must bear the responsibility. Had he gone to the Low Countries in the spring as ordered it is impossible to believe that a horde of Philip's unpaid soldiers would have sacked Antwerp on November 4th in their quest for loot, and in the process butchered some eight thousand people without distinction of age, sex, or religion. Such was the 'Spanish

[1] Quoted by Harrison, F., *William the Silent*, p. 34. London, 1910.
[2] Walsh, W. T., *Philip II*, p. 349. New York, 1937.

Fury', and Don John was to spend the remaining two years of his life endeavouring to undo its consequences.[1]

How long it took for the news of what had happened at Antwerp to reach Luxembourg it is difficult to say, but on November 5th Don John wrote to his friend, Rodrigo de Mendoza, in a vein which could hardly have been more depressed.

You will have heard of my arrival at Paris from Antonio Pérez, to whom I wrote all that had happened up to that time. On the next day I continued my journey with great haste, which was necessary, because I had been seen and recognized by all the ambassador's servants, by whom the secret could not long have been kept. So I had neither time to write, nor dared to delay; but pushed on day and night, though the roads were so villainous and so infested with plague that I had to make great detours, and to ride the same horse for two days, which greatly increased the fatigue of the journey. At last, thank God, I reached this place on the 3rd of this month, and found the worst possible tidings of these Provinces; for only this one in which I am and Friesland, of which Robles has charge, can certainly be said not to be in revolt. The rest are leagued together and calling out troops and seeking foreign aid against the Spaniards, and making and repealing laws in their own fashion, all these things being done under the name and in behalf of the King, whose name is also used while they are taking steps to admit Orange into Brussels and fitting up a house for him there.

I have written to the Council in general, and to some of its members in particular, of my having come. I know not what the reply may be, nor whether they will receive me, but am waiting to hear this and other things, which Antonio Pérez will be able to tell better than I can as yet. Such is the miserable condition of affairs here, which may God remedy, for He only can do it. I am in great anxiety to hear news from home, and what is said there about my flight, and especially what has been done since my departure in the affair which I concerted between you and your brother, and which, being a matter of such moment to a

[1] How many Spaniards there were among the troops concerned is a moot point, and the vast majority were almost certainly Germans and Walloons.

house to which I desire all good and peace, gives me much anxiety. As I desire to know what has been settled, write it to me, and with all fulness, that I may understand it clearly.

Commend me to the Duke,[1] and say that of me which I say, and what there I shall understand is that which I can write to him; and of him and his health I hope for such news as I desire. I wish to inform our Orgacio[2] that if Marina dances in the house of Antonio Pérez, she is paying for her amusements in this country, where she was mistress of all her friends, whereas she is now among strangers; and that although this is not the worst fate one can suffer, he ought to pity me, who am so much his friend, instead of me pitying him for amusing himself far more than I myself am able to do.

Ottavio has arrived with buttocks much worn, and the same thing might have happened to your lordship had you slept as little and ridden as much as we, and gone through what we have undergone and are still undergoing, after calling upon Don Rodrigo and the Count of Orgaz. I kiss the hand of my lady, and I promise her she was amongst those most invoked, and the most cherished in my memory, and ever shall be, as is due to her own remembrance. I entreat her to write now she finds herself without the presence of her lover; and moreover I inform her that what she feels is neither more nor less than absent lovers usually feel. I do not go into further explanation, because her own feeling of it will be in proportion to her true love for me. I will write to her at greater length by another courier, but as I cannot do so now, I send her what news of me I can, to oblige her to send me news in return of herself, and let her take notice of the way in which this half-message is sent to her.

Of my one-eyed[3] I kiss the hands, I do not say the eyes, until I can write to her myself to bid her remember this friend

---

[1] Inigo, fifth Duke of Infantado, b. 1536, d. 1601. Elder brother of Rodrigo de Mendoza.

[2] The Count of Orgaz.

[3] The Princess of Eboli, widow of Ruiz Gómez, and generally accounted the mistress of Antonio Pérez.

of hers, who is now so entirely her own, that he cannot in these parts offer, nor has the means to offer, her payment of all he owes her; and this message of mine is couched in such courteous language, because it is well that it should be so phrased, being sent from so great a distance. Of our cousin I do not kiss the hands, because her cousin may do it without witnesses, since for this none can be so good as he. Let her bear in mind that she is to answer to me for the happiness of my greatest friend, whom may God help, and grant him all that He can give and I can pray for.[1]

If Don John felt despondent on November 5th, it is not difficult to imagine what his feelings must have been a few days later when he was informed of the full repercussions of the 'Spanish Fury', for the reaction was such that on the 8th the Pacification of Ghent united the whole seventeen provinces. By this treaty it was agreed that the Spaniards should be expelled from the Netherlands, and that an Estates-General from all the provinces should be summoned to take measures for the common safety and the future government. The Prince of Orange was to be lieutenant admiral, and general for Philip in Holland and Zeeland. There was to be freedom of trade and communication between the provinces. All prisoners should be released, and all confiscated property restored. The placards and ordinances issued against heresy should be suspended until the Estates-General had come to a decision on the point, but no discrimination should be shown against the Catholic religion outside the provinces of Holland and Zeeland, and if the property of prelates and other ecclesiastics in the north were alienated this should not be done without compensation. The power and prestige of Spain in the Low Countries had clearly reached their nadir, and the knowledge that he was to no small extent responsible cannot have done anything to reconcile Don John to the fact.

When he left Madrid his formal instructions were not ready, and they were sent on to him to Luxembourg by the Baron of Rassenghien, a Fleming as his name implies: they were of a definitely

---

[1] cf. Stirling-Maxwell, Sir William, *Don John of Austria*, vol. ii, pp. 437-9. London, 1883.

conciliatory nature. In the French patent Don John was styled 'Messire Jean d'Austriche', instead of 'Don', by way of adopting a form of address used in the Low Countries instead of the customary Spanish title.[1] The King's instructions were that he should go to the Netherlands, which had for some years been subject to troubles and agitations 'to our great regret', in order to bring about 'by good, just, and reasonable means, a true, stable, and durable pacification therein'. To this end he was to rule with his usual 'love, gentleness, and benevolence, according to the ancient laws, rights, and customs, had and kept in the time of His Imperial Majesty, now in glory, putting an end to all causes of offence arising out of the neglect of these, and giving just and reasonable contentment to all'.

Passing from the general to the particular Philip directed that the Councils of State, both general and privy, of finances, the Assembly of Estates, administration of law, and exercise of privileges were all to be placed on the old footing, while the tribunal known to the enemies of his master and himself as the Council of Blood, was to be abolished. A general pardon – 'the most ample which before God and our conscience can be allowed' – was to be granted, and the only person to be exempted was the Prince of Orange, who is described as 'the inventor, author, and contriver of all the evils that afflict the country'. With regard to the demobilization of the troops, the King trusted to the Estates for the necessary assistance in money and credit as far as it was in their power to give it, for it was not his wish to foment the war but to bring it to an end. For this purpose Don John was either to treat with the Estates of each province separately or to convoke the Estates-General as might seem to him best, 'always and before all things maintaining the rights of the Holy Roman Catholic faith and of the Crown'. Finally, he was ordered to assume, as his predecessors had usually done, in addition to the duties of Governor-General, the government of Brabant and Flanders in particular, and to place in the castles of Antwerp and Ghent such commanders as could be trusted.[2]

[1] His official designation was Lieutenant, Governor, and Captain-General of the Low Countries and the county of Burgundy.

[2] cf. Gachard, L. P., *Correspondance de Philippe II*, vol. iv, pp. 453 and 464. Brussels, 1848–51.

As is usual on these occasions this set of formal instructions was amplified in a private letter. In it the King told his brother that Rassenghien was a man worthy of confidence, and 'one of the best conducted' of his Flemish subjects, but all the same it must not be forgotten that he was a Fleming by birth. In general the instructions were to be interpreted as meaning that Don John was to make the best bargain possible with the Provinces, shaping his course according to circumstances, and conceding as little, while saving as much, of the Royal prerogative as he could. The withdrawal of the Spanish troops was a matter of the first importance, and if by yielding on this point Don John saw his way to effecting a pacification of the country he was at liberty to do so, but in that case the Estates were to be told plainly that if they were to have their way on this point they must pay for it both by finding the necessary cash and by accepting liability for any arrears, 'a thing which they have always professed to be willing to do to be relieved of the soldiery'.[1] In an even more confidential note Philip advised his brother to be 'very careful of his soul', and 'very wary in his love affairs', from which latter observation it would appear that the King knew more about his brother's amours than the latter probably imagined.

The Pacification of Ghent marked the apogee of William of Orange, and from the moment of Don John's arrival in the Netherlands he was on his guard against the other's charm. He was from the beginning prepared to resist all Don John's blandishments, and he showed himself by no means averse to plans to kidnap, if not to murder him.[2] In the meantime he did everything to enhance his own power, and in January, 1577, the Pacification of Ghent was confirmed by the Union of Brussels. All this time Don John was kicking his heels at Luxembourg, engaged in tedious, and sometimes acrimonious, negotiations, with the Estates-General at Brussels as to the conditions in which he could enter upon his functions. It was at this time, as mentioned on an earlier page,[3] that his mother came to see him.

[1] *ibid.*, vol. iv, p. 472. Brussels, 1848–51.
[2] cf. Cabrera de Córdoba, L., *Felipe II, Rey de España*, vol. ii, p. 399. Madrid 1877.
[3] See pp. 21.

At the beginning of 1577 Don John moved from Luxembourg to Huy, a fortified town on the banks of the Meuse which belonged to the Bishop of Liège. There the negotiations with the Estates-General continued, but before long they appeared likely to founder upon a quite unexpected obstacle, namely the method by which the Spanish troops should be evacuated from the Low Countries. When the matter had first been mooted the rebels had shown themselves wholly indifferent as to the manner in which this was effected so long as their unwelcome guests left at the first opportunity, and Don John had decided that they should go by sea, since in this way, under cover of a voyage to Spain, they might be employed to further his design on England and for the liberation of the Queen of Scots. Now, however, the Estates-General insisted that the troops should be moved by land, and gave as their reason the difficulty of providing a sufficient number of transports which might necessitate the postponement of the operation until the spring – a state of affairs which did not appeal to them at all. Whether this was the reason as well as the excuse for their change of attitude may be doubted, and it is at least possible that pressure from London also played its part.

However this may be, Elizabeth had already shown signs of alarm at the prospect of a Spanish armament off the English coast, and she had instructed her representative in the Low Countries to express her uneasiness at the departure of the troops by sea, and her suspicion that in this case England, not Spain, might be their destination. Don John laughed this off in his discussions with the English ambassador, and assured him that the troops were destined for the Levant: he went even further, begged for the Queen's portrait, and expressed his intention as soon as possible of paying a private visit to England for the pleasure of kissing her hand.[1] Don John certainly had the right approach where a woman was concerned, and Elizabeth replied in like vein. He received assurances of her most cordial friendship, and he was told that she had not only refused aid to the Estates-General, but would assist Philip against them if the French took any part in the quarrel: at the same time the continuance of these friendly intentions

---

[1] Philip made a marginal note on the despatch informing him of this promise – 'This was saying a good deal.'

depended wholly on the evacuation of the troops by land and not by sea.[1]

At this point, strange as it may seem at first sight, Don John had time on his side. Spanish prospects could not be worse, and there was always the chance that they might improve; William the Silent was making little attempt to conceal his ambitions, and it was not everyone who was prepared to displace the House of Habsburg for that of Orange; and the behaviour of the more extreme Calvinists was putting a severe strain upon their Catholic allies of the Pacification of Ghent. The rebels realized this fact as well as Don John, and they determined to force the pace, so they endeavoured to put a pistol to his head by asking him two questions – would he give his approval to the Pacification, and would he consent to the immediate evacuation of the Spanish troops by land?

Orange and his supporters appear to have forgotten that young as he was the man with whom they were dealing had very considerable experience of the skilful diplomatists of the Serenissima and the Sublime Porte, and that if he was not their match he was no novice: accordingly, he neglected no opportunity of confusing the issue and prolonging the negotiation until his fortunes changed. He gave his answer to the two questions in writing on January 24th, 1577, and it proved to be in a document of no inconsiderable length. Dismissal of foreign troops, pacification, amnesty, the release of prisoners, and government on the principle of Charles V were duly promised. The King would be consulted as to the meeting of the Estates-General. On the other hand Don John required the Estates to pay the arrears due to the troops and to provide the transports to convey them to Spain, for if at all possible he was determined to hold them to their former position in this matter. The Estates were also to disband their own troops, and to produce reliable ecclesiastical and legal authority to show that the Pacification contained nothing at variance with the interests of the Catholic religion or the Royal supremacy, particularly in Holland and Zeeland. By now Don John had taken the measure of William the Silent, so he inserted a clause by which the Estates were to engage themselves that Orange would take no

[1] cf. Motley, J. L., *Rise of the Dutch Republic*, vol. iii, p. 113. London, 1856.

measure to remove his eldest son from Spain where he was in residence under some form of duress: finally, he claimed the right of surrounding himself both with troops and civil servants drawn from any nation he chose.

As may be supposed this reply was not much to the liking of the more extreme of Don John's opponents, and in particular to Orange and his immediate supporters, but there is evidence that it made an impression upon the more moderate elements among the rebels. Its immediate effect was a bitter wrangle between Don John and the commissioners who had come to see him at Huy, and during the course of it he seems to have lost his temper on one occasion in particular when he left them in no doubt concerning his personal opinion of them and their policy. Soon, however, he realized that he had gone too far, and that conciliation was essential, so he brought his personal charm to bear, and the commissioners returned to Brussels after taking a friendly leave of him. By this time, too, there were outside influences working for a peaceful settlement, notably the Empire, where Maximilian II had died in the previous October, a victim, it is to be feared, to his love of good cheer. His successor was his son Rudolf II, Don John's old friend and companion, but although he was much more sympathetic towards Spanish policy than his father had been he was also much less effective as a ruler. That he was a man of considerable culture admits of no question, and there is no reason to believe that because of his interest in the occult he was in the habit of conversing with the Evil One. We are told that the new Emperor was of 'middling stature, pleasing countenance, and his eyes sparkled with remarkable spirit and vivacity'. Furthermore, 'he was elegant in his deportment, affable and unassuming in his conversation', while, 'he was wholly devoid of that pride which is often inseparable from exalted dignity'. In short, Rudolf's real weakness as Holy Roman Emperor was 'his total inability to rule either in peace or war'.[1]

The upshot was the Perpetual Edict which was signed on February 17th, 1577, without, incidentally, the approval of William of Orange. It consisted of a long preamble, eighteen articles, and a final attesting clause. Of the articles the most

[1] cf. Coxe, W., *History of the House of Austria*, vol. ii, p. 727. London, 1807.

important were those which provided for complete oblivion where past offences were concerned; for the confirmation by Philip of the Pacification of Ghent, seeing that it had been pronounced by high authority to contain nothing prejudicial, but on the contrary to be rather advantageous, to the Catholic faith and the Royal rights; for the departure within forty days and by land, of the foreign troops, who were not to be recalled except in the event of a foreign war; for reasonable compensation for any damage done by these troops in the Low Countries; for the immediate release of all prisoners, except William's eldest son, whose case was to be dealt with as the Estates-General should determine; for the maintenance of the privileges, usages, and customs of the Netherlands; and for an oath to observe this Edict to be taken by Don John and his successors in office.

On their part the rebels promised to disband their troops, to pay 600,000 livres towards the expenses of the evacuation of the Royal troops, and to discharge the arrears of pay due to the German mercenaries; to take an oath to maintain the Catholic religion, and to receive and acknowledge Don John as Governor and Captain-General of the Low Countries. This document was signed by Don John on February 12th at Marché-en-Famine, where he had moved from Huy; it was published on the 17th of the same month in Brussels; and on April 7th, it received the King's approval in Madrid, when Philip also wrote a letter to each of the Provincial Estates thanking them for their dutiful devotion to his service. On May 1st, Don John was able to make his formal entry into Brussels.

Although Alba was highly critical of the Perpetual Edict there was a great deal to be said in its favour from the Spanish point of view. Philip had always contended that the essential principle for which he was struggling was the maintenance of the Catholic religion, and this was now conceded; furthermore, the bluff of William of Orange was called, the Catholic population which had thrown itself into his arms after the 'Spanish Fury' was drawn back into the Royal cause, and Spain had recovered a good moral position. For a brief space it appeared as if Don John had added the pacification of the Low Countries to his other laurels.

His own views can be gathered from letters which he wrote to

Garcia de Toledo and Rodrigo de Mendoza. To the first, writing on February 21st, he said, 'Some of conditions of this peace must appear hard, and to me they seem very hard; but to save religion and obedience, when this and the States themselves were lost, it has been necessary to bear with them, making account of everything as if happening by chance. For the rest, we must trust to time, that which God has given us being not a little.'[1]

To Rodrigo de Mendoza he had written four days earlier:

Now as to affairs here I will say little. Referring you for the most part to the other long letters; in substance the peace has been made in His Majesty's name between me and the Estates, and if the conditions of it are not such as might have been desired and as I strove to obtain, yet we have arrived at what was possible, which is the goal of Kings. In fine, religion and obedience being saved as is the case, the rest time must show you, and I hope in God it will show it quickly; and with this, one may account these Estates as things recovered by chance; for if we were to attempt to carry the day by arms the best that could happen to us would be the total and perpetual ruin of this country, and the worst, God knows, and the people foresee it, seeing the necessity and straitness of the times.

Yet, as I said before, time and circumstances and things settling themselves little by little will give us in the end this gain from out of what seemed, when I came here, so great a loss, God knows by the fault of so many or of whom chiefly. I owe him thanks that I am now myself dismissing people and undoing preparations for war, which I had in a state of some forwardness; and in this we begin to occupy ourselves, the Estates and I. The Spaniards are going away, and they carry my soul with them for I had rather be enchanted than see this happen. It is for God to pardon the sorcery which goes on yonder, and from which springs so much evil. In the meetings which have been held between these men and me, they have driven me on so many occasions to lose my temper, that although I have kept it in countless cases, yet there have been others when I have lost it, and have rated them roundly, telling

[1] Doc. Ined., iii, pp. 181–2.

them what they are and what they deserve, so that on every point we made ourselves useless to one another. They fear me, and consider me a choleric person; and I abhor them and consider them very great scoundrels; and so it is needful now that I should go and another come, for so sure as we meet it is certain a new disagreement will arise, and do mischief. I have therefore written home very urgently – let this be a secret between us – that I neither can nor will remain here any longer, since I have, by God's grace, accomplished that for which I came, which was to put an end to the war, according to the orders given me, when both parties were ready ranked against one another.[1]

That this last sentence represented Don John's considered opinion there is no reason to doubt: he had accomplished the task with which he had been entrusted, and he now wished to return to Spain. He clearly did not find either the Low Countries or their inhabitants attractive, and he saw no future for himself in Northwest Europe now that the Spanish troops were being withdrawn by land: had there still been a possibility of using them for a blow to liberate the Scottish Queen it is permissible to wonder whether he would have been quite so eager to quit the Netherlands at this particular moment. All this is idle speculation, for Don John had no choice in the matter, since he was Philip's subject as well as his brother, and Philip ordered him to stay at his post. As on previous occasions what the King believed to be the interests of Spain took precedence of the wishes of his own relations.

[1] cf. Stirling-Maxwell, Sir William, *Don John of Austria*, vol. ii, pp. 441–2. London 1883.

13

The Closing Scene

AT FIRST ALL SEEMED TO BE GOING WELL, AND DON JOHN
was received with great enthusiasm everywhere he went. His charm
was irresistible, and one observer wrote, 'Don John surpasses
Circe; no one comes before him without being transformed into a
worshipper. All the lords are drunk with his good graces.'[1] An
excellent example of his popularity was afforded by a visit he paid
to Louvain in the middle of April, when under his patronage the
game of popinjay was revived with unusual splendour: Don John
himself appeared with his cross-bow, and at the fifth shot brought
the popinjay down amid the delighted plaudits of the multitude.
He was thereupon proclaimed king of the bowmen for the year,
and a golden popinjay was hung round his neck, after which there
was a service in church. 'He then,' we are told, 'gave to the society
of cross-bowers a hundred crowns to drink and be merry, and ban-
queted, to his great cost and charge, the best of the town, he himself being present in person with exceeding familiarity to all men,
and getting credit marvellously by that means.'[2]

It was the same when he made his official entry into Brussels on
May 1st. Triumphal arches spanned the streets, flags waved on
every side, and the walls were hung with tapestries displaying
scenes from the battle of Lepanto. The windows and house-tops
were filled with the gayest of holiday-makers, and flowers rained
down on the hero of the day. A gilded car, drawn by two horses in
gilt trappings, was a feature of the pageant, and in it was seated a
Flemish lady representing Abundance, with the arms of the
seventeen Provinces displayed around her, and a quantity of
broken weapons at her feet to indicate the happy results that were

[1] Letter in French, without signatures or address, May 15 or 25. Public Record
Office, Flanders, 1577. No. 29.

[2] Advertisements from Brussels, April 18. Public Record Office, Flanders, 1577.
No. 29.

expected from the rule of the new Governor-General. Another car contained a galley with Turkish captives in chains to commemorate his great victory. As Dr Wylson wrote to Sir Francis Walsingham:

The pomp was great on Monday, for that the people was well disposed to bid Don John welcome, trusting him now more than they ever did mistrust him before. The next day they agreed to his admission. Upon Saturday he had his oath given him, and was established Governor with great approbation of the people. Upon Sunday there was a general procession, Don John bearing his torch bareheaded after the sacrament, the Bishop of Liège on the one side of him and the Pope's Nuncio on the other side, so many torches carried before the sacrament as their great light caused darkness with the smoke, especially to those who stood in windows as lookers-on. Upon Monday a post came out of Spain (as they said) and brought King Philip's ratification of the peace, and for all other things that Don John had agreed unto, besides assurance of money to the value of 400,000 crowns.[1]

Meanwhile the evacuation of the Spanish troops was presenting difficulties of which the financial was by no means the least important. The soldiers were ready to move before the money due under the Perpetual Edict was forthcoming, and Don John had to put his hand in his own pocket to no inconsiderable extent. Escobedo was also tireless in his efforts to raise the necessary cash, and from these transactions he emerges as an industrious and efficient official, but utterly devoid of tact, for on one occasion he writes to the King, 'I have been unable to borrow a real, nor will any man here trust Your Majesty, without holding some security,' and on another, 'People have lost all liking to deal with Your Majesty, and in truth they are not wrong.' It was outspokenness of this nature which enabled his enemies at Court to prepare the way for the fate which was so soon to overtake him. Not that he confined his acidity to his own fellow-countrymen, for after he had administered the oath to the Duke of Aerschot when the latter took command of the castle at Antwerp, he burst out, 'God with

[1] Public Record Office, Flanders, 1577. No. 29.

his angels help you if you keep your oath; if not, may the Devil carry you away body and soul.'

The soldiers themselves were proving far from easy to control, for although their fighting qualities were unimpaired, as they were shortly to demonstrate, their discipline left a great deal to be desired. They were also labouring under a considerable sense of grievance, for they were more than a little indignant at the manner in which they were being hurried out of the country to please the very rebels whom they had been sent there to subdue.[1] Then, again, Don John had ordered them to abstain from all active hostilities, and this order had been obeyed, but no such forbearance had been displayed on the other side, where sieges had been pushed on and fortresses captured in the name of Orange and the Estates. All the same early in April the troops were concentrated at Maestricht to the number of some thirty thousand, including women, children and camp-followers, and by the end of that month they were on the march to Italy.

Nor were the soldiers Don John's only difficulty, for the generals were also extremely fractious. He had wished to put Don Alonso de Vargas in command of the army on the march, but Valdes, Romero, and Dávila refused to serve under him on the ground that they were senior in rank. Don John gave way, and appointed Peter Ernest, Count of Mansfeldt, in his place; but the nomination of a foreigner aroused a further storm, in which Vargas now joined; Don John, however, refused to make any further concessions, but all the evidence goes to show that he had great sympathy with the officers and men who were being thus unceremoniously bundled out of the Low Countries, regarding them as victims of hard political necessity. His own position was extremely delicate, and in the circumstances he did not feel that it would be advisable to review the troops before they left, though he knew that this decision could not fail to give offence. 'Your Highness may send us away now,' said Sancho de Avila, who had been in command at Antwerp, 'but you will very soon have to call us back,' and there is no reason to suppose that Don John disagreed with these sentiments.

He certainly did everything in his power to make the parting

[1] cf. Montesa, Marqués de, *Julián Romero*, pp. 428–30. Madrid, 1952.

pleasant, and he wrote personal letters of recommendation to Philip with respect to several of the generals, especially Vargas whose language both with regard to the King and himself had been remarkably uninhibited. 'It may be,' he wrote, 'that in the heat of his passion he may write to Your Majesty with the freedom which he has used towards me. I therefore entreat Your Majesty not only to take no notice of it, but to show him the favour and give him the reward which he deserves, which I will take as a boon bestowed on myself; and I will also take it kind that Your Majesty will let him know that I have spoken on his behalf, and not in vain, that he may change the ill opinion which he has conceived of me.'[1]

There was one man who was under no illusions as to the significance of what was taking place, and that was William of Orange, for it was far from being in his interests that the Low Countries should return to their old allegiance. Astute as he was he had been temporarily circumvented by Don John. He had never imagined it possible that any representative of the King of Spain would accept the Pacification of Ghent, and now that the unexpected had happened, to the great joy of the nobles and the Catholics, he found himself on the horns of a dilemma: either he must repudiate his own handiwork or betray to the world that the country he had so arrogantly claimed was united under his leadership was in fact hopelessly divided. His first step was to put pressure on the deputies of Holland and Zeeland to decline to sign the Perpetual Edict, and he refused to allow its publication in those two provinces so that the inhabitants should not know the details of the pacification which had been rejected in their name. Then, skilful propagandist that he was, he issued a justification for his action. He alleged that the Estates had ratified the Edict, not indeed without waiting for his advice, but before it was possible that they could receive it; that sufficient guarantees had not been obtained for the free exercise of the reformed religion in Holland and Zeeland; that the main fortresses, instead of being razed to the ground, were to be garrisoned by the King and the Estates,

[1] *Sommier Discours de Justes Causes et Raisons qu'ont constrainct les Estats Generaulx des Paid Bas de Pourveoir a leur Deffence contre le Seigneur Don Jehan d'Austrice.* Antwerp, 1577.

which meant that in due course they would fall back into the hands of the King; and that it was unjust that not only should the Spanish troops be permitted to depart with all their plunder, but that the Provinces should be compelled to provide funds to pay men who had so long despoiled and oppressed them.

This was in reality the merest quibble, for the Pacification of Ghent, which had received the whole-hearted support of Orange, had been confirmed by the Perpetual Edict, so that Holland and Zeeland possessed all the guarantees for religious freedom which had been secured to them at Ghent. No mention of razing the fortresses had been made in the Pacification or in the discussions which preceded the Edict, and if this was as important as William maintained he, and no one else, was responsible for the omission. As for the evacuation of the Spanish troops, although the Provinces might consider it a hardship to pay for this, the alternatives were either to purchase their peaceful departure or to drive them out by force, which, even in the unlikely event of it proving possible, would unquestionably be very costly in money and lives. In effect, Orange was on very weak ground, and his policy was marked by considerable vacillation. When he found that the Edict was more popular than he had anticipated he offered to give his adhesion to it on condition that the Estates would agree that if the Spanish troops were not withdrawn by a certain date they would themselves drive them out.[1] In the circumstances of the moment this stipulation meant nothing at all, and his policy merely laid Orange open to those same charges of double-dealing which he so frequently brought against Philip.

Don John then proceeded to call William's bluff. By the advice of the Duke of Aerschot he sent one Dr Eibertus Leoninus, an eminent jurist, to him to propose terms of reconciliation with the King. Orange was told that his great power and influence would enable him at the present moment to do Philip a great service, the reward for which it would be for him to name. Don John had come to make peace, to restore the ancient prosperity and the ancient government of the Low Countries, and in the King's name to forgive all the errors of the past, as well as to promote the very objects which Orange himself had for so long been struggling to

[1] cf. Motley, J. L., *The Rise of the Dutch Republic*, vol. iii, p. 103. London, 1856.

attain. Then came a very shrewd thrust to the effect that if William had conceived it his duty to draw the sword for these objects it was now his duty for the same reason to sheathe it, and co-operate with Don John.

It would appear that at this stage Don John was of the opinion that William desired to sell himself at the highest price possible, and that he had not yet realized that his antagonist's object was to substitute himself for Philip as the ruler of the Netherlands. William, on the other hand, could hardly admit this openly, so in reply all he gave Leoninus was, not an indication of the terms upon which he would make his peace with the King, but a long and rambling statement of the reasons why no proposals to this effect could be entertained. In effect, his tactics were as shifty and tortuous as any that he blamed on his opponents.

At the same time Don John was under no illusions as to the power of his adversary, and therefore of the necessity, if at all possible, of coming to terms with him. On this point he wrote frankly – perhaps a little too frankly – to his brother.

> In the Netherlands the name of Your Majesty is as much abhorred and despised as that of the Prince of Orange is loved and feared. I am negotiating with him, and giving him every security, for I see that the establishment of peace as well as the maintenance of the Catholic religion and obedience to Your Majesty depend now upon him. Things have reached that pass that it is necessary to make a virtue of necessity. If he lend an ear to my proposals it will be only upon very advantageous conditions; but to these it will be necessary to submit rather than lose everything.[1]

Don John's adversaries were not content with a verbal opposition, and they were only too ready to proceed from words to deeds, that is to say to kidnap and later to murder him. Attempts of a similar nature had been made, and had very nearly succeeded, against Alba and Requesens, and Don John had to be constantly on his guard. To what extent Orange was privy to these plots it would probably be just as well not to inquire.

[1] cf. Gachard, L. P., *Correspondance de Guillaume le Taciturne*, Prince d'Orange, vol. iii. Pef. lii. Brussels, 1847.

Not surprisingly, Don John's health began to show signs of giving way under the strain to which it was being subjected. Ever since his arrival at Luxembourg he had worked from morning to night, often without any proper interval for meals, and about this time he had three attacks of fever, though what this signified in modern medical terms it is not easy to decide. Anyhow, we are told that he was becoming pale and thin, losing his vivacity of age and approach, as well as his natural buoyancy.

It was about this time that he was visited at Brussels by Sir Philip Sidney, his brother's godson, who had been sent by Elizabeth on the death of Maximilian II to convey the customary messages of condolence and congratulation to the new Emperor. He was returning through the Low Countries when he had his audience of Don John. 'That gallant Prince, Don John,' wrote Sir Fulke Grevil, 'when this gentleman came to kiss his hand, though at first in his Spanish haughtiness he gave him access as by descent to a youth, of grace as to a stranger, and in particular competition as he conceived to an enemy; yet after a while that he had taken his just attitude, he found himself stricken with this extraordinary planet, that the beholders wondered to see what ingenious tribute that brave and high-minded Prince gave to his worth – giving more honour and respect to this hopeful young gentleman than to the ambassadors of mighty Princes.'[1]

Such visitors must have been a welcome relief in the middle of so much official business, not least because for the first time in Don John's life a serious rift began to develop between him and his brother, almost wholly due to the machinations of Antonio Pérez, who had now been Philip's chief adviser for some four years. Pérez was said to be the illegitimate son by a married woman of one Gonzalo Pérez, a prominent civil servant in the reign of Charles V, who had legitimated him in 1542. From the moment that he entered the Royal service he applied himself to his duties unobtrusively and efficiently, while his knowledge of men and affairs, and his tact and courtesy, not only blinded those with whom he came in contact to the fact that he was a scoundrel, but were such that before long he had made himself indispensable.

[1] *The Life of Sir Philip Sidney*, p. 37. London, 1652.

His appearance was apparently in his favour, and we are told that his clothes were 'rich and very highly perfumed'.[1]

At first Philip had displayed some reluctance to employ Pérez, but he soon fell under his spell to an extent which was not the case with any other of his ministers, and which may well account for the violence of his reaction when he realized how signally his confidence had been misplaced. A contemporary observed that 'Pérez climbed so high that His Majesty would not do anything save what the said Antonio Pérez marked out for him. Whenever His Majesty even went out in his coach, Antonio Pérez went with him. When the Pope, my Lord Don John of Austria, or other lords required anything of the King, they had recourse to Antonio Pérez and by his means obtained what they solicited of His Majesty.' Another said, 'Great men worshipped him; ministers admitted his superiority; the King loved him.'[2] At what point and for what reason Pérez began to intrigue against Don John is not easy to determine in spite of the researches of Dr Marañon in our own time, and it would appear to be a safe assumption that the real object of his dislike was Escobedo, who was in any event his own worst enemy, and that in due course he proceeded to include Don John in his distrust. Nor was this all, for while claiming to sympathize with Don John's conciliatory policy, and keeping up a friendly correspondence with Escobedo, he seems to have opened up negotiations with the Dutch rebels in order to promote his own interests. The ultimate consequences were not immediately apparent, but the poison was beginning to work as early as the late spring of 1577.

Throughout May and June negotiations between Don John and Orange continued, but it was obvious that they were leading nowhere, although they were conducted in the most courteous manner. As early as May 28th, Don John expressed to his brother the fear that there would have to be a resort to arms, though at that time Philip was firmly opposed to any such action. As the situation began to deteriorate England and France became increasingly interested in it, and in addition to his other worries

[1] cf. Cabrera de Córdoba, L., *Felipe II, Rey de España*, vol. i, p. 449. Madrid, 1877.

[2] cf. Marañon, G., *Antonio Pérez*, pp. 11–13. London, 1954.

Don John had to keep an eye on those extremely experienced intriguers, Elizabeth I and Henry III.

Don John had not neglected his brother's advice to get on the best possible terms with the English Queen, and he knew enough about her to realize that no amount of flattery would be deemed excessive in that quarter as a letter from Elizabeth's representative in Brussels under date of June 11th, abundantly proves: it relates to an interview which had taken place two days before.

Then he began to declare his affection for Your Majesty, how ready he was to serve you, and how well disposed the King his brother was to maintain amity with Your Majesty, praying me to tell Your Highness that no Prince upon earth would be more assured and faithful to you than the King his brother and he would be, and therefore wished that Your Majesty would not take any other way. . . . He wished of God that he might have the leafe once to see Your Majesty, and to speak with you. I told him his wish was good, and I wished no less; for, by that means, two noble natures meeting together could not but agree in all goodness and virtue, and the one better to understand the other than by messengers and ambassadors; yea, the sight moving more by the presence than any report is able to set forth by whatsoever declaration.

And then somewhat to please him for the time I showed him Your Majesty's picture, which I had borrowed of Mr Foulke Grevil, and do send it back by this bearer, for that I could not entreat him to have it. And surely, Madame, Don John was much pleased with the sight of it, and perused it very curiously a good long time, and asked me if Your Majesty were not attired sometimes according to the Spanish manner. I told him Your Majesty used divers attires – Italian, Spanish, and French – as occasion served, and as you pleased. He said the Spanish attire was the most comely, and then he desired earnestly of me to have Your Majesty's entire stature and making, and the sooner the better.

I told him I would do my best upon my return, which I hoped would be shortly; but in the meantime I desired his whole picture, which he promised I should have in this sort upon his coming again from Mechlin to Brussels within these eight days, after the twelfth of this month that if I cause any painter come to him in my name he will sit to him for my sake, and so I shall have him. He told me he is so informed of Your Majesty that if you were in the company of your ladies, but in a black velvet French gown and a plain hood to the same, he might discern you for the Queen, although he had never seen your picture before. I told him indeed that God had done much for you, not only to call you to the place of a Queen, but also to give you such a shape fit for any Queen, and therewithall a mind endowed with such several and famous virtues, as, therefore, Your Majesty is had in admiration, and a chief spectacle to the whole world.[1]

How far this exchange of palpably insincere compliments advanced the cause of better relations between Spain and England it is not easy to see, but it is clear that Don John shared Disraeli's opinion that 'Everyone likes flattery, and, when you come to royalty, you should lay it on with a trowel.'[2]

A similar approach to the Most Christian King would not have taken Don John very far, but at the moment Henry was feeling his way in the Low Countries by means of his sister Margaret, Queen of Navarre. The proposed beneficiary was their brother, Francis, Duke of Alençon, and, since the accession of Henry to the French throne, Duke of Anjou. He was a worthless creature judged by any standard, and at no time was he more than a puppet in the hands of others. Henry realized all this as well as anybody else, and it may easily be that his main reason for putting his brother forward in the Netherlands was to get him out of France. Margaret was an ideal instrument for the purpose, for like so many women in all walks of life she was devoted to her useless brother, and only too ready to advance his interests, particularly as they appeared to coincide with those of her family and country.

She was at this time in her twenty-third year, and in the summer bloom of quite considerable beauty. She was also a somewhat lively lady, for in her *Memoirs* she tells how on the night of the

[1] Public Record Office, Flanders, 1577. No. 29.
[2] cf. Buckle, G. E., *The Life of Benjamin Disraeli*, vol. vi, p. 463. London, 1920.

Massacre of Saint Bartholomew she gave refuge not only in her bedroom but in her bed itself to a M. de Tejan who was escaping wounded from four archers of the Guard:[1] point is given to this episode when it is remembered that she had been married to Henry of Navarre a mere six days before. Margaret now decided, or it was decided by her mother and the French King for her, that it was a suitable moment to study the situation in the Netherlands on the spot, so her doctors duly prescribed for her a course of the water at Spa for a long-cured attack of erysipelas. The only difficulty would appear to have been the title by which she was to be addressed, for the bulk of the kingdom of Navarre had been incorporated in the Spanish monarchy by Ferdinand the Catholic, and her husband was only recognized in Madrid by his paternal name of the Duke of Vendôme. However, her *Memoirs* make no mention of this complication so it was probably circumvented by some subterfuge.

Margaret travelled in considerable state, with three horse-litters for herself and her chief ladies, and six coaches for the rest of the train, with ten maids of honour and a Prince of the Church also in attendance. Her first halting-place was Cambrai, where she soon made the impression she desired upon the Governor, and the same was the case at Mons, where the Count of Lalaing, the Governor of Hainault, also fell for her charms. In actual fact she could not have made her journey at a more appropriate moment from her own point of view, for Lalaing was one of the leaders of a growing third party which looked with equal mistrust upon both Philip and William, and so were prepared to regard with favour the candidature of Anjou, of whose real character they probably knew nothing. Even thus early, Don John probably suspected what was afoot, for he had originally intended to receive Margaret at Mons, and the fact that he changed their place of meeting to Namur may well have been due to what he had heard of the attitude of Lalaing.

The Queen of Navarre appears to have enjoyed her three days sojourn at Namur, and she did not fail to make an impression on Don John, always susceptible where women were concerned. She has left it on record that at a ball he never left her side, 'always talking to me, often telling me that he saw in me the resemblance

[1] *Mémoires de la Reyne Marguerite*, p. 39. Paris, 1666.

of his lady the Queen, the late Queen my sister, whom he had greatly honoured, and by all means in his power showing all honour and courtesy to me and my company, and testifying the pleasure he took in seeing me there'. She also took every opportunity of intriguing on behalf of both her brothers, and when she left Namur on July 24th she doubtless felt that she had every cause for satisfaction. Instead, however, of going to Spa she spent the next six weeks at Liège with the Prince-Bishop, where the waters were brought to her, and where she experienced the truth of the saying that pride goes before a fall, for she received a very discouraging letter from Anjou. She had gone too far, and the French King was extremely displeased with her intrigues. Anjou further warned her that Don John had become acquainted with her activities, and that she had better be careful that she was not kidnapped on her way home. In these circumstances Margaret decided upon an immediate return to France, and her journey was a good deal in the nature of a flight. Still, if she had not done a great deal in the Low Countries to further the cause of Anjou she had stimulated disaffection with Philip and Don John.

After her departure events began to accelerate towards a crisis. To what extent Don John was aware of his guest's intrigues is a moot point, and Anjou is far from being a reliable witness, but there can be no doubt that he was coming to feel isolated among enemies and very doubtful supporters: the Perpetual Edict had clearly lost all significance, the general situation was going from bad to worse, and Philip seemed quite blind to its seriousness. He was also unquestionably worried by the numerous plots to murder or kidnap him. In these circumstances he felt justified in striking out a line of his own. His immediate need was money, which Madrid had signally failed to supply, so he borrowed some from the Pope. Support of some sort from his neighbours was essential, and if the Queen of Navarre could meddle with the internal affairs of the Netherlands he could interfere in those of France, so he renewed his contacts with the Duke of Guise. The first of Don John's letters of which there is any trace is dated October 7th, but there is reason to suppose that he and Guise were in touch as early as the previous August.[1] Finally, in a perfectly bloodless

[1] cf. Mulhacén, Marqués de, *Don Juan de Austria*, p. 324. Madrid, 1944.

operation, on July 24th, he ejected the Estates' troops from the citadel of Namur, and replaced them by a force of German mercenaries upon whom he could rely. This last stroke, in spite of the storm to which it was to give rise, did at any rate mean that he could make his plans and deal with his correspondence without fear of being kidnapped by his own guards, and abducted to a Dutch or French prison.

The news of the proceedings at Namur were not at all well received in official circles in Spain, where suspicions of Don John's impetuosity were never far below the surface. Philip himself by no means approved of what had been done, and he seems to have felt that it was an attempt to force his hand to order back the *tercios*. Historians have been divided on the subject, but it is difficult to resist the conclusion that by his precipitate action Don John blazoned forth to the world that his mission in Flanders had failed. He himself continued to insist that what he had done at Namur had been dictated by necessity, and he finished a letter of justification to his sister, Margaret of Parma, with the words, 'From the citadel of Namur on August 8th, 1577, with a regiment of mutinous Germans at my gate and the populace almost in arms – that is how I am situated.'[1]

He wasted no time in putting his case before the Estates, and in explaining why he had acted as he did. His life, he declared, was not safe except in a fortress, for not only were there numbers of disbanded soldiery lying in wait for him in all parts of the country, but persons of high rank had taken part in plots for his assassination or capture. Accordingly he called upon the Estates to institute a rigorous search for these conspirators, and to bring their leaders to punishment: he also requested that both the soldiers and the civil population of Brabant should be disarmed. To strengthen his arguments he enclosed copies of two anonymous letters, which he had recently received, and in which he had been warned of a plot to seize and murder him.

By way of a reply, the Estates sent a deputation to Namur to interview Don John, and the subsequent proceedings began in a harmonious manner, with expressions by the envoys of the deepest devotion to Philip. As the discussion progressed, however,

[1] *ibid.*, p. 293.

tempers became frayed, and Don John's nerves were obviously on edge anyhow. He demanded that the Estates should cease to hold any communication with Orange should he any longer delay to fulfil the terms of the Pacification of Ghent, and that they should provide him himself with a suitable bodyguard. This was reasonable enough, but he played straight into William's hands when he went on to insist that there should be submitted to him a list of those qualified to sit in the Estates-General in order that he might know whether there were objections to any of them being allowed to take their seats. This was hardly the sort of stipulation likely to recommend him to elected representatives, and unfortunately for him he made it at a moment when Orange had a very valuable card up his sleeve which he now proceeded to play. This was the production of a packet of secret dispatches which had passed between Don John and Escobedo on the one hand and Philip and Pérez on the other: on his way through Gascony their bearer had fallen into the hands of the Huguenots, and the King of Navarre had at once forwarded them to William. In these confidential documents the writers naturally expressed views of the Estates very different from those in their public references, and in this way there was created an atmosphere which suited Orange and his supporters very well indeed.

All the same the decencies of civilized intercourse continued to be preserved for a little longer, though it was becoming obvious that the breaking-point must soon be reached. The Estates replied to Don John, after the now conventional expressions of loyalty to Philip and the Catholic faith, that they would grant him a bodyguard of three hundred foot, and that they would do everything in their power to secure the adhesion of Orange to the Pacification of Ghent. So far, so good, but they continued by firmly rejecting the pretensions of the Crown to interfere with the free election of their representatives by the nobles, clergy, and municipal corporations. Nor was even this all, for they went on to express their disapproval of the seizure of the citadel of Namur, to demand its restoration, and to inform Don John that in the parcel of intercepted correspondence they had discovered his real opinions.

Such being the case it is not surprising that the interview between the Governor and the representatives of the Estates who brought this reply should have been far from cordial, and that it should have had no practical result except mutual exasperation and estrangement. Nor was the situation improved by the contemporary failure of Don John to repeat at Antwerp the *coup* which he had successfully executed at Namur. The communications which passed between him and the Estates during the next few weeks were so barren of consequences as to be now almost destitute of interest. Neither party seemed to have much hope of influencing the other by the elaborate memoranda which were exchanged, and each was busy with preparations and negotiations which these documents were intended not to discuss but to conceal. In effect, demands and proposals were made on both sides without any expectation that they would be conceded or accepted. Yet in reviewing the proceedings of the two parties it is surely impossible to deny that Don John had every right to complain of the shifting and tortuous policy of the Estates, but the truth seems to be that their demands rose and fell according as the influence of Orange or the Catholic lords preponderated in their deliberations.

Don John was essentially a man of action, and all the evidence goes to show that these months of frustration were seriously affecting his health – certainly he was depressed as never before. Even as late as October 29th, when the *tercios* were returning, he wrote to Rodrigo de Mendoza.

> It is a thousand years since I have written, and a thousand years since I have been able to write, so many and various fortunes have I gone through that there is nothing that I have not been compelled to do; after being pushed by time, often by enemies, chiefly by my own friends and the irresolutions of the Court, often by bad health, which I also bear about me as the appropriate companion of my cares. I am now recovering from more purging and bleeding, which have been necessary.[1]

Meanwhile a new, if transient, figure had made his appearance on the stage of Netherlands politics, and this was the Archduke Matthias, brother of the reigning Emperor, Rudolf II. He was at that time a young man of nineteen, and as nothing much was

---

[1] cf. Stirling-Maxwell, Sir William, *Don John of Austria*, vol. ii, p. 445. London, 1883.

known about him he was reputed to be an attractive character, though subsequent events in the Empire itself were to prove that he was a very slippery individual indeed. He had been produced by that section of the rebels who had no wish to return to the rule of Philip or to come under that of Orange. What these people really desired was independence under a Catholic dynasty, but in this respect they were in advance of their time, for it was not until 1830 that this solution became practical politics. As for the Archduke, it never seems to have occurred to him that there was anything dishonourable in availing himself of the difficulties of his Spanish kinsman in order to deprive him of a portion of his dominions, and that it was indecent for an Austrian prince to accept a crown from the rebellious subjects of another member of his family.

On the night of October 3rd, 1577, Matthias stole out of his bed in Vienna, and disguised as a servant, with his face blackened and very few attendants, made his way to Cologne. The Emperor at once wrote to Don John telling him what had happened, and saying that it was without his connivance, which is to be doubted. That Don John did not accept Rudolf's assurances is clear from a letter that he wrote to Parma, in which he said that his own attitude would be determined by the Archduke's behaviour after he had arrived in the Low Countries: if he threw in his lot with the Estates he would be treated as an enemy.[1]

Elizabeth by no means welcomed this added complication in the already complicated affairs of the Netherlands. Her great fear was that the Provinces would fall into French hands, and Anjou was already collecting an army at La Fère, where the Queen of Navarre was also to be found. The English Queen therefore informed the Estates that Orange was the only leader upon whom they should rely, and that it was solely because of her faith in his leadership that she was willing to contribute aid either in troops or money. With this opinion in his favour William, who was every day proving himself by far the shrewdest man on the rebel side, proceeded to operate with consummate skill; he had neither originated nor approved the invitation to Matthias, but he accepted it with a good grace, welcomed the Archduke, and then ruled in his

[1] cf. Strada, F., De Bello Belgico, lib. ix. Antwerp, 1635.

name. The Orange partisans succeeded in getting William appointed Ruward, which made him to all intents and purposes dictator, with Matthias as the nominal Governor. At this point Elizabeth made a serious mistake into which she was led by her suspicion of the French. She had clearly come to the conclusion that Don John's case was hopeless, and in her fear of Anjou she came down from the fence on which she had so long been sitting, guaranteed a large loan to Orange and his party, and appeared openly in their support.

Don John reported all these events to his brother, whom he also notified of the fact that he was now devoting all his energies to the war which could no longer be postponed. Philip reacted promptly: he gave orders that all the Spanish troops which could be spared from Italy should proceed to the Netherlands, and that Parma should go with them. At the same time he informed the Estates that they must demobilize their forces, dismiss Orange, and conform to the Perpetual Edict. Their reply, on December 7th, was a proclamation deposing Don John from all the offices which he held in the Low Countries, as well as declaring him to be a breaker of the peace which he had sworn to keep, and an enemy to the commonwealth: all Netherlanders who co-operated with him were denounced as rebels and traitors. It was, however, the last time that the seventeen provinces were to speak with one voice.

Philip had been able to take this strong action because as the year 1577 drew to its close it became increasingly clear that there was no immediate threat from the Turks, whose activities he always had to take into account before committing himself too seriously on other fronts. The leaders who had been trained under Suleyman the Magnificient were dying off, and they were not being replaced by men of like calibre. Sokolli was, it is true, to be Grand Vizier for a few months longer, but his authority was being steadily undermined by a series of intrigues which resulted in the removal of his most trusted subordinates. Nor was this all, for Persia was passing through a period of temporary weakness following the death of Shah Tahmasp I in 1576, and the temptation to take advantage of this state of affairs was too great to be resisted at Constantinople: accordingly, the last months of 1577 witnessed the preparation of a large armament under Lala Mustapha, the conqueror of Cyprus, and in the following year war between the Sultan and the Shah again broke out. Philip could thus afford to concentrate on crushing the rebellion in the Low Countries.

The rebel forces were mustered at Gembloux, a small walled town to the north-west of Namur, which was Don John's headquarters. They were slightly superior in numbers, especially in cavalry, to the Spaniards, but, as was soon to be demonstrated, they were definitely inferior in quality. Orange declined a command in the field, and as he was far from being a Heaven-sent military genius he may well have been justified on grounds of competence; equally, he may have believed that defeat was inevitable, and he did not wish to bear any part of the responsibility if things went wrong. Matthias also appears to have had no desire to hazard his person or his reputation in battle, so the command was given to Anthony de Goignies, an old soldier of fortune who had served in the armies of Charles V, and notably at Saint Quentin. Soon after his appointment, it is not uninteresting to note, he had a dispute with Orange as to the enlistment of German mercenaries, who, William's critics maintained, were being introduced for no other purpose than to provide for his German friends and relatives. De Goignies would have been happier without them, and would have preferred Netherlanders, on the principle that a man's house is safest in his own keeping: the Estates, however, were under the influence of Orange, so the Germans remained.[1]

Very different feelings prevailed among the twenty thousand foot and two thousand horse whom Don John had collected at Namur. The time for action had come, and this was very much to the Governor-General's liking: he was weary of intrigue, in which he was generally no match for Orange, but now he was entering upon a sphere of activity in which he was justly renowned: evidence of his feelings at this time is afforded by the fact that he took the field under a banner of a cross emblazoned with the words, *In hoc signo vici Turcos, in hoc signo vincam haereticos.* The year he had spent in the Low Countries had told severely on his health, and when Parma arrived on December 18th, 1577, he was more than a little shocked at the change in his uncle's appearance. Yet the

[1] cf. Carnero, A., *Guerras Civiles en Flandes*, p. 125. Brussels, 1625.

troops whom he now saw mustering must have done much to raise his spirits. Of the infantry six thousand were Spanish veterans; another four were Frenchmen supplied by the Duke of Guise; five thousand were Germans; and the rest were Walloons. They were officered by the best-known commanders in Philip's service such as Mondragón, Acosta, Perroti, Vargas, and Martinengo, and, above all, Parma. The only notable absentee was Julián Romero who had fallen dead from his horse at Cremona at the beginning of the march to the Low Countries.[1] All alike, officers and men, were looking forward to wiping out the disgrace of their withdrawal from the Netherlands a few months earlier.

De Goignies does not appear to have been the exact embodiment of the offensive spirit, but as he saw Don John's forces mounting up, he decided that he had better attack them before they became any stronger: with this end in view he advanced to Saint Martin, a village about five miles from Namur, where his scouts informed him that not only were the enemy considerably stronger than he had been led to believe but that they were moving out to attack him. In these circumstances his principal officers were strongly opposed to offering battle, and when they had persuaded him to adopt their point of view they took advantage of the halt at Saint Martin, incredible as it may seem, to return to Brussels for a wedding. On this De Goignies decided to fall back on Gembloux, but some stragglers from his camp fell into Spanish hands, and his intention became known to Don John. Vacillation of this nature was highly dangerous in the face of the victor of Lepanto and of Parma, as the rebels were not long in discovering.

Don John decided to attack while his adversary was retreating, and he spent the whole of January 30th, 1578, examining the ground on which he proposed to fight. The road from Namur to Gembloux lay for the most part along the bottom of a winding valley, bounded by gentle heights, sometimes cultivated and sometimes wooded, and watered by a sluggish and muddy stream. The valley varied in width at different points, and as the season was midwinter the stream was considerably swollen, while there was mud everywhere.

[1] cf. Montesa, Marqués de, *Julián Romero*, pp. 453–5. Madrid, 1952.

Before dawn on the 31st, Don John sent Acosta with some cavalry and light infantry to reconnoitre, and, if necessary, clear the woods on the side of the road. At daybreak the main army was in motion with Ottavio Gonzaga, at the head of the cavalry, and Mondragón, with a thousand musketeers and pikemen, in the van. Next came the main body under Don John and Parma, while the rear, largely composed of Walloons, was under the command of Peter Ernest, Count of Mansfeldt. The forces of the Estates were also early astir. The leading regiments were composed of Netherlanders, but the centre was a very mixed body consisting of German, Huguenots, and English and Scottish auxiliaries. In the rear was the cavalry, with which was De Goignies himself. In some extenuation of the lack of spirit shortly to be demonstrated by his men it must be remembered that a number of the officers only recently defected from the Royal cause.

The fighting began early in the day when Acosta, who was hanging on the rebel flank, picked up a couple of prisoners whom he sent back to his main body. Shortly afterwards Gonzaga came in contact with the enemy rear, with which he had a number of skirmishes, but Don John had given him very strict orders not to become heavily engaged out of reach of support, so he fought with considerable caution. Such, however, was not the case with Perroti, who proceeded to push too far ahead for safety. Gonzaga therefore ordered him to fall back, only to receive a reply to the effect that he, Perroti, had never yet turned his back on an enemy, and even if he were willing to do so now it was impossible to disengage.

At this point Parma had ridden forward, and was with Gonzaga, when he noticed that Perroti had reached a place where the valley was narrow: the road was apparently flooded, so that both the Spaniards and the rebels were skirmishing along the higher ground. It at once occurred to him that now was the time, by a rapid advance along the flooded road, to turn the enemy retreat into a rout, and to deal an unexpected blow upon that portion of the opposing army which, being at some distance from the rearguard, considered itself in perfect security. Whether such a stroke would or would not prove successful of course depended upon the condition of the submerged road: if it were firm enough to bear cavalry, an offensive from that quarter would probably prove decisive, but if the floods had covered it with mud the horsemen who floundered in it would be an easy target for the enemy musketeers. The fact that the rebels had seen fit to deviate from it afforded presumptive evidence that the road was impassable.

All the same Parma decided to take the risk. He sent an aide-de-camp back to Don John with the order, 'Go to Don John and tell him that, like the ancient Roman, I am about to plunge into a gulf, by the aid of God and under the auspices of the House of Austria, to win a great and memorable victory.' Both the road and the ground beyond it proved to afford better footing than might have been anticipated, and when he had collected a sufficient force Parma charged the main body of the rebels, without any interference from their rearguard which was still engaged with Perroti. Upon this unexpected impact the enemy broke, their cavalry rode over their foot, and the whole army was thrown into panic, while Don John, Gonzaga, and Mondragón pushed up both mounted troops and musketeers in Parma's support. The army of the Estates disintegrated, and Elizabeth's auxiliaries behaved no better than anybody else, which is not surprising, for the English army was at a particularly low ebb at the time – as its performance in contemporary Ireland was proving, and Holinshed, who died in 1580, said that the strength of the English archers had so notoriously declined that the French soldiers were in the habit of disrespectfully turning their backs at long range, 'bidding them shoot', whereas 'had the archers been what they were wont to be, these fellows would have had their breeches nailed unto their buttocks'. Gembloux was a foretaste of what was to happen in the following year, though against much less formidable antagonists, at Glenmalure.

The losses on both sides have never been correctly estimated, but it would be no exaggeration to say that those of the rebels ran into thousands, whereas if the Spaniards lost a dozen men that was all. Thirty-four standards and colours, most of the artillery, and a great quantity of baggage and ammunition also fell into the hands of the victors. Among the prisoners was De Goignies himself, and it is said that when he was brought before Don John and asked to kiss his hand he was told to 'mark the hand of God in abasing those who revolted against religion and the King, and learn, by what had happened, in the rout of a great army by a handful of men, that God was ever on the side of Kings'. To this the defeated general replied by assuring Don John that he had never thought of taking up arms against religion, after which he was taken away into captivity at Namur. As to the fate of the other prisoners, the evidence is conflicting: Strada says that they were disarmed, and released on a promise that they would not bear arms – the Flemings at any time and the foreigners for a year – against the King.[1] Cabrera stated that Don John set six hundred Scots at liberty, 'showing them his clemency'[2]; but Tassis avers that most of them were put to death by drowning.[3] Whatever may be the truth of these conflicting statements according to the rules of war at the time Don John would have been justified in putting any English and Scots to death since their countries were at peace with Spain, just as Elizabeth's generals a little later did not hesitate to massacre the prisoners taken at Smerwick even though they had surrendered under promise of mercy.

After his victory Don John assembled his senior officers, and thanked them for their services. At the same time, while expressing his special gratitude to Parma, he administered a slight reproof for his daring: he ought to remember, the uncle reminded the nephew, that he had been sent to the Low Countries not as a private soldier, but as one whose advice was at His Majesty's service. To this Parma tactfully replied that no man could be a good captain until he had first proved himself to be a good soldier, more particularly when he was serving under so great a general as Don John.

The battle of Gembloux secured for the Spaniards the valley of the Sambre, forced Orange and the Archduke to abandon Brussels, and dealt a heavy blow to the rebel cause in the southern provinces. On the other hand in the north the fear which it inspired served rather to advance the interests of William. In March, his brother, John, was elected Governor of the province of Gelderland, and

---

[1] *De Bello Belgico*, lib. ix. Antwerp, 1635.

[2] *Felipe II, Rey de España*, lib. xii. Madrid, 1877.

[3] *Commentariorum de Tumultibus Belgicis sui Temporis Libri Octo*, vol. iv, p. 294. The Hague, 1743.

in May the supporters of Orange succeeded in overthrowing the Catholic magistrates of Amsterdam, thus securing that city for the insurgent cause. In spite of his victory Don John was himself a victim to a melancholy which was itself evidence of his declining health, and on February 23rd, he wrote to Rodrigo de Mendoza.

I suppose you will have received that which I wrote from St Argenton about the victory which God had given us. God Himself knows how troubled I am to find myself so utterly unable to prosecute the victory so far as it might have been carried, after I had trusted that His Majesty would have so provided me with what was needful; for, if I had been so provided, I am sure Brussels would have been his own, and with it the greater part of these Provinces. But now they have taken their resolution; and therefore little trifling villages are defending themselves against us, in such fashion as to cost us the blood of brave men. And on this account I send Monsieur de Billi with this despatch, to ensure that I leave no stone unturned, and that His Majesty should understand what is going on, and what it befits him to do, and that we understand what his orders are. . . .

I am well, God be thanked, and that is no small matter considering the bodily fatigue I undergo; but chiefly considering what I suffer in spirit, compelled thereto by this miserable present world, mortal enemy of the poor absent, wherein you have to make excuses for very loyal services which are not held to be so unless you let yourself be taken and destroyed like a beast. So I am told there is no lack at Court of people who say, if I should be taken prisoner, what would be lost, or what would it signify? Let him come here who holds that opinion, contrary to that which I think should be the opinion of a friend, that by what he avoids for himself he may know what I have to do, and how I shun no dangers except the contemptible ones, nor can ever withdraw myself from others; and if he should come, he would perhaps see that happen in spite of him, which from afar he condemns.[1]

[1] cf. Stirling-Maxwell, Sir William, *Don John of Austria*, vol. ii, pp. 457 and 459. London, 1883.

A month later Don John had an added cause for worry in the murder of his secretary in Madrid. The affair is still one of the most mysterious in Spanish history, but the main outlines are clear. Escobedo had been sent to Spain to put before the King and Pérez the difficulties of his master's position in the Low Countries, and he seems to have behaved with very considerable indiscretion, which, in view of his character, was only to be expected: in particular he criticized the King with reckless freedom in front of the Princess of Eboli, who clearly passed his observations on to Pérez, whence we may be sure that they were not long in reaching Philip himself, doubtless without losing anything in the telling. Some historians have taken the view that more than political considerations were at issue in this somewhat unsavoury episode. They would have us believe that Escobedo was horrified when he discovered the footing upon which Pérez and the Princess of Eboli stood with one another, and that when the guilty pair found that he was aware of their secret they were terrified that he would betray it to Philip, who, according to the scandal-mongers, was among the Princess's lovers. Another school of thought holds that Escobedo discovered some underhand intrigues in which Pérez was engaging with the rebels in the Low Countries.

In any event, as we have seen, the minister had for some months been putting Don John's actions in as bad a light as he could to the King, and it was not a very difficult operation, for the Governor-General was inclined to pursue a somewhat personal foreign policy; he negotiated with the Pope and he intrigued with the Guises without previously informing his brother, and Philip suspected that he was being egged on by Escobedo, a view in which he was much encouraged by Pérez. Such was the position on the night of March 31st, 1578, when Escobedo was waylaid by five men in a side street in Madrid, and murdered.

That he was done to death on the instructions of Pérez there would appear to be little doubt, but the complicity of the King is more difficult to prove, though not a few historians have taken it for granted. Philip had long regarded the dead man as his brother's evil genius, and as such had wished him out of the way, but to wish a man out of the way is not the same thing as having him murdered. It was not, of course, until after Don John's death, and the return of his State papers to Spain, that Philip realized the extent to which he had been misled by Pérez, and from that moment the minister's fate was sealed. In all the circumstances it is most probable that if the King did not definitely order the killing of Escobedo the murder certainly did not displease him. In any event it could be justified for reasons of State, as a recent historian has justified the murder of the Guises by Henry III.[1]

All the same the news of his secretary's death was interpreted by Don John as a sign of the way in which the wind was blowing in Madrid, and he came to the conclusion that he had lost his brother's confidence, which added greatly to the depression in which he was increasingly becoming plunged. That he had a pretty good idea who was at the bottom of the affair would seem to be indicated by a letter which he wrote to Philip on April 20th.

With greater grief than I can describe, I have heard of the unhappy death of the Secretary Escobedo, for which I cannot find, nor shall I ever find, any consolation; because Your Majesty has lost such a servant as I know him to have been, and I such a one as Your Majesty also knows that he was. And although there is in this sufficient cause for the sorrow which I feel, above all else I lament that at the end of so many years and services he should meet with a death so unworthy of him, and caused by his having served his King with so much truth and love, and without any of those other aims and without the craft which are now in fashion. Even in the worst matter, it is my opinion that nothing should be rashly judged; but yet I do not think that in this I incur blame when I say that I point at no one in particular, but believe that there is no doubt the affair is as I have said. As one to whom so many opportunities of knowing were given, and who did know the independent manner in which Escobedo bore himself in the service of your Majesty, I am much afraid of the quarter whence the blow came. After all, I do not certainly know it, nor, knowing it, would I say more than this, that for the love of Our Lord I entreat Your Majesty as lovingly as I can that you will not permit such an outrage to happen in your Court, or so great an affront to be done to me as

[1] cf. Erlanger, P., *Le Massacre de la Saint-Barthélemy*, p. 226. Paris, 1960.

that which has been done to me also, without using every possible diligence to know whence the blow came and to punish it with the rigour it deserves. And although I believe Your Majesty has already done this very completely, being so Christian and justice-loving a Prince, yet I nevertheless beg it of you, feeling that I ought as a gentleman to take care of the honour of one who so truly deserved it of me, as did Escobedo, and to whom I am under obligations so great that I may with just reason consider myself to have been the cause of his death, as Your Majesty knows better than any other person.

May Your Majesty therefore be pleased, I pray, to approve of my not only reminding you of the affairs of the deceased, but soliciting you, as I will do by every post, with regard to them until entire justice shall have been done, and remuneration for his services made, and of my even letting other things stand still, as I ought, as a gentleman, to do. All this I once more entreat Your Majesty as humbly and as earnestly as I can, and that Your Majesty will be pleased to order answers to be sent me on these various points; for I confess to Your Majesty that nothing can now happen to trouble my spirit like this death, until everything which concerns the deceased has been arranged. As to his affairs I do not yet know how he has left them, so of none of them can I speak in particular; but I pray Your Majesty will remember the desire of Escobedo, which was ever to serve Your Majesty honourably and with clean hands, and the poor house which he leaves behind him, and that you will show the kindness which they deserve to those who remain in it; and especially that you will confer upon his eldest son the places and emoluments possessed by his father. That these will be well bestowed upon Pedro de Escobedo, and that he is a man whose merits will every day grow with the employment and favour which he may receive, no one knows better than Your Majesty.

Considering the position Escobedo was obliged to maintain, and his small income, I think it likely that he may have left some debt, which may trouble his soul, and also his children and his wife. I therefore ask Your Majesty to make them a grant by which these debts may be paid. But my chief request is, that as I find myself in the place of father, as it were, to the eldest son, you will do me the signal favour of giving him all which his father enjoyed. As to the debts, I can easily arrange to defray the most of those which are for food and clothing, and to provide for the payment of those which are most pressing, which is the least that I can do for the case of one who laboured until his death, and died, to afford me repose and that good assurance as to the service of Your Majesty, in all matters that passed through his hands, which I have ever desired and shall desire all my life. It is for Your Majesty to see whether these obligations deserve that these offices should be given, and whether I have a right to be confident that the favour which I beg will be granted to me, in regard to all that I have sued for and shall continue to sue for, until that justice and grace are obtained for which the blood and services of the dead are always pleading. May Our Lord keep Your Majesty in the welfare and ease which I desire and need.[1]

It was not long before Don John discovered that political murder was not the prerogative of the King of Spain alone, for the Spanish ambassador in London sent him the picture of one Ratcliffe, who had been a prisoner in the Tower until Walsingham released him on condition that he murdered Don John. In due course he made his way to Tirlemont, and with an accomplice got into the room where his intended victim was giving audience. Don John, however, recognized the man's face from the portrait, and Ratcliffe and his companion were duly arrested, when they both made a full confession. Their lives were spared by the humane Governor-General, but after his death Parma had them executed. There are various versions of this incident, and Father Antonio Ossorio goes so far as to say that Ratcliffe received his instructions from Elizabeth in person.[2] Why she should have been so desirous of Don John's removal is not immediately obvious since no English interest was involved, but she may have encouraged the would-be murderer as a woman rather than as a queen:

[1] Brit. Mus., Bibl. Egerton. Papeles Varios.
[2] *Vida de Don Juan de Austria*, pp. 282–4. Madrid, 1946.

there had been some wild suggestions that Don John should marry her instead of Mary, and to these he had been singularly unresponsive; Elizabeth was also quite uninterested in them, but Hell proverbially holds no fury like a woman scorned.

When Don John wrote to Philip on the morrow of the murder of Escobedo he had less than six months to live. During this time his health was rapidly declining, and he was compelled to entrust the military command to Parma, with the most satisfactory consequences, for within twenty days he reduced to obedience the whole province of Limburg with the loss of about twenty of his own soldiers. The summer of 1578 also saw a revival of the intervention of Anjou in the troubled politics of the Low Countries. for the Catholic nobles, still firmly opposed to Orange, turned to the Valois prince in their disillusionment with Matthias. An already confused situation thus became even more confused. William no more favoured the Frenchman than he had the Austrian, but he did not deem it politic to oppose him, for he knew that Anjou's arrival would irritate Elizabeth, who might thereby be induced to give increased aid to the rebels to prevent them from becoming wholly dependent on the French. He was fully justified in the belief that the English Queen would regard Anjou's appearance on the scene as an affront, and on May 22nd she wrote to William Davison from Greenwich of the Estates that 'if they do well look into the course which they are entered into, they shall find that this French aid is more like to turn them to hurt than help, which kind of declining we see to be of so ill consequence; that were it not for the love we bear to those countries and the care we have of their safety, we should not only be discouraged from further dealing with them, but also be driven to join with Don John'.[1] A plain hint which Davison almost certainly passed on to the appropriate quarter.

These last weeks of Don John's life were marked by a certain amount of desultory fighting and by a good deal of very insincere negotiating. At Rijnemants on the first of August he clashed with a superior rebel force, against the advice of Parma, and a drawn battle was the result. Unfortunately for him Philip was not able to

[1] Harrison, G. B. (editor), *The Letters of Queen Elizabeth*, p. 127. London 1935.

give him much assistance at this time. The situation in the Mediterranean was once more causing anxiety, for although the Turks were occupied with the Persians there was danger much nearer home, in Morocco. Sebastian of Portugal had invaded that country at the end of June, and on August 4th he went down to disaster at Alcazar-el-Kebir. Philip had never at any time believed that his nephew was likely to be successful in his Moroccan campaign, and so the confirmation of his fears did not take him by surprise, but this triumph of the Crescent on his very doorstep compelled him to take precautions which necessarily limited the assistance that he could afford his brother in the Low Countries.

By this time Don John was fully convinced that no useful purpose would now be served by reopening negotiations with the rebels, but Philip, embarrassed as he was by the course of events in Morocco, was desirous of a peaceful settlement with the Estates if one could be reached, so his brother was compelled to adopt a policy which was personally distasteful to him. The prime mover in this last attempt at a compromise would appear to have been Elizabeth.

As we have seen she had all through played Philip, Orange, and the French off against one another with a cynical disregard for anything except what she might get out of the prevalent troubled conditions. Her position in the matter was to all intents and purposes that while respecting Philip's theoretical sovereignty in the Netherlands she wished to weaken it, but not to such an extent that it would be overthrown. Any open assistance to rebels against their rightful monarch was contrary to her principles, and to this extent she was sincere. For the rest she was only defending abroad the local liberties and the religious freedom which she refused at home. She did not wish to see Spain completely dominant in the Low Countries, for that might constitute a menace to herself: her aim was to keep Philip so fully occupied with suppressing insurrection that he would have neither time nor money to spare for other enterprises.

The overthrow of Spanish rule, as she saw it, might well let the French in, and that would be a remedy much worse than the disease. With these ends in view she supported Orange only just enough to enable him to keep on worrying Philip, and she was even induced in due course to give some assistance to Anjou, so long as his effort remained a private enterprise, and was not pushed too far; but she wished neither of them to be successful. Such a policy was neither heroic nor was it morally defensible, but it was unquestionably in the interests of the weak England of those days. Had the Queen followed the wishes of the more hotheaded of her advisers war with Spain would have been inevitable, and probably also with France, who would never have allowed England to become entrenched on her northern frontier. It was a policy which called for the utmost finesse, but any other would have resulted in disaster.[1]

Accordingly under pressure from the English Queen commissioners from both sides met at Louvain in August, and they were assisted in their deliberation by representatives of the Emperor and Elizabeth – in the case of the latter by Lord Cobham and Sir Francis Walsingham. In spite, however, of the advice of these Imperial and English mediators the Estates would offer no conditions that could possibly be accepted, for they would have left the King with nothing more than a titular sovereignty over the Provinces, and in reply Don John contented himself with an assertion of the pacific intentions and desires of his brother and himself, while he threw all the blame for the war, past and future, upon the refractory and unreasonable people of the Netherlands. Finally, he asked Cobham and Walsingham what they thought of the terms pressed upon him. 'Indeed,' replied Walsingham, 'they are too hard; but, bad as they seem, it is only by pure menace that we have extracted them from the Estates.' 'Then,' said Don John, 'you may tell them to keep their offers to themselves. Such terms will not do for me.' He then went on to say that such inadmissible conditions having been put before him, he hoped it would appear to the Queen of England 'that he had reason to refuse the same'.[2]

Walsingham was one of the shrewdest judges of character in contemporary Europe, and he was much impressed by Don John, for he wrote to Burghley, 'In conference with him, I might easily

[1] cf. Maynard, T., *Queen Elizabeth*, pp. 248–50. London, 1943.
[2] MSS., Flanders, 1578, no. 32. Public Record Office.

discern a great conflict in himself between honour and necessity. Surely I never saw a gentleman for personage, speech, wit and entertainment comparable to him. If pride do not overthrow him, he is like to become a great personage.'[1] That was written on August 27th, and what Walsingham did not realize was that he and Lord Cobham were dealing with a dying man, so cleverly did Don John apparently disguise the fact. He had again been attacked by the fever which seems to have been lingering in his system for some weeks, and his last illness is considered to have commenced on September 17th. From Namur he had himself carried to the lines of the Regiment of Figueroa which were outside the town, and where he thought the air would be healthier; with characteristic self-sacrifice he refused to allow any of the senior officers to leave their quarters on his account, and in these circumstances an old pigeon-house was selected as the only apartment suitable for him. It was hastily cleaned, its rough walls and roof were covered with some rich hangings, and curtains were placed over the holes which served as windows, while a wooden staircase was constructed to replace the ladder by means of which the upper storey was normally reached. From the very beginning of this last illness Don John would appear to have despaired of his recovery, and on September 28th he appointed Parma, in the event of his own death, to be Governor-General and Commander-in-Chief in the Low Countries until Philip's pleasure was known.

For nearly three weeks in all he struggled against what he felt to be the inevitable, rapidly losing strength the whole time, but there then came a day when he was seized by the most violent pains, and had to take to his bed. He soon became delirious, and talked of battlefieds and trumpet-calls; he gave orders to imaginary lines of battle; and finally relapsed into unconsciousness. After two days of muttering delirium he awakened, and took extreme unction. Next day the dying flicker continued, and he heard the priest say mass; though his sight had failed and he could not see, he had himself raised in the bed, feebly turned his head towards the elevation of the Host, and adored the body of Christ with his last glimmer of consciousness. He then fell back unconscious, and

[1] MSS., Holland. Public Record Office.

sank into a state of coma from which he never rallied. At one o'clock in the afternoon on October 1st, 1578, he died.

From that day to this the cause of Don John's death has been a matter of dispute among historians and doctors. The Orange propagandists have hinted, and would like to have us believe, that he was murdered by his brother's orders, for which there is not a shred of evidence, and which is inconceivable in view of the relations which had always existed between them. Another school of thought will have it that he died of venereal disease contracted during the time that he was in Italy, but here, again, evidence is lacking. The more romantic have claimed that he died of a broken heart for the lady whom he mentions in his letters to Rodrigo de Mendoza, but it is difficult not to agree with Rosalind that 'men have died from time to time, and worms have eaten them, but not for love'.[1] More probably the late Dr MacLaurin was nearer the truth when he wrote that 'this young man's brave life was terminated by that curse of young soldiers – ruptured typhoid ulcer in ambulatory typhoid fever. His army was dwindling with pestilence; he himself walked about feeling feverish and "seedy" and losing weight rapidly for a fortnight; he was just at the typical age, in the typhoid time of the year, and in typhoid conditions; his ulcer burst, causing peritonitis; the tremendous shock of the rupture, together with the toxaemia, drove him delirious and then unconscious; being a very strong young man he woke up again as the first shock passed away; as the shock passed into definite peritonitis unconsciousness returned, and he was fortunate in being able to hear his last Mass before he died.'[2]

Don John's funeral took place with such pomp and circumstance as was possible under active service conditions. The honour of actually carrying the body was distributed by Parma among the different regiments to prevent dissension, for the Spaniards had claimed it on the ground that the dead man was the brother of their King, the Germans because he was by birthplace their fellow-countryman, and the Flemings because he was their Governor-General. It was accordingly carried to the gate of the

[1] *As You Like It*, Act IV, sc. i, I, 110.
[2] *Post Mortem*, pp. 131–2. London, 1923.

camp by members of the State Council and the gentlemen of the household, and from there to Namur by six senior captains of various regiments. At the head of the procession marched that of Figueroa, the crack unit of the Spanish Army, with trailing colours and arquebuses reversed. Parma was the chief mourner.

The actual funeral service took place in Namur cathedral, but only the intestines were finally buried there, for in the following spring the body was disinterred by the order of Philip for removal to Spain, but in the conditions then existing it was decided that this had better be done secretly. Accordingly leave was obtained from the French Government for the passage through France of certain members of Don John's household who were returning to Spain, but the real object of the journey was not stated. Meanwhile the body had been cut in pieces at the joints, and placed in three leather bags, which were carried on the pack-saddle of a horse like any other baggage. On arrival in Spain the severed portions were reassembled, and the body was interred at the Escorial where that of Charles V had been buried four years earlier.

The career of Don John of Austria recalls the lines of Dr Johnson on Charles XII of Sweden:

> He left the name at which the world grew pale
> To point a moral or adorn a tale.

Perhaps his early death was in the best interests both of himself and of his country. There was nothing for him to do in the Low Countries which Parma could not do better, for events had already proved that his nephew was a more competent soldier and the future was to show that he was an incomparably more adroit politician. At the same time it must be admitted that Parma had the advantage of succeeding to the Governorship of the Netherlands at a moment when Philip was becoming alive to the intrigues of Antonio Pérez, and there can equally be no doubt that his path had been rendered easier for him by his predecessor. Yet when all is said and done the great days of Don John were when he was commanding the armaments of the Holy League, for he was a superb leader of men: also, he was then supported by a highly competent staff and by extremely capable admirals and generals, which was not the case in the Low Countries until the last months of his life. His main weakness was that he by no means always realized where the true interests of Spain lay, and if they clashed with his own ambitions he tended to ignore them. In these circumstances it was well for his country that his master and brother was Philip II, so well termed 'The Prudent'.

Index